EZEKIEL

AN INTRODUCTION AND COMMENTARY

by

JOHN B. TAYLOR, M.A.

Vice-Principal, Oak Hill College, London

INTER-VARSITY PRESS
Downers Grove, Ill. 60515

Printed in Great Britain by
Billing & Sons Limited, Guildford and London

GENERAL PREFACE

THE aim of this series of *Tyndale Old Testament Commentaries*, as it was in the companion volumes on the New Testament, is to provide the student of the Bible with a handy, up-to-date commentary on each book, with the primary emphasis on exegesis. Major critical questions are discussed in the introductions and additional notes, while undue technicalities have been avoided.

In this series individual authors are, of course, free to make their own distinct contributions and express their own point of view on all controversial issues. Within the necessary limits of space they frequently draw attention to interpretations which they themselves do not hold but which represent the stated conclusions of sincere fellow Christians. While he has done all this, the author of this commentary has shown that it is possible to make a book of the Bible – often little read and studied outside a few well-known passages – stand out afresh in its historical and prophetic setting, yet with meaning, relevance and application for the serious reader today.

In the Old Testament in particular no single English translation is adequate to reflect the original text. The authors of these commentaries freely quote various versions, therefore, or give their own translation, in the endeavour to make the more difficult passages or words meaningful today. Where necessary, words from the Hebrew (and Aramaic) Text underlying their studies are transliterated. This will help the reader who may be unfamiliar with the Semitic languages to identify the word under discussion and thus to follow the argument. It is assumed throughout that the reader will have ready access to one, or more, reliable rendering of the Bible in English.

There are signs of a renewed interest in the meaning and message of the Old Testament and it is hoped that this series will thus further the systematic study of the revelation of God and His will and ways as seen in these records. It is the prayer of the editor and publisher, as of the authors, that these books will help many to understand, and to respond to, the Word of God today.

D. J. WISEMAN

CONTENTS

AUTHOR'S PREFACE

COMMENTARIES may be divided into two classes. Some are designed to help readers of the Bible to understand better the parts which they read. The others are designed to help the same people to tackle the parts they would otherwise ignore. The present commentary is intended to fall within this second category. To those who have grappled confidently with the problems of Ezekiel's visions and who can spend happy hours working out the fulfilment of his prophecies, these pages have little to offer. But those who have done no more than dip tentatively into his forty-eight chapters will, I hope, be encouraged to be more venturesome. For their benefit I have tried to avoid undue technicalities and, even when I have felt it necessary to make reference to the original Hebrew, I have tried to make my comments clear and readable so that the complete layman will never feel himself at a loss. My success will be judged, therefore, not so much by the number of people who read this book as by the number who read Ezekiel as well.

I am most grateful to Professor D. J. Wiseman both for his personal encouragement and for a number of helpful suggestions and improvements he has made; to the Rev. Arthur Cundall for carefully checking the manuscript and pointing out inaccuracies which I may never have spotted; and to Mr. Alan Millard for help in preparing the chronological table in the Introduction. My thanks are also due to Mrs. Valerie Everitt and Mrs. Joy Hills for their invaluable help in typing the manuscript. Most of all I should like to express my gratitude to my wife and children, who have willingly made sacrifices so that this book should be written and who have encouraged me more than I can say.

Easter Day 1969   JOHN B. TAYLOR

CHIEF ABBREVIATIONS

Akk.	Akkadian
ANEP	*The Ancient Near East in Pictures* by J. B. Pritchard, 1954.
ANET	*Ancient Near Eastern Texts relating to the Old Testament*[2] by J. B. Pritchard, 1955.
ARI	*Archaeology and the Religion of Israel*[3] by W. F. Albright, 1953.
AV	English Authorized Version (King James).
BA	*Biblical Archaeologist.*
BASOR	*Bulletin of the American Schools of Oriental Research.*
Bertholet	*Hesekiel*[2] by A. Bertholet (*Handbuch zum Alten Testament*), 1936.
BJRL	*Bulletin of the John Rylands Library.*
BZAW	*Beihefte zur Zeitschrift für die alttestamentliche Wissenschaft.*
Cooke	*A Critical and Exegetical Commentary on the Book of Ezekiel* by G. A. Cooke (*International Critical Commentary*), 1936.
Cornill	*Das Buch des Propheten Ezechiel* by C. Cornill, 1886.
Davidson	*The Book of the Prophet Ezekiel* by A. B. Davidson (*Cambridge Bible for Schools and Colleges*), 1892.
de Vaux	*Ancient Israel: Its Life and Institutions* by Roland de Vaux, Eng. tr. 1961.
DOTT	*Documents from Old Testament Times* edited by D. Winton Thomas, 1958.
EB	*Encyclopaedia Biblica* edited by T. K. Cheyne and J. S. Black, 1899–1903.
Eissfeldt	*The Old Testament, an Introduction* by Otto Eissfeldt, Eng. tr. 1965.
Ellison	*Ezekiel, the Man and his Message* by H. L. Ellison, 1956.

ET	*Expository Times.*
EVV	English Versions (used where AV, RV and RSV agree).
Fohrer	*Ezechiel* by G. Fohrer (*Handbuch zum alten Testament*), 1955.
GK	*Hebrew Grammar*[2] by W. Gesenius, E. Kautzsch and A. E. Cowley, 1910.
HDB	*Hastings' Dictionary of the Bible.*
Hengstenberg	*Commentary on Ezekiel* by E. W. Hengstenberg, Eng. tr. 1869.
Herntrich	*Ezechielprobleme* by V. Herntrich, 1932.
Hitzig	*Der Prophet Ezechiel* by F. Hitzig, 1847.
Howie	*Ezekiel, Daniel* by C. G. Howie (*Layman's Bible Commentaries*), 1961.
HUCA	*Hebrew Union College Annual.*
IB	*The Interpreter's Bible*, Vol. 6. *The Book of Ezekiel*. Introduction and Exegesis by H. G. May; Exposition by E. L. Allen, 1956.
IDB	*The Interpreter's Dictionary of the Bible*, in four volumes, 1962.
JB	*Jerusalem Bible*, 1968.
JBL	*Journal of Biblical Literature.*
JSS	*Journal of Semitic Studies.*
JTS	*Journal of Theological Studies.*
Keil	*Biblical Commentary on the Prophecies of Ezekiel*, by C. F. Keil, Eng. tr., no date (2 vols.).
Kliefoth	*Das Buch Ezechiels* by Th. Kliefoth, 1864–5.
Klostermann	*Studien und Kritiken* by A. Klostermann, 1877.
Knox	*The Holy Bible*[2] translated by Ronald Knox, 1956.
Koehler	*Lexicon in Veteris Testamenti Libros* by L. Koehler and W. Baumgartner, 1953.
Kraetzschmar	*Das Buch Ezechiel* by R. Kraetzschmar (*Handkommentar zum Alten Testament*), 1900.
Lat.	Old Latin Version.
LXX	The Septuagint (pre-Christian Greek version of the Old Testament).

May	See *IB*.
mg.	margin.
Moffatt	*A New Translation of the Bible* by James Moffatt, 1935.
MS	manuscript.
MT	Massoretic Text.
NBD	*The New Bible Dictionary* edited by J. D. Douglas, 1962.
OTMS	*The Old Testament and Modern Study* edited by H. H. Rowley, 1951.
PEFQ	*Palestine Exploration Fund Quarterly Statement.*
Peake	*Peake's Commentary on the Bible* edited by Matthew Black and H. H. Rowley, 1962. Section on Ezekiel by J. Muilenburg.
RSV	American Revised Standard Version, 1952.
RV	English Revised Version, 1881.
Skinner	*The Book of Ezekiel* by John Skinner (*The Expositor's Bible*), 1895 (2 vols.).
Stalker	*Ezekiel* by D. M. G. Stalker (*Torch Bible Commentaries*), 1968.
Syr.	Syriac Version.
TB	Babylonian Talmud.
Toy	*Ezekiel* by C. H. Toy (*Polychrome Bible*), 1899.
VT	*Vetus Testamentum.*
ZAW	*Zeitschrift für die alttestamentliche Wissenschaft.*
Zimmerli	*Ezechiel* by W. Zimmerli (*Biblischer Kommentar: Altes Testament*), 1955 onwards.

INTRODUCTION

I. THE BOOK OF EZEKIEL

FOR most Bible readers Ezekiel is almost a closed book. Their knowledge of him extends little further than his mysterious vision of God's chariot-throne, with its wheels within wheels, and the vision of the valley of dry bones. Otherwise his book is as forbidding in its size as the prophet himself is in the complexity of his make-up.

In its structure, however, if not in its thought and language, the book of Ezekiel has a basic simplicity, and its orderly framework makes it easy to analyse. After the opening vision, in which Ezekiel sees the majesty of God on the plains of Babylon and receives his call to be a prophet to the house of Israel (1–3), there follows a long series of messages, some enacted symbolically but most expressed in spoken form, foretelling and justifying God's intention to punish the holy city of Jerusalem and its inhabitants with destruction and death (4–24). Then, at the half-way mark in the book, when the fall of Jerusalem is represented as having actually taken place (though the news has still not percolated through to the exiles), the reader's attention is diverted to the nations that surround Israel and God's judgment on them is pronounced in a series of oracles (25–32). By this time the reader is prepared for the bombshell of the news of Jerusalem's destruction, and 32:21 tells of the fugitive's statement, 'The city has fallen!' But already a new age is dawning and a new message is on Ezekiel's lips. With a renewed commission and a promise that God is about to restore His people to their own land under godly leadership by a kind of national resurrection (33–37), Ezekiel leads on to describe in apocalyptic terms the final triumph of the people of God over the invading hordes from the north (38, 39). The book concludes, as it began, with an intricate vision, not this time of the Lord's chariot-throne moving over the empty wastes of Babylon, but of the new Jerusalem with its temple court and inner sanctuary where God would dwell among His people for ever (40–48).

It is not surprising, therefore, that most older commentators regarded Ezekiel as being free from the literary fragmentation that was imposed by critics upon the prophecies of Isaiah, Jeremiah and some of the twelve minor prophets. A. B. Davidson's introduction to his commentary on Ezekiel (1892) began with the oft-quoted verdict: 'The Book of Ezekiel is simpler and more perspicuous in its arrangement than any other of the great prophetical books. It was probably committed to writing late in the prophet's life, and, unlike the prophecies of Isaiah, which were given out piecemeal, *was issued in its complete form at once*.'[1]

Twenty years later G. B. Gray could still draw the conclusion that 'no other book of the Old Testament is distinguished by such decisive marks of unity of authorship and integrity as this'.[2] But by the time McFadyen wrote his *Introduction to the Old Testament* (1932 edition), he was having to use more cautious language: 'We have in Ezekiel the rare satisfaction of studying a carefully elaborated prophecy whose authenticity has, till recently, been practically undisputed.'[3] The phrase 'till recently' refers to the work of scholars like Kraetzschmar, Hölscher, C. C. Torrey and James Smith. But before we consider their views, let us briefly summarize the arguments on which the traditional view of the unity of Ezekiel has been based.

There are six main reasons for ascribing the book to a single author, the prophet Ezekiel.

1. The book has a balanced structure, as we have already observed, and this logical arrangement extends from chapter 1 to 48. There are no breaks in the continuity of the prophecy, except where (as in the case of the oracles against the nations, 25–32) this is done for deliberate effect. The only part that could readily be separated from the rest, the vision of the new temple (40–48), appears neatly to balance the opening

---

[1] Davidson, p. ix (my italics).
[2] G. B. Gray, *A Critical Introduction to the Old Testament* (1913), p. 198.
[3] McFadyen, p. 187.

vision of chapters 1–3 and is better regarded as a fitting conclusion to the whole, although manifestly of somewhat later date (*cf.* 40:1).

2. The message of the book has an inner consistency which fits in with the structural balance. The centre-point is the fall of Jerusalem and the destruction of the Temple. This is announced in 24:21ff. and reported in 33:21. From chapter 1 to 24 Ezekiel's message is destructive and denunciatory : he is a watchman set to warn the people that this is the inevitable consequence of the nation's sins. But from chapter 33 to 48, while he still regards himself as a watchman with a message of individual retribution and responsibility, his tone is encouraging and restorative. Before 587 BC his theme was that the deportation of 597 BC, in which he himself was one of the victims, was certainly not the end of God's punishment upon His people : worse was to come, and the exiles must be prepared to face it. But after it had come, and the worst had happened, God would act to rebuild and restore His chastened Israel.

3. The book shows a remarkable uniformity of style and language. This is largely due to the repetitious phraseology used throughout the book. May[1] gives a list of no fewer than 47 typical Ezekielian phrases which appear periodically in its pages, and many of these are peculiar to this prophet. This does not of course prove anything about the actual authorship, because an editor could easily have picked up phrases typical of Ezekiel and woven them into the additional material he incorporated, but it is strong evidence for the unity and coherence of the book in its final stage, and it suggests that the editor of the finished work, if he was not Ezekiel himself, identified himself closely with Ezekiel's outlook and beliefs.

4. The book has a clear chronological sequence, with dates appearing at 1:1, 2 ; 8:1 ; 20:1 ; 24:1 ; 26:1 ; 29:1 ; 30:20 ; 31:1 ; 32:1, 17 ; 33:21 ; 40:1. No other major prophet has this logical progression of dates, and only Haggai and Zechariah among the minor prophets afford any comparable pattern.[2]

---

[1] *IB*, pp. 5of.
[2] The chronology of Ezekiel is studied more closely under section III of the Introduction, below, p. 36.

5. Unlike Isaiah, Jeremiah, Hosea, Amos and Zechariah, which all combine material in the first and third persons singular, a feature which is usually regarded as a sure sign of editorial compilation, Ezekiel is written autobiographically throughout. The only exception is the duplicate introduction (1:2, 3), which looks very much as if it was an editor's explanation of an opening verse which clearly needed some kind of interpretation for his readers (see Commentary, p. 52). But this is the only such instance.

6. The picture of the character and personality of Ezekiel appears consistent through the whole of the book; there is the same earnestness, the same eccentricity, the same priestly love of symbolism, the same fastidious concern with detail, the same sense of the majesty and transcendence of God.

Despite this evidence there has never been lacking a handful of critics who have been sceptical about the unity of Ezekiel. Josephus' statement[1] that Ezekiel left behind him two books must not be made to shoulder too much of the blame for this. A century ago Ewald distinguished two elements in Ezekiel, the former representing spoken prophetic oracles and the latter being the literary production of a writing prophet. He did not, however, feel that this division demanded that the unity of the book should be abandoned. Some years later Kraetzschmar argued strongly against literary unity on the grounds that he could detect numerous inconsistencies in the text, doublets and parallel versions, which led him to postulate two recensions of the book, one in the first person and the other in the third person. The weakness of Kraetzschmar's conclusion was that the only passages in the third person were 1:3 and 24:24 (where Yahweh says : 'Thus shall Ezekiel be to you a sign'), and not surprisingly he received scant support for his theory. Scholars like Herrmann,[2] who saw the validity of Kraetzschmar's evidence but rejected his conclusion, preferred the more conservative estimate of Ezekiel

[1] *Antiquities*, x. 5. 1 : '. . . Ezekiel also, who was the first person that wrote, and left behind him in writing two books, concerning these events' (W. Whiston's translation).

[2] *Ezechielstudien (Beiträge zur Wissenschaft vom Alten Testament*, 1908) and *Ezechiel (Kommentar zum Alten Testament*, 1924), both by J. Herrmann.

as being a unity compiled by the prophet's own hand, but with later editorial accretions.

In the same year that Herrmann produced his commentary on Ezekiel, however, Gustav Hölscher published a study[1] reversing his own conservative views of ten years earlier[2] and subjecting the book of Ezekiel to what Rowley has described as 'the most dramatic dismemberment it has yet suffered'.[3] He took as his starting-point the belief that Ezekiel was a poet and therefore that it was unlikely that he would have written many of the prose passages in the book. He also excised poetical passages that were not in what he regarded as Ezekiel's characteristic metre. Out too went passages where symbolism was mixed in with concrete facts, for he argued that a true poet would not do such a thing. Even more arbitrary was his view that the doctrine of individual responsibility must be post-exilic, so these passages also had to be relegated to redactors. The result of this drastic analysis was that Ezekiel the prophet was left with a bare 170 verses out of a total of 1,273 contained in the book named after him. Although Hölscher's conclusions were revolutionary, his methodology was not original (Duhm had given much the same treatment to the book of Jeremiah in 1903[4]) and before very long an American scholar, W. A. Irwin, came to similar conclusions through different reasoning.[5] Irwin began with a detailed study of Ezekiel 15, deducing from this that there was a discrepancy between the oracle itself and its interpretation which amounted to sheer misunderstanding. The interpretation could not therefore be Ezekiel's work. Applying this principle to the rest of the book he left Ezekiel with about 250 genuine verses, or only one-fifth of the whole book.

Radical as these assessments may be, they appear almost

---

[1] G. Hölscher, *Hesekiel, der Dichter und das Buch* (1924).
[2] G. Hölscher, *Die Profeten* (1914), pp. 298ff.
[3] The essay by H. H. Rowley, 'The Book of Ezekiel in Modern Study', *BJRL*, XXXVI, 1953–54, pp. 146–150 (now more readily available in his book, *Men of God: Studies in Old Testament History and Prophecy*, 1963), from which this quotation is taken, is an admirable survey of the extensive literature on Ezekiel which can only be touched on in this Introduction.
[4] B. Duhm, *Das Buch Jeremia übersetzt* (1903).
[5] W. A. Irwin, *The Problem of Ezekiel* (1943).

conservative in comparison with the view of C. C. Torrey,[1] who deleted Ezekiel altogether. For him Ezekiel was a fictitious character, invented originally about 230 BC by an author who was attempting a pseudepigraph purporting to be by one of the prophets who preached in Jerusalem during the reign of Manasseh (*c.* 696–642 BC; *cf.* 2 Ki. 21:1–17). His reasoning was that 1–24 dealt primarily with Jerusalem and probably had its origin there (we shall find this problem recurring later on), and that the idolatries described in Jerusalem (8:1–18) could not have occurred after Josiah's reforms had taken place in 621 BC. The present form of the book, with its Babylonian setting, was the work of a later, anti-Samaritan editor who reshaped it and added chapters 40–48 as the plan of a new temple which would surpass in splendour that built by the Samaritan sect on Mount Gerizim. James Smith[2] also attributed the ministry of Ezekiel to Manasseh's reign, but regarded him as a historical character whose ministry was exercised partly in Palestine and partly among the exiles of the northern kingdom of Israel (compare Ezekiel's many references to 'the whole house of Israel'). He may even have been the priest referred to in 2 Kings 17:28. Like Torrey, Smith postulated a later editor who transformed the book and gave it its Babylonian environment.

Herntrich[3] drew on the work of both these men to give Ezekiel a Palestinian setting for the whole of his prophetic ministry. He did not follow them in referring this back to Manasseh's reign but concentrated it into the years 593–586 BC. A disciple of Ezekiel later clothed his work in Babylonian dress and added chapters 1 and 40–48, as well as other editorial material. Herntrich's work was important and influenced a number of writers,[4] chief of whom was the German, Alfred Bertholet, whose second commentary on Ezekiel[5] incorporated the classic statement of the view that

[1] C. C. Torrey, *Pseudo-Ezekiel and the Original Prophecy* (1930).
[2] J. S. Smith, *The Book of the Prophet Ezekiel: a New Introduction* (1931).
[3] V. Herntrich, *Ezechielprobleme* (*BZAW*, 1932).
[4] *Cf.* Oesterley and Robinson, *An Introduction to the Books of the Old Testament* (1934), p. 325; J. Battersby Harford, *Studies in the Book of Ezekiel* (1935).
[5] A. Bertholet, *Hesekiel* (*Handbuch zum Alten Testament*, 1936). His earlier

Ezekiel exercised a double ministry. From 593 BC, the date of his call, Ezekiel prophesied in Jerusalem until its fall; he was then taken into captivity and continued his ministry in Babylonia. Fischer[1] modified Bertholet's view to the extent that he believed Ezekiel received his initial call in Babylon, not Jerusalem, which involved too much dislocation of the text, but that his call was to go to the house of Israel and this he did by making the journey to Jerusalem described in 8:3. Among others who subscribe to the view of a double ministry in Palestine and Babylon are Pfeiffer,[2] Wheeler Robinson,[3] Auvray[4] and May.[5]

Against this view G. A. Cooke[6] stood out for the more traditional interpretation, as provided by the biblical text, of an exclusively Babylonian locale for Ezekiel's ministry, explaining along psychological lines the problems of Ezekiel's acute awareness of events in Jerusalem and, more particularly, the strange account of Pelatiah's death (11:13). For a long while his was a lone voice, but Howie's monograph, published in 1950,[7] returned whole-heartedly to the conclusions that were accepted so widely at the beginning of the century. This was no mere conservatism for its own sake, but the result of a careful examination of the earlier theories which led him to the conclusion that there were fewer difficulties in accepting the traditional view than in postulating extensive editorial alterations of the text. Howie has been followed in broad outline by several post-war commentators, such as Georg Fohrer,[8] Walter Zimmerli,[9] Eichrodt,[10] Muilenburg[11] and

---

commentary was published in 1897 as *Das Buch Hesekiel* (*Kurzer Hand-Commentar zum Alten Testament*).

[1] O. R. Fischer, *The Unity of the Book of Ezekiel* (1939) (unpublished).

[2] Robert H. Pfeiffer, *Introduction to the Old Testament* (1941).

[3] H. Wheeler Robinson, *Two Hebrew Prophets* (1948), pp. 75, 81ff.

[4] P. Auvray, *Ezéchiel* (*Témoins de Dieu*, 1947).

[5] *IB*, p. 52.   [6] Cooke, pp. xxiiif.

[7] C. G. Howie, *The Date and Composition of Ezekiel* (*JBL* Monograph Series IV, 1950).

[8] G. Fohrer, *Ezechiel* (*Handbuch zum Alten Testament*, 1955).

[9] W. Zimmerli, *Ezechiel* (*Biblischer Kommentar*, 1955 onwards).

[10] W. Eichrodt, *Der Prophet Hesekiel* (*Das Alte Testament Deutsch*, 1959 and 1966).   [11] Peake, pp. 568f.

Stalker,[1] as well as by writers like Orlinsky,[2] Rowley[3] and Eissfeldt.[4]

Muilenburg expressed his conclusions in the following terms: 'That the book passed through a long and complicated literary history can scarcely be questioned, and that it represents a compilation of traditions of great diversity is apparent. But the weight of evidence seems to fall in favour of a view not greatly unlike that held by scholars of previous generations. The considerable disagreement in the results achieved by recent scholars does not inspire confidence in their validity. While the presence of expansions and supplements may well be admitted, even here the difficulty is that the passages are so similar in style and content that absolute certainty concerning their secondary character is excluded. . . . Our conclusion, then, is that the book as a whole comes from him.'[5] This is the standpoint adopted in the present commentary. Attempts to isolate Ezekiel's own work from his editor's have been eschewed as being too uncertain an occupation.[6] The homogeneity of the whole book is such that we are inclined to the view that the prophet could well have been his own editor.

The average reader, however, regards this as a matter of small consequence, and he comes to the book of Ezekiel anxious to understand the message of this book and to hear the word of the Lord speaking to his own generation as it did to the Jews of the sixth century BC.

II. EZEKIEL THE MAN

Ezekiel was the son of Buzi; he was a priest and probably the

[1] D. M. G. Stalker, *Ezekiel* (*Torch Bible Commentaries*, 1968).
[2] In *BASOR*, CXXII, 1951, pp. 34–36.
[3] Rowley, *Men of God* (1963), pp. 209f.
[4] Eissfeldt, p. 372, comments: 'So far as the period and place of the prophet's activity is concerned, we must be satisfied with the remark that there are no really decisive arguments against the reliability of the tradition which finds expression in many passages in the book.'
[5] Peake, p. 569.
[6] *Cf.* S. Mowinckel, *Prophecy and Tradition* (1946), pp. 84f.

son of a priest.[1] He was taken captive in 597 BC, when the armies of Nebuchadrezzar, king of Babylon, captured Jerusalem after a brief siege. With the young king Jehoiachin and 'all the princes, and all the mighty men of valour, ten thousand captives, and all the craftsmen and the smiths' (2 Ki. 24:14), he was removed from the Temple, which was to have been his life, and resettled on the dusty plains of Babylonia. In the fifth year of his exile, *i.e.* 593 BC, the call of God came to him to exercise a prophetic ministry to the house of Israel. If we are right in thinking that 'the thirtieth year' referred to in 1:1 was the thirtieth year of his age, it follows that Ezekiel was a young man in his mid-twenties when the exile began and this would allow for the considerable period of time over which his ministry extended. The latest date that is given to one of his oracles is the twenty-seventh year of the exile (29:17), and this would take him to the age of 52. Nothing is known of his life apart from what is contained in the book which bears his name, nor is there any tradition to tell us when or how he died. We know that he was married and that his wife died at the time of Jerusalem's fall (24:18). He was a man of influence, being consulted by the elders among the exiles (8:1 ; 20:1) ; and although this may be due to his prophetic ministry and the reputation which he quickly acquired, it is just as likely that it is attributable to his social standing derived through his father, Buzi.

Apart from his visionary visit to Jerusalem (8:3 – 11:24), the only location with which Ezekiel is connected is either his house or the plain (or 'the valley' ; 3:22f. ; 37:1), near to the river Chebar at a place called Tel Abib. The river Chebar has been tentatively identified with the *naru kabari*, or 'great river', referred to in two cuneiform texts from Nippur. It was the name given to an irrigation canal which brought the waters of the Euphrates in a loop south-eastwards from

---

[1] The fact that this information is found in 1:2, 3, the passage in the third person singular which may well have been an editorial interpolation, does not in any way invalidate the truth of the statements. If we had not been told that Ezekiel was a priest we should almost certainly have guessed that he was.

Babylon via Nippur and back to the main river near Uruk (biblical Erech). The modern name for it is Shatt en-Nil. About Tel Abib nothing geographical is known except that it probably represents Akk. *til abûbi* ('mound of the deluge'?). The first word is a common description given to a mound over the remains of a succession of buried cities (*cf.* Tell el-Amarna, Tell es-Sultan, *etc.*), and a comparison with Ezra 2:59 (where some of the returning exiles came from places like Tel-melah and Tel-harsha) suggests that the Judean captives may have been allowed to build their exilic communities on old ruined sites of this sort, which to this day are scattered over the plains of Babylonia. Of Ezekiel's house we can deduce that it was made of mud-bricks typical of the locality, and this suggests a tolerably settled way of life for the exiles.[1]

The prophet seems to have had reasonable freedom of movement to come and go as he wished, and the evidence both of the fugitive's arrival (33:21) and of Jeremiah's correspondence with the exiles (Je. 29) indicates that theirs was no prison-camp existence. Restrictions there must have been, but community organization (*i.e.* the existence of elders, 8:1; 20:1), agriculture, worship and instruction, marriage and communication-links with Jerusalem were all permitted them. Almost certainly they were able to visit some of the great cities of the land, chief of which was Babylon with its world-famous hanging gardens, its vast fortifications and the magnificent Ishtar Gate. Ezekiel would have seen the stepped ziggurats, or temple-towers, reminiscent of the tower of Babel, and perhaps he was conscious of their formal similarity with the great stepped altar of Solomon's Temple which he incorporated with only slight modification in his own temple of the future (43:13–17; Fig. IV). He would have been made aware of the strange, composite sphinx-like creatures which were depicted everywhere, either as deities or as guardians of the gods, and it is not impossible that the sight of these encouraged his imagination to think in similar terms when

---

[1] The brick mentioned in 4:1 was of this sort, and the action of digging through the wall in 12:5 suggests this kind of building.

describing the visions that he saw, though it must never be forgotten that his priestly training at the Jerusalem Temple would have introduced him to the cherubim depicted there. His most striking impression, however, would have been of the combination of excessive idolatry and worldly splendour. The multiplicity of temples, the incredible prosperity of the city, the hive of industry and culture, all this would have made any Hebrew captive feel how small his home country was and how great were the all-conquering gods of Nebuchadrezzar. But once Ezekiel had experienced his vision of the *merkabah*, the chariot-throne of Yahweh, confirming to him that the God of Jerusalem was alive and triumphant even in this heathen, polytheistic land of Babylon, it is not surprising to find that his recurring theme is the majesty of the Lord and his reiterated message is that the house of Israel, the exiles, the nations of the world, even the forces of darkness, should all 'know that I am the Lord'. To judge from the frequency of its use (over fifty times in all), this aim was Ezekiel's consuming passion.

All this presupposes that Ezekiel's ministry took place in Babylon. Against this view the advocates of a partial or total Palestinian ministry for Ezekiel argue that his intimate knowledge of the idolatries that were being practised in the Temple (8:1–18), his apparent confrontation with Pelatiah (11:1–13) and his telepathic awareness of events such as the beginning of the siege of Jerusalem (24:2) and its eventual fall (33:22), indicate that it was far more likely that he was there on the spot in Jerusalem for some or all of the time. Further, they would argue that his commission was to the house of Israel, that many of his messages concerned Jerusalem (4:1 – 5:17) and were addressed to the people of Jerusalem and Judah (6:1 – 7:13; 16:3ff.; 21:1–17, *etc.*), and that it is difficult to contemplate (in Cooke's words) 'a prophet in Babylonia hurling his denunciations at the inhabitants of Jerusalem across 700 miles of desert'.[1] However, no-one has yet insisted that Ezekiel's oracles addressed to the foreign nations should have been delivered on Ammonite territory or

[1] Cooke, p. xxiii.

in Tyre or Egypt, and there is no need to suppose that his oracles addressed to Jerusalem must therefore have been delivered in the holy city and not in front of the exiles. As Ellison[1] rightly points out, 'Ezekiel was in fact prophesying *of* but not *to* Jerusalem.' Although several years had passed since their deportation had taken place, the exiles still lived for Jerusalem and home. It was the centre of their interests and hopes; every snatch of news that came through to Babylon was treated like a grain of gold-dust. Apart from the duration of their stay in exile, events in Jerusalem were the only supremely relevant factor in their thinking. It would be strange indeed if Ezekiel did not give it the prominence it deserved in his ministry to the exiles.

This still does not resolve the problem of Ezekiel's trance-like visit to Jerusalem. But here we are up against the problem of the ease of communication between Babylon and Jerusalem. It is highly unlikely that Ezekiel would have been allowed to return from exile to Jerusalem, and Bentzen's suggestion[2] that permission may have been granted in order that Ezekiel could be used as the pawn of Babylonian propagandists has little to commend it. If a Palestinian setting for any of Ezekiel's ministry is demanded it is preferable to argue that this should have followed an original call in Palestine and not in Babylon. But to postulate an original call in Palestine involves considerable dislocation and rearrangement of the text as we have it in chapters 1–3. A study of the efforts made by commentators to separate two distinct strands in chapters 1–3, one belonging to an original Palestinian call and the other being a later Babylonian recommissioning, will be enough to convince most readers that the ingenuity and emendation that are needed for the task condemn the theory as highly implausible. And Orlinsky pertinently asks: 'What could Ezekiel (or a redactor) have hoped to gain by shifting the locale of the initial call from Judah (if so it was) to Babylon?'[3] Orlinsky's question has not been satisfactorily answered, but

[1] Ellison, p. 20.
[2] Aage Bentzen, *Introduction to the Old Testament* (1948), Vol. II, p. 128.
[3] *BASOR*, CXXII, 1951, p. 35.

the exponents of a double ministry argue in reply that their theory provides a better explanation of the problems associated with Ezekiel's apparently telepathic powers.

It seems, however, to the present writer that those who take this view are trying too hard to reduce Ezekiel to a level of complete normality. Abnormality of some sort was an essential feature of the Old Testament prophet's charismatic ministry. He was uniquely aware of God, whether from a supernatural, visionary experience which constituted his call or from the inner consciousness of having a message from God implanted in his mind. He was a man for whom the miraculous held no surprises, especially when this was connected with the fulfilment of words that he had spoken under divine constraint. If Ezekiel's extrasensory powers had operated over-frequently or been switched on to order, we could feel suspicious; but they give the impression of having been rare, memorable and concerned only with events of crucial importance. At the same time we must beware of making too much of these powers, for much of the knowledge Ezekiel shows of the state of affairs in Jerusalem could well have come to him through normal channels of information, particularly as he would have been one of the first to receive confidential news of Temple affairs.[1] The real 'coincidences' appear to be Pelatiah's death (11:13) and the start of the siege of Jerusalem (24:2).

The case of Pelatiah is set in the context of Ezekiel's vision in which he felt himself transported to Jerusalem. Still in vision he sees twenty-five elders by the east gate of the Temple and he is able to identify two of them, Jaazaniah the son of Azzur and Pelatiah the son of Benaiah. It is reasonable to suppose that these were well-known characters, known by name both to Ezekiel and to the elders of the exiles in whose presence Ezekiel is supposed to have had this vision, and to whom he subsequently described it all (11:25). While Ezekiel prophesies, Pelatiah falls down dead. The text does not stipulate that it was *because of* Ezekiel's word that he died (as in the case of Ananias and Sapphira in Acts 5:5, 10), but the

[1] Note the use of the phrase 'came to *me*' in 33:21.

coincidence was enough to make Ezekiel shocked and frightened (11:13b). The significance of the event is twofold. First, it is significant that Ezekiel was able to be aware of a striking occurrence which took place hundreds of miles away in Jerusalem at the same time as he was in a trance-like state in Tel Abib. Secondly, when news of this event reached the elders in exile it would have been powerful confirmation of Ezekiel's supernatural powers and would authenticate him and his message in their eyes. The importance of this incident is not therefore to show that Ezekiel had the power to strike a man down with a single word at a range of 700 miles, as some have interpreted it. It was the last thing that Ezekiel wanted or intended to happen. Rather it illustrates his *awareness* of a major event taking place far away and is therefore exactly parallel to the other examples of this same power in relation to the timing of the siege and fall of Jerusalem. To want to deny occasional exhibitions of such power to a prophet of God shows a lack of understanding of the power of God's Spirit in a man, and to deny it to Ezekiel of all people is to attempt to make him other than what he was.

In our judgment it is equally mistaken to try to categorize Ezekiel, especially at this remove, in modern psychological terms. His unusual behaviour and highly imaginative symbolical acts have been accounted for in a number of ways. Stalker comments : 'Ezekiel has been called a cataleptic, a neurotic, a victim of hysteria, a psychopath, and even a definite paranoid schizophrenic, as well as being credited with powers of clairvoyance or levitation.'[1] To transfer his ministry to Jerusalem may remove the stigma from some of these accusations but it does not satisfactorily solve the problem, for as we have seen it raises more problems than it solves. Much of Ezekiel's 'abnormal' behaviour is a matter for interpretation. To begin with, as we have already observed, for a prophet a certain degree of 'abnormality' was normal ; he was caught up in ecstasy and frequently reinforced his oracles with dramatic acts (*cf.* Zedekiah the son of Chenaanah, 1 Ki. 22:11 ; and Jeremiah, Je. 13:1–14 ; 19:10–13). Ezekiel

[1] Stalker, p. 23.

was also a priest by training and upbringing, and therefore
symbolism on a grand scale was second nature to him,
especially a symbolism that combined word and deed.
Whatever we may think about the strangeness of some of his
actions, about his silent grief on the death of his wife, his
dumbness, his long periods of lying on his side, he comes over
to us as a supremely controlled personality, in the grip of a
passionate zeal for God rather than of some mental illness.
'He is best understood', writes Howie, 'as a sensitive human
soul caught in the crosscurrents of history, driven by a burning
zeal for God, painfully aware of the tragedy in which his
people were involved.'[1] His sensitivity may be judged by the
brief description of his feelings for his wife (24:15–18), by his
earnest plea that God will spare His people and not destroy
them completely (9:8; 11:13), and by the tenderness of his
description of God as the Shepherd of His sheep (34:11–16).
This balances the harshness of many of his prophecies of
judgment and the cold logic that characterizes his insistence
that God will act 'not for your sake . . . but for the sake of my
holy name' (36:22).

For Ezekiel everything had a meaning. The actions he
performed, the words he used, all were directed towards an
end. His dumbness is typical of his personality. It could not
have been a literal dumbness, or we should have to displace
all the oracles that were attributed to him before 33:22.
Certainly the editor of the finished work did not mean us to
interpret his dumbness in this way. The only alternative is
that this was a 'ritual dumbness', an imposed and willingly
accepted proscription of any speech unless it was a pronouncement given him from the Lord. Understood like this,
it can be seen how much additional regard would have been
given to his symbolic actions and the oracles that accompanied them. His visions were classic examples of this symbolical sense. The inaugural vision of the chariot-throne held
meaning in every line; much of it is lost on us today but the
broad outline can nevertheless be still discerned. It attempted
to describe the indescribable and to say in the language of

[1] Howie, p. 15.

spiritual experience something about the character of the God it represented. The vision of the new temple, on the other hand, used priestly symbolism to say what this God required of His worshippers. It is bound up with concepts of holiness and the demand for order and perfection, reverence and symmetry.

As a writer Ezekiel is often ponderous and repetitive.[1] A limited number of phrases and themes recur frequently and this can be daunting for modern readers who are not acquainted with the conventions of ancient writing. Occasionally he uses poetry, but for the most part he writes in prose; not a colourful, descriptive prose, but a sombre, prophetic prose with a cadence but no discernible metre. When he recites a poem it is frequently an elegy or lamentation (Heb. *qînâ*; see note on 19:1), a poem set in the mournful 3:2 rhythm. Sometimes he picks up a snatch of a song, like the song of the sword (21:9, 10) or the song of the cooking-pot (24:3-5), and he interprets them in his own way. He shows a vivid imagination in his lament over the kings of Israel (19:1-14) and in his description of the sinking of the good ship Tyre (27:3-9, 25-36), as well as in the vision of the valley of dry bones (37:1-10), but on other occasions he shows a remarkable lack of imagination. The one thing he does not lack is a passionate intensity – towards God, towards his message and towards his hearers. Everything was subordinated to his almost overwhelming sense of obligation and responsibility. He was a watchman, and if he failed to warn the people, their blood would be upon him. To this end he was prepared to listen to the prevailing mood among the exiles and to answer their objections. He took up popular proverbs (11:3; 12:22, 27; 18:2) and showed they had no validity. He answered the unexpressed bewilderment that was in men's hearts (18:19,

[1] Examples of phrases frequently used by Ezekiel in a variety of forms are: 'they (you) shall know that I am the Lord' (66 times); 'I will vindicate the holiness of my great name' (8 times); 'I (the Lord) have spoken (and I will do it)' (49 times); 'as I live, says the Lord' (15 times); 'I will scatter you among the nations and disperse you through the countries' (9 times); 'I will gather you out of the countries . . .' (10 times); 'I will pour out my wrath (satisfy my fury) upon you' (16 times); 'the word of the Lord came to me' (49 times); 'because . . . therefore . . .'(37 times).

25 ; 20:32). In short, he combined in a unique way the priest's sense of the holiness of God, the prophet's sense of the message that had been entrusted to him, and the pastor's sense of responsibility for his people.

III. HISTORICAL BACKGROUND

The early period of Ezekiel's life saw the ending of the dominance of the Assyrian Empire, a brief interim spell of Egyptian influence in Judah's affairs and then the growing control of Babylonian kings over Near Eastern politics. The kings of Judah under whom he lived were :

Josiah	640–609 BC
Jehoahaz	609 BC
Jehoiakim	609–597 BC
Jehoiachin	597 BC
Zedekiah	597–587 BC

Josiah's extensive programme of Temple repairs and religious reformation is well known to every reader of the Old Testament (2 Ki. 22:1 – 23:30 ; 2 Ch. 34 ; 35). His reign was a watershed in Judah's spiritual development. Although his reforms were based on the finding of the book of the law during the reconstruction work on the Temple (almost certainly this was Deuteronomy in whole or in part), his freedom to carry them through was partly due to political considerations. In the Ancient Near East vassalage frequently involved the inferior partner in an obligation to accept the worship of the overlord's gods, as well as the payment of tribute or other dues. Thus the cult of astral deities or the setting up of idols by earlier kings of Judah was often a mark of submission to Assyrian authority. Religious reformation was therefore not simply an internal act, born out of spiritual awakening, but it could be interpreted as a rebellious move against the patronage of a powerful ally. It was Assyria's weakening influence which allowed Josiah to carry through the reforms which both his own desires and the discovery of the long-neglected scroll encouraged him to do.

Assyria's collapse may be dated by the fall of Nineveh in 612 BC, and Babylonian supremacy was sealed seven years later by Nebuchadrezzar's crushing defeat of the Egyptian army at Carchemish on the Euphrates in 605 BC. Between these dates there took place the mysterious death of the ill-starred Josiah at the hands of Pharaoh Necho II of Egypt. The AV account (2 Ki. 23:29) suggests that Necho was going to fight *against* Assyria, and it is a mystery why Josiah should have wanted to oppose him on Assyria's behalf. From the Babylonian Chronicle,[1] however, we know that Egypt was going *to the aid of* Assyria against the Babylonian menace, and this is reflected in the RSV translation of this verse, and so the problem changes to why Josiah should have taken an apparently pro-Babylonian stand. It is unlikely that he was already in alliance with Babylon and so we can only suppose that he felt that an Egyptian victory would do more ultimate harm to Judah than a Babylonian one. Anyway, his suicidal action cost him his life and Jehoahaz, his son (also called Shallum), became king in his place. Necho's campaign against Babylon was unsuccessful and so, in an effort to establish his hold on Syria and Palestine, he had Jehoahaz deported to Egypt after a reign of only three months,[2] and replaced him with his brother, Eliakim. At the same time he demonstrated his authority and Eliakim's vassalage by giving him the throne-name of Jehoiakim and by laying a heavy burden of tribute upon the land (2 Ki. 23:31–35).

Jehoiakim was a thoroughly irresponsible ruler as far as his people were concerned and he earned Jeremiah's utter contempt, especially for his grandiose scheme for palace improvements and the imposition of forced labour to carry it through (see Je. 22:13–19). The religious reforms of Josiah were allowed to lapse, no doubt encouraged by that good king's tragic death, which must have seemed to many to

---

[1] The Babylonian Chronicle is a reliable, factual account of the annals of the Babylonian Empire from 626 to 539 BC. The parts which are extant cover the years 626–622, 610–594, 556, 555–539 BC, and they frequently shed light on Old Testament chronology. Some relevant sections are to be found in *DOTT*, pp. 75–83.

[2] For an elegy on Jehoahaz, see Je. 22:10–12; Ezk. 19:2–4.

have been a contradiction of the faith he had stood for, and all kinds of idolatrous practices crept back into Jerusalem life. The pagan cults referred to by Ezekiel in 8:1–18 were but the continuation of a movement which began with Jehoiakim's accession. In Jehoiakim's fourth year Necho's army, which had been maintaining a cautious watch on the northern frontiers of Syria near Carchemish, was completely crushed, first at Carchemish (605 BC) and then again when in full retreat at Hamath. Shortly afterwards Jehoiakim became tributary to Nebuchadrezzar (2 Ki. 24:1), but at the first sign of weakness on the Babylonians' part (an indecisive battle between Necho and Nebuchadrezzar in 601 BC caused the latter to return home to reorganize his army), the Judean king rebelled. He was allowed only a temporary respite. While Nebuchadrezzar was busily occupied dealing with other troubles, he sent smaller contingents of his forces, along with raiding bands from his Syrian, Ammonite and Moabite vassals (2 Ki. 24:2; Je. 35:11), to harry Judah. Then in December 598 BC he moved with all his army on Jerusalem. At the same time Jehoiakim died, possibly by assassination,[1] and his eighteen-year-old son, Jehoiachin (also called Coniah or Jeconiah, Je. 22:24, 28; 1 Ch. 3:16), had to choose between resistance or surrender. The expected help from Egypt failed to materialize (2 Ki. 24:7) and after a three months' siege the young king gave himself up on the second day of Adar 597 BC, *i.e.* 16th March. Together with the queen mother and the palace retinue, and all the leading citizens of the land (the princes, the mighty men of valour, the smiths and the craftsmen are specifically mentioned; 2 Ki. 24:14), he was taken into captivity to Babylon where he apparently lived out his days. Only one further reference is made to him, in 2 Kings 25:27–30, which concluded the account of the monarchy by adding that in his thirty-seventh year of exile, the accession year of Evil-merodach king of Babylon (*i.e.* Amel-marduk, 562–560 BC), he was freed from prison or

[1] Jehoiakim died before the Babylonian armies reached Jerusalem, and the statement in 2 Ch. 36:6 may indicate that he was kidnapped by a pro-Babylonian party.

house arrest, as it more likely was, and was made a life pensioner at the king's table.

A remarkable shaft of light was thrown on Jehoiachin's captivity by the discovery by R. Koldewey of a large number of cuneiform tablets stored in the palace vaults of Babylon not far from the Ishtar Gate. These appeared to be records of rations of oil and barley issued to prisoners by the chief store-keeper. Although discovered at the beginning of the century and brought back to the Kaiser Friedrich Museum in Berlin, it was not until the mid-1930s that an Assyriologist, E. F. Weidner, began to read and translate them. In the course of this work he came upon the name *Ya'u-kinu*, Jehoiachin, and the identification was confirmed by the description 'king of the land of Yahudu'. The ration-tablet conveys little information by itself,[1] but the significance lies in the description of Jehoiachin as king. Apparently he was still regarded by the Babylonian administration as the rightful claimant to the throne, and Zedekiah was thought of as nothing more than a temporary regent. If this was so (and one of the tablets mentioning Jehoiachin's name can be dated in 592 BC,[2] *i.e.* in Zedekiah's time), it gives added grounds for the exiles' confident expectation that his return to Judah and their repatriation were imminent.[3] It also helps us to understand why Ezekiel, while not sharing the exiles' optimism, rejected Zedekiah's kingship, scrupulously avoiding giving him the title of king (*melek*), and dating all his oracles by the exile of 'King Jehoiachin' (so described in 1:2).

Back in Judah Zedekiah the brother of Jehoiakim, who had been appointed puppet-king in Jerusalem, was a weakling and quite unable to cope with the political cross-currents of his time. Although he was the Babylonian nominee and owed allegiance to Nebuchadrezzar, there were strong pro-Egyptian forces at work encouraging him to rebel. One of his advisers was Jeremiah, whose advocacy of a policy of sub-

---

[1] For a translation and assessment of it, see *DOTT*, pp. 84–86.

[2] W. F. Albright, 'King Joiachin in Exile', *BA*, V, 1942, pp. 49–55.

[3] This expectation was also held in Jerusalem and was fostered by the words of prophets like Hananiah (Je. 28:1–4).

mission to Babylon earned him much popular hatred. Zedekiah attempted to protect him, but the description of his efforts given in Jeremiah 37 and 38 indicates that the real power lay with the war party and the king's power was severely limited. A political crisis occurred early in his reign when there was apparently a move on the part of Judah's neighbours (Moab, Edom, Ammon, Tyre and Sidon were involved)[1] to unite in rebellion against Nebuchadrezzar, but this was strongly opposed by Jeremiah and appears to have come to nothing.[2] Eventually, however, public enthusiasm for revolt was fanned by the political hotheads and, with the support of Egypt's Pharaoh, Psammetichus II (593–588 BC), Zedekiah rather unwillingly took the plunge.[3]

Retaliation was swift. By January 588 BC the Babylonian army was at the gates of Jerusalem, and before long only Lachish and Azekah, of all Judah's fortified cities, were still resisting. In a collection of letters, written both to and from the garrison commander at Lachish and discovered there in 1935, the fall of Azekah is vividly described.[4] In the summer of 588 the approach of an Egyptian army caused a temporary lifting of the siege of Jerusalem but it was soon driven back and the siege was resumed.[5] In July 587 the walls were breached and Zedekiah took the opportunity to make his getaway, but he was overtaken near Jericho and carried

[1] Je. 27:2ff.

[2] The rebellion may well have been prompted by news of the revolt in Babylonia in 595/4 BC, in which many of Nebuchadrezzar's troops had to be put to death before it could finally be quelled. If that is so, Zedekiah's visit to Babylon in 594/3 BC (Je. 51:59) may have been to allay suspicions and to affirm his personal loyalty to the king.

[3] The only other country which supported the revolt was Tyre, and it is noteworthy that Ezekiel's strongest condemnations were directed against Egypt and Tyre (Ezk. 26–32). The gloating over Jerusalem's fall, which Ezekiel attributed to Ammon, Moab, Edom and Philistia (Ezk. 25), may be a hint that these countries had either withdrawn from the rebellious alliance or had actively sided with Nebuchadrezzar when they saw how events were going.

[4] These letters provide fascinating contemporary records of events in Judah at this time and should be read in *DOTT*, pp. 212–217. In his Tyndale lecture, *The Prophet in the Lachish Ostraca* (1946), Professor D. Winton Thomas discusses the evidence for identifying the prophet referred to in the letters with Jeremiah.

[5] See Jeremiah's warning of this in 37:5–10.

prisoner to Riblah, Nebuchadrezzar's battle headquarters. His punishment was to watch his sons killed and then to have his eyes gouged out and to be taken in chains to Babylon where he died. A month later Jerusalem was burnt to the ground to the accompaniment of further executions of civil and military leaders, and a further deportation to Babylon.

What little there was left of Judah was incorporated into a Babylonian province and a member of Zedekiah's cabinet, Gedaliah, was appointed governor. As his father, Ahikam, had once saved Jeremiah's life (Je. 26:24), it is not impossible that Gedaliah too was a friend of Jeremiah's and had supported him in his policy of appeasement to Babylon. This would account for his nomination to his new office, but he was regarded by many as a collaborator with the enemy and before long (it may have been a few months or a few years) he was assassinated at Mizpah by a group of men under Ishmael, a member of the royal family. This was the signal for a general exodus from Judah, probably through fear of reprisal; and much against his will Jeremiah was taken with these political émigrés to Egypt where he ended his days (Je. 40–44).

Before attempting to fit Ezekiel's chronology into this historical survey it is worth asking the question why Jeremiah and Ezekiel make no explicit reference to each other. Although separated in distance they were both outstanding men in the same sphere of prophetic religion, they dealt with similar themes and frequently their teachings coincided or overlapped quite remarkably. Some have suggested that the two men were opposed to each other, that Jeremiah classed Ezekiel with prophets in exile like Ahab the son of Kolaiah and Zedekiah the son of Maaseiah, whom he roundly condemned in 29:15, 20–23, and that Ezekiel's criticism of the leaders in Jerusalem concealed an allusion to Jeremiah. But the evidence for this is totally lacking. That two contemporary prophets should fail to name each other need cause no surprise : Amos and Hosea, Isaiah and Micah, Haggai and Zechariah, are additional examples of silence without any implied animosity. It seems to the present writer that these two prophets of the exile betray their knowledge of each other by numerous allusions to the other's teaching, or at least to the same themes which occupy the other's attention. Both of them seemed to be taking a lone stand for the truth, one in Jerusalem and the other in Babylon : they both insisted that the future of Israel lay with the exiles and not with those left behind in Jerusalem ; they both rejected the fatalism of those who quoted the proverb about the fathers eating sour grapes and the children's teeth being set on edge ; they both inveighed against the shepherds of Israel who failed to care for the flock ; they both emphasized the principle of individual retribution and the need for individual repentance ; they both looked forward to a lengthy exile, followed by a restoration under godly leadership ; they both spoke in terms of a new covenant which would be inwardly and personally appropriated ; and they both spoke against the false prophets who prophesied peace when there was no peace.

These parallels and similarities between Jeremiah and Ezekiel do not answer the question that was originally posed, but they do suggest that the two men were almost certainly aware of each other's existence and probably in sympathy with each other. If, of course, a Palestinian setting for Ezekiel's ministry were postulated, the problem of their ignoring each other, while living and preaching as near neighbours to each other, would be considerably aggravated, but we have already rejected that possibility on other grounds. Finally, we must remember that while we know by name only these two great prophetic personalities of the exile, along with the names of a few shadowy figures like Uriah (Je. 26:20–23) and Hananiah (Je. 28:1–17), there must have been scores of men in Israel who claimed to be prophets, and it would not always have been easy for the true to be distinguished from the false. Among these there were doubtless a few of the calibre of Uriah, but many others would have been of Hananiah's sort at whom chapters like Jeremiah 23 and Ezekiel 13 were directed. We must therefore beware of drawing unwarranted conclusions from slender evidence, and we must also be careful not to build major problems out of instances where the Bible appears to have no comment to make.

Ezekiel's chronology

Ezekiel is unique among the Old Testament prophets for his orderly sequence of dates for many of his oracles. These may be tabulated in the following chart:

Reference	Event described	Ezekiel's date [1]			Date by Julian Calendar [2]		
		Day	month	year	Day	month	year
1: 1	Ezekiel's call	5	4	30 }			
1: 2	Ezekiel's call	5	(4)	5 }	31	July	593
8: 1	Vision of idolatry in Jerusalem	5	6	6	17	Sept.	592
20: 1	Deputation of elders	10	5	7	9	August	591
24: 1	The siege begins	10	10	9	15	Jan.	588
26: 1	Oracle against Tyre	1	(11)	11	12	Feb.	586
29: 1	Oracle against Egypt	12	10	10	7	Jan.	587
29:17	From Tyre to Egypt	1	1	27	26	April	571
30:20	Pharaoh's broken arm	7	1	11	29	April	587
31: 1	Oracle against Pharaoh	1	3	11	21	June	587
32: 1	Lament over Pharaoh	1	12	12	3	March	585
32:17	Pharaoh in Sheol	15	(12)	12	17	March	585
33:21	'The city has fallen'	5	10	12	8	Jan.	585
			or better				
		(5	10	11)	19	Jan.	586
40: 1	Vision of the new Jerusalem	10	1*	25	28	April	573

*lit. 'beginning of year'

It will be seen from this chart that if one abstracts the collection of oracles against the nations (25–32), which incorporates no fewer than seven of the fourteen dates, the remaining dates are in a precise, logical order. This is true whether one follows the MT on the news of the fall of Jerusalem (33:21) or emends 'the twelfth year' to 'the eleventh year', as seems preferable (following Albright, Howie). Of the dates in

[1] Dates in brackets are those which have been assumed in the commentary where MT is not explicit or where variants occur.

[2] These dates are based on the tables given in R. A. Parker and W. H. Dubberstein, *Babylonian Chronology, 626 BC – AD 75* (1956), p. 26. They must not be taken too dogmatically because they assume questions on which there is more than one interpretation. For instance, we cannot be sure whether Ezekiel followed a calendar which ran from autumn to autumn or from spring to spring. The dates given above assume that we are dealing with a vernal calendar.

chapters 25–32, two have no mention of a month (26:1; 32:17), but the oracle following 26:1 presupposes that Jerusalem has fallen and it must therefore be dated later than the date given at 33:21, and the suggestion to supply the eleventh month seems not unreasonable. This makes the oracle against Tyre come less than a month after the news of Jerusalem's fall had reached Tel Abib. The oracles against Egypt are in chronological sequence with the exception of 29:17, which is manifestly an afterthought inserted deliberately at that stage in the sequence, and of 32:17, though if the omitted month is taken to be the twelfth, this too fits in to the ordered pattern.

The problem outstanding is the interpretation of the thirtieth year in 1:1. Many scholars have resorted to textual emendation, the most well known being that of Herntrich,[1] who emended it to the third year, and he has been followed more recently by C. F. Whitley.[2] Bertholet's suggestion that it should be emended to the thirteenth year, in which he has been followed by Auvray and Steinmann,[3] is related to his reshaping of Ezekiel's ministry so that the vision marked the inauguration of the second (Babylonian) period, but he has been strongly refuted by both Fohrer and Zimmerli. Those who have sought to understand the text as it stands have suggested (i) that it was the thirtieth year after Josiah's reformation, *i.e.* about 591 BC; (ii) that it was the thirtieth year of Ezekiel's age, an idea going back to Origen; (iii) that it was the thirtieth year of the exile of Jehoiachin, and that the reference was not to Ezekiel's inaugural vision but to the date of final editing or compilation of the whole book (so Berry,[4] Browne,[5] Albright,[6] and Howie).

The first of these suggestions may be discounted because there is no evidence for any similar dating from an event,

[1] Herntrich, p. 63.
[2] C. F. Whitley, 'The "thirtieth" year in Ezekiel 1:1', *VT*, IX, 1959, pp. 326–330.
[3] J. Steinmann, *Le prophète Ezéchiel et les débuts de l'exil* (1953).
[4] *JBL*, LI, 1932, p. 55.
[5] L. E. Browne, *Ezekiel and Alexander* (1952), p. 10; but he interprets the whole book as a late fourth-century commentary on Alexander's campaigns, and the thirtieth year is dated from the succession of Artaxerxes III.
[6] *JBL*, LI, 1932, p. 96.

however important, without specific reference being made to it. The mention of the reign of King Jehoiachin in 1:2 indicates that if the thirtieth year from Josiah's reform was intended, the editor missed the point, and if he failed to understand it we wonder if any contemporary reader would have been more successful. [1]

The arguments for the 'year of compilation' theory are attractive and fit well with the later pattern of dates, viz. the twenty-fifth year for the vision of 40–48, and the twenty-seventh year for the prediction of Nebuchadrezzar's advance on Egypt after his failure at Tyre. There being no point of reference given in the text, it seems highly reasonable to infer the same point of reference as is applied to all the other dates in the book. The arguments for this interpretation are well put in Howie's monograph. [2] On the other hand, they demand a modest rewriting of verses 1–3 of Ezekiel 1, and they reject the editor's effort at harmonization in his reference to the fifth year of Jehoiachin in 1:2. If Howie is right, the editor could not have been Ezekiel himself (as he supposes), for the muddle of the dates in verses 1 and 2 would have been too apparent for an intelligent compiler to allow. As it has come down to us 1:2 can be no other than an explanatory gloss on the unattached date in 1:1 and, what is more, the problem of 1:1 must have been so fully recognized by the editor that it did not even cross his mind that it referred to the compilation of Ezekiel's oracles in the thirtieth year of Jehoiachin's exile. To the editor, at any rate (and we can get no nearer to our original source than him), the thirtieth year and the fifth year of the exile were identical.

We are left therefore with the possibility either that these numbers represent two alternative systems of dating, [3] an idea which has attracted little or no support from present-day

---

[1] The same objection must also apply to variants of this theory, *e.g.* that it was the thirtieth year of Jehoiachin's life (Snaith, *ET*, LIX, 1947–48, pp. 315f.); or of Manasseh's reign (C. C. Torrey, *Pseudo-Ezekiel and the Original Prophecy* (1930), pp. 63f.); or of a Jubilee period (S. Fisch, *Ezekiel*, *Soncino Bible*, 1950, p. 1).

[2] C. G. Howie, *The Date and Composition of Ezekiel* (*JBL* Monograph Series IV, 1950).

[3] So Cooke, pp. 3f., following Begrich.

specialists in Old Testament chronology, or that the thirtieth year was Ezekiel's thirtieth year. This has much to be said for it. First, it is *prima facie* most likely that when a personal reminiscence is being recorded in the first person singular any reference to a particular year, unless otherwise described, would signify the year of the writer's age. Secondly, there is the evidence of Genesis 8:13 that this was an acceptable form of Hebrew expression.[1] Thirdly, there is good reason to suppose that the thirtieth year of a man's life was the age when he could assume the full duties of the priesthood. This is argued on the grounds that the same was true for the Levites, according to Numbers 4:3 and 1 Chronicles 23:3, though there were stages of preliminary training for the work dating from the twentieth[2] and the twenty-fifth years.[3] The evidence of later Judaism is strangely silent on the subject of the age of initiation to the priesthood, but thirty recurs as the age of full maturity and it is not without its significance that thirty was the age of our Lord at His baptism and the commencement of His ministry.[4] If this is so, the significance of his thirtieth year, in Ezekiel's autobiographical introduction, would not be lost on his readers and something of the pathos of his disappointed hopes of Temple service would come through. It may therefore be assumed that it was by way of compensation for his loss of privilege through the exile that the Lord called Ezekiel to the ministry of prophet and watchman in the fifth year of King Jehoiachin.

IV. THE MESSAGE OF EZEKIEL

The total impact of a book is often much more than the message intended by the author, and by the same token the message that the book of Ezekiel contributes to God's revelation in Holy Scripture is much more than Ezekiel's bare

---

[1] 'In the six hundred and first year, in the first month, the first day of the month, the waters were dried from off the earth.' The reference is to Noah's life, as 7:6 and 7:11 make clear. I am indebted to S. G. Taylor, *Tyndale Bulletin*, 17, 1966, pp. 119f. for this reference.

[2] 1 Ch. 23:24.   [3] Nu. 8:24.   [4] Lk. 3:23.

words to his fellow-exiles. If it were nothing more than that, we could sum up his teaching in two phrases : *God will destroy* and, after 587 BC, *God will restore and rebuild*. But to relate this to the needs of men and nations today, as is the task of biblical exposition, one must look beneath the surface at the underlying principles of the nature of God and of His dealings with men, which the prophet appreciated and applied in the way that he did to the situations of his own time. For the Old Testament prophet was essentially an interpreter, applying what he knew of God's nature and laws to the social, political and religious conditions of the day. His was therefore a hazardous task. He had to weigh up facts and draw the right conclusions. He had to speak fearlessly, knowing that he could well be opposed or misunderstood. He had to speak loudly and memorably, for his communication problems were far greater than ours are today. Above all, having few precedents to go on and no Bible to hide behind, he had to make doubly sure that the words he spoke were not his but the words of Him that sent him. And he had to do all this against the background of the words of other men who professed to be prophets but who were chanting out their oracles without the authority that came from experiencing the word of God within themselves.

Much of Ezekiel's language is repetitive. This sometimes makes for tiresome reading, but it helps to highlight his recurrent themes. Five of these have been chosen for comment here. Like the stars that make up a constellation, they are the fixed points around which the pattern of his message can be built up.

a. *The otherness of God*

All prophecy begins with the character of the God who inspires it. In the case of Ezekiel, who was brought up in priestly circles in Jerusalem, it is inevitable that the aspect of God which he felt most deeply was His holiness. This was not a moral quality, though it could and did show itself in moral actions (*cf.* Is. 5:16b). It was a word expressing relationship. The root meaning of *qōdeš* (holiness) is 'to be separate', and so to be cut off from ordinary relationships and use for the sake of serving a peculiar function, one belonging to God, the Holy One. The God of Israel did not simply possess this quality; He *was* it. Everything connected with Him derived holiness from Him. So there could be a holy place where He was worshipped, holy people who acted as His ministers, holy garments that they wore and holy equipment that they used. His name also was holy, His people Israel were holy (even when they were living unrighteously), and the place which He made His dwelling was His holy mountain.

The vision of the Lord riding upon His chariot-throne (1–3) typified this sense of otherness and majesty. It was unutterably splendid, mysteriously intricate, superhuman and supernatural, infinitely mobile but never earth-bound, all-seeing and all-knowing. This is how God revealed Himself to Ezekiel, not by propositions regarding His character but in personal encounter. The rabbis who insisted that no-one under the age of thirty should read this part of Ezekiel's book were conscious that here they were standing on holy ground. So was Ezekiel. Like Simon Peter when confronted by the supernatural ability of Jesus (Lk. 5:8), he could only fall down on his face as one dead. This was the setting for his commission to prophesy, and from it he carried with him through the whole of his ministry a sense of awe and holy fear. It is the true prophet's hallmark in every generation. The false prophet can chatter glibly about God, because he has never met Him. The man of God comes out from His presence indelibly marked with the glory of his Lord.

Ezekiel must have known that the God of Israel was the God of the whole world, as its Creator and Sustainer. His priestly traditions would have taught him that He was the God of all the nations, and their Judge. But there must nevertheless have been great comfort for him and for the exiles to know that this God whose dwelling-place was on Mount Zion could appear to them by the river Chebar, amid all the sordid heathenism and idolatry of Babylonian life. If any Israelite ever felt that he was cut off from his God as well as from his Temple (*cf.* Ps. 137:4), this theophany in Babylon could be taken as a sign that God still cared for His people, even in the punishment of their exile.

b. *The sinfulness of Israel*

Ezekiel was faced with conflicting reactions to the nation's recent disasters. Some felt that the punishment due to them for their disobedience had been exhausted by the events of 597 BC and there remained nothing to do but wait for re-patriation. Others took the fatalistic line and regarded them-selves as the unfortunate heirs to their forefathers' sins for which an unjust God was now punishing them. Most felt a measure of security in that, as they were Yahweh's own people, He could never punish them too drastically without losing face in the eyes of the heathen. A few felt that Yahweh had lost face and had been shown to be impotent before the gods of Babylon. The prophet's treatment of these views, as shown in the commentary on chapters 12–24, demonstrates his ability and willingness to meet his hearers on their own ground and to answer the objections that they raise. But for the most part his aim is to convince the people of their utter unworthiness of any consideration from God, in order to shame them into true repentance.

He does this in two ways, the general and the specific. In the first instance he uses allegory to describe historically the story of Israel's persistent unfaithfulness to the gracious covenant of God. Three passages deal with this: 16:1–63; 20:1–31 and 23:1–49. Each of them schematizes the past in a slightly different way. The parable of the foundling (16:1–63) begins with Israel, or perhaps Jerusalem, as an unlovely outcast child ('weltering in your blood'), but as she grew to maidenhood and reached the age of love the Lord entered into a covenant with her, purified and beautified her, and lavished queenly riches and honours upon her. In return for this, Israel trusting in her beauty played the harlot with foreigners and despised her divine benefactor. Chapter 20 sees Israel's history as a cycle of disobedient acts each followed by a gracious decision of God not to punish but to withhold His hand. It is remarkable for its repeated phrase, 'I acted for the sake of my name, that it should not be profaned in the sight of the nations among whom they dwell' (20:9, 14, 22). God's action in revealing Himself to Israel, making a covenant with them, and even chastening them, was initially for their benefit ('that they might know that I am the Lord', *etc.*; 20:12, 20, 26), but ultimately His dealings with Israel looked beyond that nation's own interests to the concern that God's name should be known and respected the whole world over. This was a doctrine which put Israel's election-pride firmly in its place. Finally the allegory of the two sisters (23:1–49) discounts even the possibility of Israel's original innocence. Oholah and Oholibah played the harlot in Egypt in their youth. They could hardly be described as fallen women because they had never been anywhere but in the gutter. Their only characteristic was an insatiable appetite for fornication, and their punishment would be correspondingly complete.

The intention of these surveys was to shame and to horrify. If scholars are right in supposing that a regular feature of Israelite worship was a liturgical recital of the sacred traditions of the past, the 'wondrous works' (*niplā'ôṭ*) of the Psalter, then Ezekiel could almost be accused of parodying them with these monstrous distortions of his. But the closer they were looked at the more evident would it appear that they were not in fact as distorted as some might think. Our Lord's version of Jewish history was no more distorted, and His hearers recognized it as being uncomfortably true to the facts (Lk. 20:9–19).

More specifically, Ezekiel cites in chapter 8 the wrong-doings that he knew to be going on in the Temple. These were of course religious deviations and they included bare-faced idolatry, animal worship, nature worship, and sun worship. Although some features of his description suggest that these may have been typical rather than actual episodes, they nevertheless illustrated the degree of syncretism that was affecting the worship of God in Jerusalem. They also constituted abundant justification for God's decision to punish the people of Jerusalem with a slaughter reminiscent of the

Passover plague (9:5f.) and to rain destruction upon the city as in the days of Sodom and Gomorrah (10:2). Both here and in the three surveys of the past, the sins of Israel have in the main been religious sins. The people have been idolatrous, they have made alliances and played the harlot with foreign powers (and this involved religious subservience as well, as we have seen), they have not fulfilled their covenant responsibilities, they have not kept to the ordinances and judgments which the Lord gave them at Sinai (5:6f.). In a word, they had profaned God's holy name (20:9 ; 36:20–23) ; and because for Ezekiel God was holiness, this was the most heinous sin. In comparison with this, the social sins which Amos had attacked two centuries before get scarcely a mention.

c. The fact of judgment

This was no new doctrine for an Old Testament prophet. Messages of judgment had been the regular output of prophets for many a year. But that very fact made Ezekiel's task more difficult. There was a great deal of difference between threats of judgment and a message that judgment was imminent. This was why Ezekiel felt so acutely his responsibility to act as a national watchman to Israel to give warning of the disaster that was about to strike. God's message to him was that the God who spoke would also act : 'I the Lord have spoken, and I will do it' (17:24 ; 22:14 ; 24:14 ; 36:36 ; 37:14). God had spoken the word of judgment, and men were no longer to shrug it off with the excuse that though the prophets had threatened, nothing had happened so far (12:22), or that it all referred to the distant future (12:27). God's word now was, 'The word which I speak will be performed' (12:28).

d. Individual responsibility

Von Rad[1] has pointed out that Ezekiel's position as a watchman was 'almost contradictory, since it is Jahweh who both threatens Israel and at the same time wishes to warn her so that she may be saved'. The possibility of the salvation of a remnant is frequently held out, even in the predictions of

[1] G. von Rad, *Old Testament Theology*, vol. II (Eng. tr., 1965), p. 230.

destruction (*e.g.* 5:3, 10; 6:8; 9:4), and Ezekiel's intention in acting as watchman is that the wicked man may turn and save his life (3:18). This is more explicitly stated in 18:1–29, where in a context of temptation to fatalism (18:2f.) Ezekiel is at pains to say that every man is treated as an individual by God. What happens to him is not dependent purely on heredity (his father's sins), nor yet on environment (the nation's sins), but is conditioned by personal choice. The choice that matters is commitment to God. So the wicked man can turn from his wickedness to God, proving his commitment by obedience to the commandments, and his wickedness will not be held against him. Conversely, the righteous man has to be warned not to trust in his righteousness as an excuse for playing with evil; if he does so, he is showing that his true commitment is not to God, and his righteousness will not be credited to his account. This is no statement of justification by works; it is saying that a man's life is a matter of his heart. God does not average out a man's life; it is the direction of his commitment that counts. And basic to Ezekiel's analysis of the whole issue is that the Lord has no pleasure in the death of the wicked (18:23, 32); He wants him to turn and live.[1]

This is a thoroughgoing individualism which more than outweighs the sense of corporate responsibility and corporate guilt which was typical of much pre-exilic popular thought. It appears again in 14:12–20, where the point is made that no-one can hide behind the righteousness of others, not even of men like Noah, Daniel and Job, in the destruction that is about to fall upon Jerusalem. Salvation will be on a purely individual basis. (Compare the exempting mark that was put upon the foreheads of those who groan over all the abominations that are committed in the city: 9:4.[2]) It does not follow from this that Ezekiel was virtually the inventor of individual religion, the protestant among the prophets, and that every-

---

[1] An excellent exposition of this passage is to be found in von Rad, *op. cit.*, vol. I, pp. 393f.
[2] The relationship between this passage and Abraham's intercession for Sodom is discussed briefly in the commentary, *in loc.*

thing before him was collectivistic. Not only Jeremiah, but many of the individual psalms and the personal experiences of patriarchs and kings bear witness to the reality of individual piety and a personal awareness of God. It was Ezekiel's genius to spell out the application of the principle of individual responsibility in the face of the corporate judgment that was about to overtake Jerusalem. Destruction was coming, but men could repent and be saved. Ezekiel the watchman was also Ezekiel the evangelist.

e. *The promise of restoration*

Although repentance is for the individual, salvation is to be enjoyed by him as a member of a restored community. The new Israel is to be brought to life miraculously by the working of God's Spirit, who alone can make dry bones live (37:5). It will be a community without the old divisions of Israel and Judah to tear it apart (37:17). It will enjoy the blessings of an everlasting covenant, and the covenant watchword, 'they shall be my people, and I will be their God', will be written into its constitution (11:20; 14:11; 36:28; 37:23, 27). At its head will be 'my servant David', the Messiah King (37:24f.). No attempt is made to identify this person and we search the book of Ezekiel in vain for any elaboration of this particular theme. He, however, will be entitled to be called the king (*melek*) of Israel, as well as being its prince (*nāśî'*), a term which in the future Messianic age will have lost its pejorative overtones (*cf.* 37:25; 45:7, *etc.*). He will rule justly and conscientiously, caring for the weak and crippled among the flock (34:23). The land will prosper and flourish, and from out of the sanctuary in the new Jerusalem will flow the symbolical river of life to water the waste places of the earth (47:1–12). All this, however, is but the external aspect of the restoration that God promises to His righteous remnant. Internally, He holds out the offer of a new heart and a new spirit for the individual Israelite, so that he may be made clean from the defilement of his sins and the uncleanness of the exile and may be motivated from within to live after God's commandments (36:24–28). In these words Ezekiel gives added definition to Jeremiah's prophecy of the new covenant (Je. 31:31–34), which he appears to have known about in some detail, and in particular he explains how this hope can be effected through a spiritual transplant, by God's gift of a heart of flesh in exchange for man's heart of stone. The message is clear : man's greatest stumbling-block is in himself and nothing can resolve this problem except the gracious action of God in renewal and spiritual regeneration.[1]

V. THE TEXT

The Hebrew text of Ezekiel has suffered more than most books of the Old Testament in the process of transmission, and the RSV footnotes bear witness to the many occasions on which the translators had to resort to the Versions or to conjecture in order to make sense of a particularly obscure sentence. This is not surprising, because Ezekiel used a number of rare words and architectural terms which later copyists could not be expected to know. It is unwise, however, to correct too readily what may be difficult Hebrew on the basis of a much more intelligible LXX rendering, because we can never be sure that the LXX translator was not improving on his original without adequate grounds for doing so. The LXX remains, of course, an invaluable aid to all who would attempt to find out the best Hebrew text. It represents a translation made into Greek, probably around the end of the third century BC, and bears witness therefore to a much earlier stage in the transmission of the Hebrew text than the MSS from which our English Versions are translated. But before its readings are accepted as superior to those of the later Hebrew text, the scholar must be sure of the following points : (i) he must be sure that the LXX reading is the correct one and has not itself suffered corruption in course of transmission ; (ii) he must judge accurately what the Hebrew text was that lay behind the LXX translation ; (iii) to do this he needs to know the

[1] For a full and penetrating study of Ezekiel's message, which unfortunately appeared after this Introduction was written, see W. Zimmerli, 'The Message of the Prophet Ezekiel', *Interpretation*, XXIII, 1969, pp. 131–157.

capabilities of the LXX translator, *e.g.* whether he knew Hebrew well or only indifferently, whether he translated it slavishly or idiomatically, whether he was not averse to incorporating a theological bias of his own, and so on.[1]

In the case of the LXX of Ezekiel, it seems likely that the translation was done by two or even three hands, though with an over-all editor who produced a unifying effect upon the whole book.[2] These did their job competently, but on a number of occasions they paraphrased instead of translating; they omitted what they considered to be repetitious phrases or inserted explanatory comments on no authority but their own; and there are instances where they altered the translation to make it accord with their own viewpoint. So the need for great care in interpreting the LXX is underlined. In the present commentary, the policy has been one of caution, and emendation on the basis of the LXX has been followed only where the Hebrew has seemed to be either unintelligible or obviously corrupt. The other Versions, Syriac, Old Latin and Vulgate, have only limited value in correcting the Massoretic Text because they are all heavily dependent upon the LXX.

The LXX of Ezekiel is well represented in the main codices, but in recent years particular interest has been focused upon the Scheide papyri, which contain an early third-century AD witness to the Greek of Ezekiel 19:12 – 39:29.[3] An interesting result of these studies has been the suggestion that the unusual form of the divine name in the book of Ezekiel, 'the Lord God' (*'aḏōnāy yahweh*), was brought about by the expansion of an original *yahweh* by scribes who were averse to pronouncing the holy name of God and who inserted *'aḏōnāy* as a guide to the reader on its pronunciation. The pronunciation later became standard without the need for any insertion in the text, but it remained in the transmitted Hebrew text of Ezekiel.

[1] This of necessity begs the basic question of so-called proto-Septuagintal studies, viz. the issue of whether an original LXX text is discoverable or whether a number of parallel recensions have always existed side by side. For a summary of the position, see *OTMS*, pp. 250–252.

[2] See H. St. J. Thackeray, *The Septuagint and Jewish Worship* (Schweich Lectures, 1921); Nigel Turner, 'The Greek Translators of Ezekiel', *JTS*, VII, 1956, pp. 12–24.

[3] For a bibliography of these studies, see *IB*, p. 68, note 77.

ANALYSIS

49

COMMENTARY

I. EZEKIEL'S VISION, COMMISSION AND MESSAGE
(1:1 – 5:17)

a. Introduction (1:1–3)

These introductory verses consist of two distinct statements, one in the first person and the other in the third person. The first verse gives a date – *in the thirtieth year,* but we are left to guess how this is to be reckoned – and describes what happened to Ezekiel by the river Chebar in the phrase *the heavens were opened, and I saw visions of God.* This naturally links up with verse 4 where the content of the vision is described also in autobiographical form. Verses 2 and 3 appear at first sight to be unrelated to their surroundings. They repeat the location of Ezekiel's prophetic ministry, *by the river Chebar*; they introduce a new date, with the same day of the month but a different year, though this time it is anchored in a recognized system of dating; and they describe what happened to Ezekiel, not in terms of visionary experience, but in the more traditional prophetic phrases, *the word of the Lord came* and *the hand of the Lord was upon him.* Some would argue from this that we are dealing here with two superscriptions to the prophet's work which come from different original collections. However, verse 1 is so clearly a part of the chapter that follows on from verse 4 onwards that it is preferable to see this as Ezekiel's own way of introducing the vision which constituted his call, and to take verses 2 and 3 as a parenthetic note, possibly supplied in order to explain the puzzlingly indefinite *thirtieth year* with which the book begins.

As the book has come down to us verses 2 and 3 are integral to the whole, because they provide not only a historical setting for Ezekiel's vision but also a necessary title to the work giving the customary information about the author's identity. This material has been discussed more fully in the Introduction,[1] where we noted that the date was probably the

[1] See pp. 37ff.

thirtieth year of Ezekiel's age which coincided with the fifth year of Jehoiachin's captivity, namely 593 BC. And if we are right in assuming that this was the age at which a priest would have entered upon his duties at the Temple, it is clear that Ezekiel regarded his vision and call to be God's spokesman to the exiles as coming at a crucial point in his life. It was in a sense a compensation for the priestly ministry which the misfortune of exile had snatched away from him. When his moment of ministry was due to begin, God summoned him to another sphere of work. The priest was commissioned as a prophet.

There is no contradiction between the ideas of visionary experience, expressed in verse 1, and of *the word of the Lord* coming to Ezekiel in verse 3. The latter is, of course, the most frequent expression associated with the Old Testament prophet (1 Sa. 15:10; 1 Ki. 12:22; Is. 38:4; Je. 1:2; Ho. 1:1; Joel 1:1). But the Israelite prophet was also a seer (Heb. *rō'eh* or *ḥōzeh*). The first is used in 1 Samuel 9:9 to denote the name formerly given to the *nāḇî'*, 'prophet', but it is by no means restricted to archaic usage : Isaiah uses it in 30:10, and the Chronicler describes both Samuel and Hanani by this term. The second carries more the meaning of 'to see in a vision' and is also used, especially by the Chronicler, as a title for prophets of the past like Gad, Iddo and Asaph. Its use by Amaziah, the priest of Bethel, when he contemptuously told Amos to return to his native land of Judah and to prophesy there ('Begone, you visionary'; see Am. 7:12) is not typical. Indeed, Isaiah's prophecy begins with the words, 'The vision (*ḥāzôn*) of Isaiah . . . which he saw (*ḥāzâ*) concerning Judah and Jerusalem.' The visionary experience was then as natural and as recognized a mark of the prophet as was the compulsive word of the Lord within him. These two aspects of the revelation of God to the prophetic consciousness are to be found side by side in, for example, 1 Samuel 3:21 : 'The Lord revealed himself to Samuel at Shiloh by the word of the Lord.'

On the location of *the river Chebar*, see the Introduction, p. 21.

b. The vision of the Lord's chariot-throne (1:4–28)

The theophany which Ezekiel now describes must have been experienced by him when he was alone on the sandy plain at some distance from the main encampment of the exiles which was his home. This much is indicated by 3:14f., and those verses also illustrate the degree of freedom to wander which he and his countrymen apparently enjoyed in Babylonia.

4. Alone with his thoughts, and doubtless sharing the gloomy views of his fellow-exiles about their separation from the presence of God in Jerusalem, he suddenly was aware of a black storm-cloud gathering in the north. It is possible that in his actual experience he began by observing some such natural phenomenon, from which there developed the supernatural vision of the glory of the Lord which occupies most of this chapter. The physical and visible led into the spiritual and the visionary. Alternatively, the whole thing from beginning to end was a vision experience with no starting-point in reality. At all events, the description of the vision moves from the normal to the supranormal, beginning with a thunder-cloud, black and threatening, with the brightness of the desert sun lighting up its edges and with lightning-flashes streaking across the darkened sky. The last phrase of verse 4 begins to show that this is more than the usual desert hurricane : its appearance is graphically described as being 'like the gleam of glowing bronze from out of the fire'. The rare Hebrew word *ḥašmāl*, used here and in verse 27 and in 8:2, is not *amber* (AV, RV) but some kind of shining metal (*cf.* RSV's *bronze*) : in every case it is descriptive of the Lord's dazzling splendour, and so it prepares the way for the supernatural features of the vision that follow.

5–11. The prophet's attention is first focused on the four grotesque *living creatures* which supported the platform or *firmament* (22f.) on which stood Yahweh's throne. These were basically of human form, which presumably means that they stood upright (*cf.* verse 7 : *their legs were straight*, RSV), but they each had *four faces* looking in four different directions, *four wings* in addition to human hands, and the soles of their feet were like *a calf's*. This last reference seems to have no discernible significance and some translators have therefore re-pointed the word to read it as 'rounded', but that scarcely helps. Possibly the calf typified nimbleness (*cf.* Ps. 29:6 ; Mal. 4:2), or else we must conclude that any meaning it had is now lost on us.

10. The *four faces* represented the highest forms of life to be found among the different realms of God's creation : *man* as supreme came first and faced forwards ; the *lion* and the *ox* were the kings among wild beasts and domestic animals (what the writer of Genesis 1 calls 'cattle' and 'beasts of the earth') ; and the *eagle* was the chief of the birds of the air. The creeping things and the fishes of the sea were not represented ! The living creatures formed a square and, as each faced outwards with its human face, the effect of this symmetrical pattern was that whichever way one looked at the four creatures, a different face was seen from each and so all four faces were visible at the same time from any angle. The one nearest to the viewer would be showing as a man, the one on the left would face him as an ox, the one on the right as a lion, and the creature at the rear would be showing its eagle's appearance. It is tempting to search for some kind of proto-type for these creatures among the composite animal figures carved on Babylonian temples and Hittite city-gates, but there is no evidence for anything more than a general in-fluence from Egyptian and other Near Eastern art-forms with which Ezekiel must have been familiar.[1] Almost certainly the final form is Ezekiel's own, and it reflects his passion for the symmetrical which we shall see again in the architecture of the future temple.

The hollow square which these creatures made up was achieved by their being linked together at their wing-tips. Only two of their four wings were extended for this purpose, the others being used to conceal their bodies (11). In Isaiah 6 the seraphim had six wings, two of which were used to cover the face in adoration, two to cover the feet in modesty and with the other two they flew. In Ezekiel there was no need

[1] The closest comparison which archaeology affords is with the cherub-figures which flank the throne of Hiram, king of Byblos (see *IDB*, vol. 1, pp. 131f.; also *NBD*, figs. 56, 167).

for movement and the motionless outstretched wings simply served as supports for the platform above. Although they were not worshipping Yahweh, the holiness of the divine presence was nevertheless enough to demand that their naked human bodies should be decently covered over. In addition to wings, they also had *hands* which would be put to good use later (10:7). It is best to translate verse 8 with Cooke thus : 'And the hands of a man were upon the sides of the four of them.' The Hebrew bears this meaning and it spares us the necessity of attributing four hands to each creature, which EVV would seem to imply.

12–14. In the midst of the hollow square were the *burning coals* (13), a feature which Isaiah shared in his vision, though his were heaped upon the altar. For Ezekiel, the fire symbolizing judgment was at the heart of God's presence and it periodically flashed forth in bursts of lightning. (*Cf.* Pss. 18:8 ; 50:3 ; and for the reference to the *torches*, Gn. 15:17 ; Ex. 20:18.) The result of having this fiery core was that wherever the creatures went, they *darted to and fro, like a flash of lightning* (14, RSV). However, there was no such thing as independent movement for the creatures : the whole chariot-throne of which they were a part moved uniformly together under the impulse of *the spirit* (12 ; Heb. *rûaḥ*). This word has been variously understood as (*a*) the Spirit of God, (*b*) the wind which brought the great cloud from out of the north, (*c*) the spirit within the living creatures, and (*d*) the 'vital energy or impulse by which God from His throne acted upon them'.[1] All of these meanings can be borne by the Hebrew wording. The similarity of the phrase in verse 20, 'the spirit of the living creatures', suggests that one of the last two meanings is to be preferred. But of these (*c*) implies almost that the creatures moved at their own inner impulse, and this is less likely than that they were motivated by the impulse of God acting within them.

15–18. Beside each creature was a *wheel* and it was this which made contact with the ground. In appearance it was like *chrysolite* (16 ; Heb. *taršîš*), a stone which Petrie identified

[1] Cooke, p. 15.

as yellow jasper,[1] but which most commentators prefer to call 'topaz', following Myres.[2] The ancient Versions translated it as 'chrysolite', and this is followed by RSV, but it still leaves the question of its geological identity unsolved. The *beryl* (AV, RV) is a greenish stone and is quite different. Verses 16b and 17 suggest that each wheel consisted of two wheels, probably solid discs, which bisected each other at right angles, thus allowing movement in any of four directions without being turned. Translate in verse 17 'towards their four sides', *i.e.* the four directions which the creatures faced, and not *upon their four sides* (as AV, RV).

The RSV gratuitously emends the text of verse 18 to translate, *The four wheels had rims and they had spokes*. The Hebrew as it stands means 'As for their rims, height to them and fear to them', *i.e.* they were high and terrifying, a description apparently borne out by their being *full of eyes*. The Hebrew is not easy and the Versions had difficulty in translating it, but the MT can give sense and it is better to accept that than to try to improve on it in the way that many western scholars find irresistible.

19–21. The description thus far prepares the way for what is to follow. The Deity is, as it were, carried aloft on the platform, supported by the representatives of His creation. Man, for all his superiority to the animal kingdom, is one with them in acting as his Lord's guardian and servitor. But he performs his duties without movement and apparently without effort. The wheels move, but the creatures are still, and yet the whole palanquin speeds lightly over the ground in whatever direction the guiding impulse directs. And, as if to show that God is not earth-bound, the chariot-throne can lift itself into mid-air and fly. So effortlessly mobile is the God of Ezekiel's vision.

22, 23. The translation *firmament* is not a good rendering for the Hebrew *rāqîaʻ* in verse 22. It arises out of the Vulgate *firmamentum*, which is a literal rendering of the Greek *sterōma*, which in turn is trying quite correctly to indicate the Hebrew meaning of something 'made firm' by beating or stamping, *e.g.* a hammered piece of metalwork. It usually refers to the curve

[1] *HDB, s.v.* 'Stones, Precious'.   [2] *EB*, col. 4807.

of the heavens, which to an observer on the ground appears like a vast inverted bowl of blue. In passages like Genesis 1:6 ; Psalms 19:1 ; 150:1 ; Daniel 12:3, it clearly has this meaning, but in Ezekiel it has the sense of a firm, level surface or plat-form. In the book of Revelation this same phrase becomes 'a sea of glass, like crystal' before the throne of God (Rev. 4:6). The mention of *crystal* in verse 22 is derived from the LXX, which so renders the Hebrew *qeraḥ*, ice or hoar-frost. The EVV follow LXX, but in fact the accompanying adjective *awesome* (RSV mg.) is more in keeping with 'ice' than with 'crystal', and so it is best to understand what Ezekiel saw as 'something like a plat-form, gleaming dreadfully like ice, spread out over their heads'.

24, 25. As it moved there was a strange whirring sound, as the four outstretched pairs of wings vibrated powerfully. The noise was like a mountain torrent (*many*, RSV, or *great*, AV, RV, *waters*) or like rolling thunder (*the voice of the Almighty*, AV, RV) or like the sound of an army on the move. LXX omits all but the first of these three expressions, but they are graphic similes and convey well the idea of God's awefulness, heard with the ear as well as seen by the eye. In addition to the sound of movement, the prophet also mentions the *voice* of God which can be heard from above the platform. No words are quoted in verse 25, but the God of the vision will later be speaking to Ezekiel and so the sound of a voice is mentioned at this early stage of the description.

26–28. At last, the prophet can lift his eyes upwards to describe what is on top of the platform. He has been approach-ing this with the utmost caution, beginning with the features farthest away, but eventually he comes to describe the throne (like *sapphire*, or 'lapis lazuli', a stone highly prized in the ancient world) and the One who sat upon it. Here either his eye or his nerve fails him. Whereas the four living creatures could be described in detail, all he could say of God was that He had human form and *the appearance of fire* (27). To say even this, however, was incredibly bold, for was not Yahweh invisible and therefore indescribable? It was an idea deeply written into Israelite thinking that no ordinary person could set eyes on God and live to tell the tale. Hagar, Jacob, Moses,

Gideon and Manoah, all had remarkable experiences which proved the rule (Gn. 16:13 ; 32:30 ; Ex. 33:20–23 ; Jdg. 6:22 ; 13:22 ; *cf.* Dt. 5:24), but in their case they met what at first seemed to be a human being who subsequently turned out to be an angel or some other manifestation of God. Their sense of shock was based on being wise after the event and therefore on not having given the divine messenger due deference. With the prophets, however, some kind of experience of God, either purely auditory or, as with Isaiah and Ezekiel, in a vision, was almost a necessity in order to authenticate their later ministry. For Moses, God spoke out of a burning bush (Ex. 3:1–6). Jeremiah had no visual experience, though his call was associated with two messages based on the sight of an almond-rod and a boiling pot (Je. 1:11ff.). Isaiah, however, had a most impressive vision, all of which he recounts (Is. 6), except for the actual appearance of the Lord whose 'train filled the temple'. Ezekiel opens the door a little further and lets God be seen in a human outline but with so dazzling a splendour that nothing more could be seen or said. It is left to Daniel to go all the way and to describe in detail the features of the Ancient of Days (Dn. 7:9ff.).

Is this just another instance of anthropomorphism? Does it indicate that the image and likeness of God in which man was made was in fact the physical appearance, and not his spiritual capacity? Even though Ezekiel knew the early chapters of Genesis and used their language and imagery (especially in chapter 28), there is nothing to indicate that this was so. It was a deeply-held tenet of Israelite religion from Moses onwards that God could not be visibly expressed, and for that very reason idolatry was out. But given the possibility of a theophany, no form but the human form could conceivably have been used to represent the Deity. It was, however, no mere human that Ezekiel saw : His radiance was surrounded by the glory of a rainbow, and the prophet could show his awe in no other way than by falling on his face in the dust before his God (28).[1]

---

[1] For a further comment on the meaning of this vision to Ezekiel, see the Introduction, p. 41.

c. The commission to be the Lord's spokesman to the house of Israel (2:1 – 3:15)

1. The first words that God addresses to Ezekiel appropriately put the prophet in his rightful place before the majesty which he has been seeing in his vision. The phrase *son of man* is a Hebraism which emphasizes Ezekiel's insignificance or mere humanity. 'Son of' indicates 'partaking of the nature of' and so when combined with *'āḏām*, 'man', it means nothing more than 'human being'. In the plural it is a common phrase for 'mankind'. Other examples of this usage are Isaiah 5:1, where the 'very fertile hill' is literally 'a hill, son of oil', and Jonah 4:10, where the Lord says of the plant that sheltered Jonah for so short a time that it 'was a son of a night and it perished a son of a night'. The same construction is reflected in Luke 10:6, where Jesus warned the seventy to stay only at a house where there was 'a son of peace', meaning a man of good will, who would welcome them peaceably.

From this, its simplest and non-technical use, which occurs over 90 times in Ezekiel and is characteristic of the prophet's self-conscious sense of human frailty before the aweful might and majesty of God, the phrase 'son of man' takes on special significance through its use in Daniel 7:13, 14 to describe the personification of spiritual Israel, 'the saints of the Most High' (verse 18). In itself this is not yet a Messianic title, because in Daniel it simply indicates the qualitative distinction between the kingdoms of the world, represented by four great beasts, and the kingdom of the faithful, represented by a human being. But by the time the *Similitudes of Enoch* were written (46:1, 2) the Son of man had come to mean specifically the Messiah. Our Lord's use of the title seems to have taken advantage of the ambiguity between the simple and the technical meanings, so that in one sense He could not be accused of making any overt claim to Messiahship, while in the other sense He did not debar those with the requisite spiritual insight from accepting the fuller significance of His person.

2. Despite Ezekiel's prostration, he was summoned to his feet to hear God's commission. On verse 1, Davidson well comments : 'Not paralysis before him is desired by God, but reasonable service. . . . It is man erect, man in his manhood, with whom God will have fellowship and with whom he will speak.'[1] God's words revived him and 'spirit' entered him – not necessarily *the Spirit*, as in RSV, but spiritual energy which he felt within him, strengthening him and infusing his whole body.

3. Ezekiel's ministry was to be *to the children of Israel, to nations that are rebellious, which have rebelled against me* (RV). The extent of his actual ministry is discussed more fully in the Introduction,[2] where reasons are given to justify the contention that Ezekiel prophesied only in Babylon to the exiled Israelites who were there with him. While it is not impossible that the influence of his ministry could have extended back to Jerusalem, at least before its total destruction in 587 BC, as far as he was concerned the house of Israel was co-terminous with what he saw of it on foreign soil, namely the exiled remnant. If the word *nations* (3, RSV mg.) is not to be omitted (with LXX and Lat.) or emended to a singular form (as with Syr., followed by RSV), it must have some contemptuous significance, because normally it never refers to Israel and Judah but only to the nations of the world, the heathen. This is by no means impossible here, associated as it is with the idea of their rebelliousness against God. It is a characteristic of Ezekiel's message that he saw nothing good in Israel's past history (*cf.* chapters 16 and 23), and so to describe the people as both 'heathen' and 'rebellious' (*i.e.* idolatrous) at the very outset of God's word of commissioning is quite in keeping with the outworking of the prophet's message in the rest of the book. Toy aptly comments that the term 'expresses with peculiar exactness Ezekiel's conception of the national career, which he regards as one unbroken apostasy'.[3]

4, 5. The people are further described as *impudent and stubborn* (4, RSV; lit. 'hard of face and firm of heart'). The first phrase suggests the shameless attitude of the man who will not lower his gaze but prefers to brazen it out ; the second describes the stubborn, unyielding will that refuses point-

[1] Davidson, p. 15.   [2] See pp. 21ff.   [3] Toy, p. 97.

blank to give way even when found guilty. The similar phrase, 'stiff-necked' (lit. 'hard of neck'), is found several times in the Pentateuch (Ex. 32:9; 33:3, 5; 34:9; Dt. 9:6, 13; 31:27) but does not occur in Ezekiel. For the same idea, compare Isaiah 48:4, 'I know that you are obstinate, and your neck is an iron sinew and your forehead brass' (RSV). It appears therefore that Ezekiel entertained little or no hope that he would have a sympathetic hearing accorded him. In his vision God made it clear that only two things were really important. First, that Ezekiel's message was to be *Thus says the Lord God*, the distinctive mark of all true spokesmen of the Lord from the days of Moses to the present time; and secondly, that the consequence of his prophesying was not so much repentance or belief, or even paying attention to his words, but that they should *know that there has been a prophet among them* (5). The faithful witness of the messenger was more important than a successful response from his hearers. A similar forecast was made in the case of Isaiah at his commissioning (Is. 6:9f.), and Jeremiah, even though he was not explicitly warned that the same thing would happen to him, soon learned that he was almost doomed to be disregarded or misunderstood.

6, 7. Ezekiel is scarcely given an opportunity to make excuses for himself, in the tradition of Moses (Ex. 3:11 – 4:17) and Jeremiah (Je. 1:6), for God immediately forestalls any hesitations by giving him an exhortation to take courage (2:6–8), followed by a foretaste of his message (2:9 – 3:3). This in turn is followed by the promise of the power to persevere in the face of opposition (3:4–9). To judge from his subsequent ministry, Ezekiel does not give the impression of being anything but fearless. It is almost as if he is immune to the many human reactions of fear and inadequacy and sorrow that dog most of God's servants. It is therefore all the more illuminating to see the repeated way in which God has to tell him to be free of his natural fears and not to be *dismayed at their looks*. The verb here is a very strong word, meaning 'to be shattered'. And the Israelite exiles are described as *though briers and thorns are with you and you sit upon scorpions*. The prophet's feelings will be painfully hurt by the cruel and rancorous treatment he must expect to receive from the exiles in response to his oracles. But it will be easier for him to bear it if only he realizes that such reactions are entirely in character as far as his hearers are concerned, *for they are a rebellious house* (6, RSV; *though* of AV, RV is misleading).

8–10. Then comes the strange command to *eat* the scroll which in the vision is held out to him. Once again natural hesitancy is forestalled by the words, *be not rebellious,* for disobedience at this stage would identify the prophet with the rebellious house to whom he was to speak the word of the Lord. To be effective Ezekiel had to be different from his hearers at least in this respect. In the event he did obey and so acted in conformity with the Servant of the Lord who could say, 'The Lord God has opened my ear, and I was not rebellious, I turned not backward' (Is. 50:5). The test of obedience was successfully passed.

The scroll *had writing on the front and on the back* (10, RSV), an unusual feature because scrolls were normally inscribed only on the inside. Perhaps it was meant to imply that God had a great deal for Ezekiel to say. The idea is taken up again in Revelation 5:1, but no clue is given to the meaning of this aspect of the scroll's description. Medieval commentators were less reticent. Cooke quotes Nicholas of Lyra as saying, 'The book was written within and without : without in respect of the literal meaning, but within in respect of the mystical meaning that lies concealed beneath the literal (sub littera latentem)' ![1] Ellison's suggestion is more likely, that there was no room left for any additions by the prophet himself. The writing consisted of *words of lamentation and mourning and woe,* which is a fair reflection of the contents of Ezekiel's preaching during the period up to the fall of Jerusalem. But to say that Ezekiel was nothing but a prophet of doom is to draw an unwarrantable conclusion. This, however, is what Hölscher has done on the basis of this verse, denying to the 'genuine' Ezekiel all statements and oracles connected with restoration or hope. See the Introduction[2] for a fuller statement of his views. The point of this description is

[1] Cooke, p. 35. [2] See p. 17.

63

rather to emphasize the contrast between the apparently
unpalatable contents of the scroll and the honey-sweet taste
that it left in the prophet's mouth. This sweetness had nothing
to do with the nature of the contents, but came simply from
the fact that these were the words of God, who makes the
bitterest experience of life sweetly satisfying. Jeremiah
expressed the same thought when he wrote : 'Thy words
were found, and I ate them, and thy words became to me a
joy and the delight of my heart' (Je. 15:16 ; *cf.* also Pss. 19:10 ;
119:103).

3:1-3. The eating of the scroll was associated with the
command to *go* and *speak* the words of God to the house of
Israel. Even though this commission was repeated three
verses later, after the scroll had been eaten, it must not be
thought that the eating and the speaking were two separated
acts. Implicit in the reception of God's word, symbolized
by the eating of the scroll, was the acceptance of the responsibility to utter it at God's direction. The word of God
which was prevented from being uttered would become, as it
became for Jeremiah, 'in my heart as it were a burning fire
shut up in my bones, and I am weary with holding it in, and
I cannot' (Je. 20:9). The true prophet, sent and inspired by
God, invariably had this sense of inner compulsion. In much
the same way Peter and John testified before the Sanhedrin :
'We cannot but speak of what we have seen and heard'
(Acts 4:20).

4-9. The wording of God's charge to Ezekiel in these
verses is at first sight confusing, because it appears to repeat
much of what has already been said in 2:3-7. To understand
it, it must be appreciated that the earlier section constituted
the commissioning of Ezekiel : these later verses represent the
equipping of the prophet with the qualities that he will need
in order to fulfil his commission. At first, God seems to be
saying that Ezekiel's assignment is not a particularly difficult
one : he is going to compatriots and not to foreigners whose
speech would be as incomprehensible to him as his would be
to them. *You are not sent to a people of foreign speech and a hard
language* (5) : the Hebrew is literally 'deep of lip and heavy of

64

tongue'. Both phrases occur once elsewhere : the former is found in Isaiah 33:19, where it also refers to foreign peoples 'stammering in a tongue which you cannot understand' ; the latter is a phrase used by Moses in Exodus 4:10 to describe his own lack of eloquence and translated by RSV as 'slow (of speech and) of tongue'. In the first phrase 'deep' has the meaning of 'unfathomable' ; in the second the word 'heavy' can cover both the idea of 'sluggish, dull' (as Moses professed to be) and also the sense of 'burdensome' and tiresome to be understood.

But having said that, God's words then turn back on themselves and indicate that a commission to preach to barbarians would be a relatively easy thing to undertake, for *Surely, if I sent you to such, they would listen to you* (6). The language is of course metaphorical and there is no need to see here any connection with the events of the Day of Pentecost : in any case Peter's hearers were not barbarians, but Jews of the Dispersion and Gentile proselytes. The words are used to point the contrast between the excusable inability of people of a foreign language to understand and the quite inexcusable stubbornness of Ezekiel's Israelite hearers. The interpretation of this sentence is slightly complicated by variations in rendering the words 'surely, if' (Heb. *'im lō*). Some older commentators, such as Keil, would take it as an adversative : 'Not to many nations . . . ; *but* to them [the Israelites] have I sent thee, they can understand thee.' But this rendering loses the powerful contrast that the EVV retain, and it is doubtful whether the phrase *they would listen to you* can be translated in the way that Keil would want. The RSV is therefore to be followed. The opposition that Ezekiel is warned to expect, however, is not to be regarded either as unusual or as directed against him personally. *But the house of Israel will not listen to you; for they are not willing to listen to me* (7). After so many years of persistent deafness to the voice of God through inspired prophets and through national disasters, it is hardly likely that the people will soften before the preaching of Ezekiel. All God can offer is the ability to withstand them to their face, and accordingly He hardens his face and his forehead.

The repetition of the word *hard* in verses 8 and 9 (Heb. *ḥāzāq*) may be a deliberate play on the prophet's name, for Ezekiel means 'God strengthens' or 'God hardens' (Heb. *yᵉḥezqēʾl*). It was certainly a characteristic mark of his ministry that he was able to outlast his opponents and not to be worn down by their apparent intransigence. To that extent, at any rate, he was well named.

The word translated *adamant* (9) is the Hebrew *sāmir*, which is used frequently by Isaiah meaning 'thorn-bushes'. Unless we are dealing with two separate words, the only connecting link with the present use is that of sharpness, which comes out clearly in Jeremiah 17:1, 'With a point of diamond it is engraved'. From there it is used as a byword for hardness, both literal and metaphorical (*cf.* Zc. 7:12). The word *flint* usually referred to knives made of flint (*cf.* Ex. 4:25; Jos. 5:2f.; Ps. 89:43).

10, 11. In the concluding words of his vision Ezekiel hears his sphere of ministry specifically defined as the people in exile (lit. 'to the Gôlâ, to the sons of thy people'). For all practical purposes the exiles *were* the house of Israel as far as Ezekiel was concerned; and they were *his* people for whom he had a responsibility. He was not to be influenced by their reactions to his words, but he was to declare authoritatively a message that was not his own, *Thus says the Lord God*. At the same time the phrase *all my words that I shall speak to you* allows for the possibility of further revelations that are yet to come to Ezekiel for him to assimilate and to pass on to his hearers.

12, 13. Still in the context of his visionary experience Ezekiel was aware of being *lifted up* by the same divine impulse that had earlier raised him to his feet (2:2). This was no psychic levitation, but a subjective experience of feeling airborne, which was coupled with the audible sounds of the whirring of wings and rumbling of wheels *like a great earthquake* (RSV), which the prophet had noticed in 1:24. The MT suggests that with this great noise there came the sound of a paean of praise, *Blessed be the glory of the Lord from his place* (12, AV, RV). The expression has been retained in Jewish devotions and is to be found in the morning service of the

Jewish Prayer Book, but there are the following strong grounds for not retaining it in the original text : (a) If the words were intended as a doxology uttered by the living creatures, one would have expected some indication to that effect : the words immediately follow *I heard behind me the sound of a great earthquake* (RSV). (b) The natural interpretation of the great noise is the sound of the chariot-throne beginning to move, and so to incorporate some wording uttered from an unspecified source is both unnecessary and unexpected. (c) The phrase has no parallel in biblical Hebrew and is particularly awkward followed by 'from his place'. To translate the benediction almost as a parenthetic insertion and to link 'from his place' with the main sentence, as Keil does, only emphasizes the need for some rearrangement of the text. He translates : 'And a wind raised me up, and I heard behind me the voice of a great tumult, "Praised be the glory of Jahweh," from their place hitherward.' It is therefore best to read the word *bārûk*, 'blessed', as *berûm* (the letters *kaph* and *mem* are easily confused in the old Heb. script) and to translate with RSV, *as the glory of the Lord arose from its place, I heard behind me. . . .*

14, 15. All this took place while Ezekiel was in his state of trance, but with verse 15 we find the prophet returning from the place of the theophany to the settlement at Tel Abib.[1] The effect of his vision had not however completely left him, because he uses phrases like *the hand of the Lord was strong upon me* (14 ; cf. verse 22) which are typical of prophetic ecstasy, and this would account for the seven-day period when he sat among the exiles *overwhelmed*,[2] overcome with a mixture of horror and wonderment at what he had seen and heard.

---

[1] See Introduction, p. 24.

[2] The word is a Hiphil participle from the root *š-m-m*, 'to be appalled', 'desolated'. *GK* describes it as inwardly transitive (§53d) and classifies it with a number of other verbs which express 'the entering into a certain condition and the being in the same'. Keil compares Ezra 9:3f. and translates 'rigidly without moving' and therefore 'motionless and dumb'. Koehler retains the causative force of the Hiphil and takes it as 'causing (his onlookers) to be awe-struck, disconcerted'. But it is far more likely that the verb describes the state in which Ezekiel found himself, and so RSV is to be preferred.

Ezekiel describes his first reactions as he was led away from the scene of his vision with the words *I went in bitterness in the heat of my spirit.* LXX omits the word 'bitter' and translates 'I set off at the impulse of my spirit', but this does little justice to the strong language of MT. Hebrew *mar*, 'bitter', can express fierce temper or anger, as of a bear robbed of her cubs (2 Sa. 17:8); discontentment, as of the Adullamites (1 Sa. 22:2); or wretchedness, as of Job (Jb. 3:20) and Hezekiah (Is. 38:15). Of these possible meanings the associated phrase 'heat of spirit' points to anger as the dominant emotion in Ezekiel's heart. It is not impossible that he was roused to such bitterness by the prospect of being committed to a patently unsuccessful ministry of the word of the Lord. His natural feelings rebelled against his calling and so the hand of the Lord had to be heavy upon him to subdue and control him. The more usual interpretation, however, is to regard this as an example of the prophet's being caught up into the righteous anger of God against His people so that he enters into the burden of the 'lamentation and mourning and woe' which constituted the message of God to Israel (2:10). Skinner merely comments on these verses that Ezekiel was left 'in a state of mental prostration'.[1] This, of course, was perfectly true, and it is confirmed by the use of the word *overwhelmed* in verse 15, but it does not seem adequately to solve the problem of this particular phrase. Davidson is probably right in comparing Jeremiah 6:11 and commenting : 'The prophet was lifted up into sympathy with God and shared his righteous indignation against Israel.'[2]

On the period of *seven days* (15), compare Ezra's experience of sitting in a state of horror until the evening sacrifice (Ezr. 9:4). Job's friends sat with him for seven days and seven nights without speaking a word to him (Jb. 2:13). Saul of Tarsus needed three days without food and vision to recover from his Damascus Road experience (Acts 9:9). Perhaps it is not without significance that seven days was the period for the consecration of a priest (Lv. 8:33) and Ezekiel may have regarded this as the preparation for his ordination to a

[1] Skinner, p. 52. [2] Davidson, p. 21.

prophetic priesthood. Certainly he was not yet ready to open his mouth in prophecy. A period of readjustment was needed as he sat with his fellow-exiles and allowed the vision and the message to sink in. The message that he had received was a horrifying one, of judgment and misery and bloodshed. What made it even more horrifying was that he had to proclaim it not just to the winds, but to real people whom he knew and liked, who had suffered with him on the long journey from Jerusalem to Babylon, and with whom he had learnt to live in the strange new community of the exiles. 'Zeal for God becomes tempered and humanized in actual service' (Davidson).

d. The silent watchman (3:16–27)

16–21. Just as Habakkuk took his stand upon the watchtower (Hab. 2:1), so Ezekiel is appointed as *a watchman* to the people of Israel (17). The expression used is literally 'I have given you to be a watchman', signifying that the appointment of Ezekiel as a prophet to warn the exiles of their impending doom was in fact an act of grace on God's part. The term *watchman* was a common one for the true prophets of Yahweh (*cf.* Is. 56:10; Je. 6:17; Ho. 9:8). Their function was to be alert to the situation around them, to hear the word of God whenever it came to them, and to speak it accurately to the people. Inevitably this meant that the prophets as often as not acted as messengers of judgment to an erring people, and Ezekiel was no exception. His message was about the serious consequences of sin. To the wicked, that is to say, the man who not only did not fear God but lived a life in open defiance of His commandments, his message was *You shall surely die* (18). The righteous man too needed to be warned : if he had fallen away from the path of righteousness he needed warning just as much as the wicked did, and even if he was maintaining his righteousness he still needed the constant ministry of being warned not to sin. The saint needs the watchman's warnings as much as the sinner does.

To say, however, that Ezekiel by his warnings would save

his *soul* (19, 21, AV) is most misleading. The Hebrew word *nep̄eš* has a wide range of meaning, from 'throat' to 'person', but it means 'soul' only in the sense in which we call a person 'a soul'. Hebrew has no knowledge of a soul as a part of a man's make-up. Man was *nep̄eš*, a person, a unity. RSV is therefore right to translate *you will have saved your life*.

What is meant by the *righteous man* (20)? We must be careful not to read New Testament doctrine back into the Old and interpret this in the full light of Pauline justification. The *righteous* (Heb. *ṣaddîq*) was essentially the man who showed by his good living his adherence to the covenant. It went without saying that he was dutiful in carrying out the requisite religious observances, but the 8th-century prophets make it clear that many performed these enthusiastically and yet were far from righteous. However, within the sphere of the covenant community, which included every Israelite there was, some would be counted 'in the right' before the imaginary tribunal of God's justice and so possess righteousness (Heb. *ṣeḏeq*), while others would be condemned and classed with the wicked. There was no easy rule of thumb to guide a man in making this assessment and there could therefore never be anything approaching a Christian doctrine of assurance. To presume upon the covenant was notoriously the first step on the path to condemnation. At its most basic the qualification for righteousness was adherence to the Ten Commandments, the stipulations of the covenant. But in practice these were so little observed, and the cultic requirements of the Mosaic law were given proportionately so much more regard, that the prophets had each to reiterate the underlying moral and spiritual requirements of the covenant for the benefit of an ill-taught generation. So the constant demands of God's righteousness were set forth: 'Wash yourselves; make yourselves clean; remove the evil of your doings from before my eyes; cease to do evil, learn to do good; seek justice, correct oppression; defend the fatherless, plead for the widow' (Is. 1:16f.). Or again, 'Seek good, and not evil, that you may live. . . . Hate evil, and love good, and establish justice in the gate; it may be that the Lord, the God of hosts, will be gracious to the remnant of Joseph' (Am. 5:14f.). Or again, 'He has showed you, O man, what is good ; and what does the Lord require of you but to do justice, and to love kindness, and to walk humbly with your God ?' (Mi. 6:8). This was no new teaching, but a call back to the old covenant requirements of Yahweh, the God of Israel, which stemmed from the days of Moses and Mount Sinai. It was a demand for righteous actions which reflected a heart (*i.e.* total personality, incorporating mind, will, emotions and attitudes) that was humble before God and in a state of peace (Heb. *šālôm*) with Him. In view of this it is clear that righteousness was not thought of as an indelible characteristic : it could all too easily be lost, and then the man's former righteous acts counted for nothing.

The warning that the sinner would *die* had a purely temporal reference. As far as we can see Ezekiel had little or no concept of resurrection, still less of eternal life, and the threat that was inherent in this word of warning was that the wicked man would meet with an early or a violent death. Death that came at the end of a long life was no hardship, especially if a man had children and grandchildren to continue his name after him. But a short life and an untimely end were punishments indeed. If this happened as a result of the prophet's failing in his duty to warn the sinner to turn from his ways, God said, *His blood I will require at your hand* (18, 20). This allusion to the principle expressed in Genesis 9:5f. implies that, just as the blood of a murdered man demanded requital through the next-of-kin taking vengeance on the murderer, so a man dying unwarned would be regarded virtually as the victim of a murder committed by the watchman who failed in his duty. It is of course put metaphorically, but it none the less emphasizes the overpowering responsibility with which Ezekiel was entrusted. The Christian's responsibility to warn a lost generation is surely no less terrifying.

The word *stumbling-block* (20 ; Heb. *mikšôl*), like its New Testament Greek counterpart, *skandalon*, means an occasion for stumbling, either literally or in an ethical sense. It does not here indicate that God deliberately sets out to trip up the righteous and bring him crashing to the ground, but that He leaves opportunities for sin in the paths of men, so that if their heart is bent on sin they may do so and thus earn their condemnation. There is no sense in which stumbling is inevitable : it always involves moral choice, and there was also the watchman's word of warning to point out where and what the stumbling-blocks were.

22–27. Again under the effect of the trance, Ezekiel goes out *into the plain*. The word means literally a 'cleft', and therefore an area between mountains : some would translate it a 'valley-plain'. It may well refer to a specific site which Ezekiel frequented in his periods of solitude, and it was doubtless the place where he was to have his vision of the valley (same word) of dry bones (*cf.* 37:1).

The phrase *the glory of the Lord stood there* (23) sums up, not just a part, but the whole of the vision which the prophet had seen in chapter 1. The abiding recollection was not of the accoutrements of the heavenly chariot-throne, but of the One who sat upon it. Ezekiel also indicates that this was a different location from his original vision *by the river Chebar*. For comment on *the spirit entered into me* (24) *cf.* on 2:2.

It is not clear whether this added vision of the glory of the Lord followed on almost immediately from his commission to be a watchman or whether, between verses 21 and 22, there was a period in which Ezekiel prophesied in accordance with the terms he had been given. If he did so, it would explain the apparent reversal of his commission which the following verses contain. He had spoken God's word of warning ; he had not been heeded ; and so he was now commanded to be house-bound and silent. The difficulty is that the chronology of these early chapters scarcely allows any time for this. The difference between the dates of 1:1 and 8:1 is only one year and two months, and if that has to include the 390 days of his lying on his left side for the punishment of Israel (4:5), there remains little enough time for anything but the briefest ministry as a watchman. It seems therefore preferable to regard 3:22–27 as the final episode in a protracted period of commissioning which lasted some days and in which there were these various high-point experiences, when God spoke to Ezekiel and the course and pattern of his ministry were gradually unfolded. It would be unlikely for a prophet in one theophany to get a grasp not only of his call, but also of his message and the awful responsibility of his task, and of the way in which he was to fulfil it. For Ezekiel all this came by stages, and only when the last stage was reached was he called upon to make his first public pronouncement in the symbolical drama of the siege-works against Jerusalem (4:1).

Those who advocate an abortive ministry between these two sections would argue that the phrase *they shall lay bands upon thee* (25, RV) refers either to physical restraint which was placed upon Ezekiel by his opponents, or metaphorically to the silencing of his oracles by less violent but equally effective forms of opposition. The same kind of interpretation cannot, however, be given to the prophecy of his dumbness and it is therefore better to think of a self-imposed restraint rather than one dictated by opposition to earlier oracles. RSV interprets in this way by taking the verb 'they shall lay' as an impersonal plural, signifying the passive voice, thus : *cords will be placed upon you, and you shall be bound with them*. It is important to realize that both the binding with cords and the dumbness were 'not to prevent the exercise of his vocation, but, on the contrary, to make him fitted for the successful performance of the work commanded him' (Keil).[1] The limitations imposed on him were part and parcel of his message : they were a ritual demonstration to the people of Israel that they were *a rebellious house* (26, 27).

And I will make your tongue cleave to the roof of your mouth, so that you shall be dumb and unable to reprove them (26, RSV). The silence was not intended to be absolute : from time to time God would speak with the prophet and permit him to pass on a message to his people. This was therefore no dumbness of the kind that occurred to Zechariah, the father of John the Baptist (Lk. 1:20). It was to last for a limited time, until the fall of Jerusalem was announced to the exiles some six years later. Then it would come to an end (33:22). Other references

[1] Keil, p. 65.

to it occur in 24:27 and 29:21, but nowhere else. In the meantime Ezekiel had cause to make many pronouncements, some in conjunction with his silent acted messages and others as straightforward oracles. On one occasion (20:3) he refused to answer some elders who came to him 'to inquire of the Lord', but he did not do so without a full explanation of his reasons for not satisfying their curiosity. In other instances where elders came to him to ask his advice there is no suggestion but that they expected him to be able to answer them perfectly normally (*cf.* 8:1 ; 14:1). We have already[1] noted various suggestions to the effect that Ezekiel suffered from a catalepsy or some serious nervous disorder, and we have seen that no such explanation, introducing either organic or psychological malfunctioning, satisfactorily gets over the problems posed by a literal acceptance of these words. It is far more satisfying and realistic to understand this as a ritual dumbness, or a divinely commanded refusal to make public utterances except under the direct impulse of God's word. From that moment onwards, Ezekiel was to be known as nothing but the mouthpiece of Yahweh. When he spoke, it was because God had something to say ; when he was silent, it was because God was silent.

The two Hebrew words, *haššōmēaʿ yišmāʿ*, lit. 'let the hearer hear', or 'he who hears will hear' (27), are the prototype for our Lord's favourite formula : 'He who has ears to hear, let him hear.' The message spoken is calculated to confirm men in their attitude to the God who inspired it : they will either hear it and obey, or ignore it and be condemned. The hearer's response is dictated by his inner being.

e. Four enacted messages (4:1 – 5:17)

i. The siege of Jerusalem (4:1–3). We must imagine that the strange actions which Ezekiel was now told to perform were to be carried out either just inside his house or, more likely, on the open space in front of his doorway. The actions were pointless unless they could be watched by a large

[1] See the Introduction, p. 26.

number of people, and we must suppose that it was not long before the word got around that Ezekiel was doing some unusual things near his home. In a close-knit community like that of the Tel Abib exiles nothing could be kept secret for long. Stories about life in prisoner-of-war camps during the Second World War have shown quite clearly how news could spread like wildfire among thousands of internees. Ezekiel's trance-like state, described in 3:15, had obviously been noted and so it was not surprising that some supernatural or ecstatic pronouncement or sign should follow.

The centrepiece of his silent charade was a large, rectangular, sun-baked *brick* (RSV; AV *tile*; Heb. *lᵉbēnâ*), on which he had drawn the easily recognizable outline of the fortifications of Jerusalem, dominated by the roof-line of Solomon's Temple. This he placed on the sand for everyone to see. Then he prepared to *put siegeworks against it*. How this was done must be a matter for conjecture. To suggest that all the details of verse 2 were drawn upon the one brick seems too unrealistic: for the message of this drama to be understood it had to be on a large scale.[1] More than likely, these were depicted either by the use of models made to surround the central representation of Jerusalem, or simply by markings in the sand which could readily be made to give the appearance of siege-towers, mounds and military encampments.

The word translated *fort* in AV and *siege wall* in RSV is a collective noun, *dāyēq*, always occurring in the singular. It appears in 2 Kings 25:1 (=Je. 52:4), where it seems to mean a chain of offensive towers built around the besieged city. It must be distinguished from the *mound*, *sōlᵉlâ*, which was the rampart of earth 'heaped up' (Heb. root *s-l-l*) outside a city wall so that the besiegers were on a level with the defenders on the walls. Some of the Assyrian bas-reliefs mentioned in footnote 1 illustrate towers similar to the *dāyēq*, manned by

---

[1] Some commentators compare Assyrian sculptured slabs depicting siege warfare (as in *NBD*, figs. 89, 94), but this is not the natural meaning of Heb. *lᵉbēnâ*. If it could be translated 'brickwork', this could of course be an instruction to Ezekiel to depict the whole scene on the outer wall of his house.

archers and sometimes movable and equipped with a built-in battering-ram. (*Cf.* Ezk. 21:22 ; 26:8f.)

When all this was done Ezekiel was told to *take an iron plate, and place it as an iron wall* (3, RSV) between himself and the city. The iron plate (AV, RV, *pan*) was probably the large, saucer-shaped piece of metal which was used by the Israelites for baking bread. When placed upside down over a fire of red-hot embers it soon heated up to form a serviceable, convex hot-plate on which the flat barley-loaf, or griddle-cake (Heb. *'uḡâ*), could be cooked. Ewald understood it as a symbol of the powerful fortifications of Jerusalem against which the siege was laid, in which case Ezekiel was supposed to be representing the besiegers who *press the siege against it*. Alternatively it could have symbolized 'the implacable and iron severity of the siege' (Davidson), but that would still leave the prophet in the role of the besieger. It seems more in keeping with the symbolism of Ezekiel as the Lord's prophet that he was in fact representing Yahweh in this drama, and the iron wall stood for Yahweh's determined hostility towards the holy city. It was God's act to be bringing armies against Jerusalem ; it was Jerusalem's God who had rejected her and would soon bring her to the ground. In this way, not only the symbolical action but Ezekiel's part in it became *a sign for the house of Israel*. This was one day going to happen.

At this stage it is necessary to consider the extent to which Ezekiel's symbolic activity may be classified as sympathetic magic. This is a name given to a recognized form of behaviour of a primitive kind, in which an individual performs certain acts, often with the help of models or effigies, which are intended to produce the effect which the action symbolizes. The crudest form is the method of cursing, known in classical times, which was effected by writing the name of one's victim on a potsherd and then smashing it against a wall.[1] This was not simply a method of venting one's hatred ; it was seriously intended to bring upon the victim the shattering which his name suffered. More sophisticated versions would include burning wax effigies of one's enemies in order to

[1] Compare the Egyptian execration texts; *ANET*, pp. 328f.

destroy them. Many of the practices of sorcery and divination used in ancient Egypt, Assyria and Babylonia followed this principle and, on the basis of the general similarity of Near Eastern culture patterns, some would see the Israelite prophets, who frequently used symbolical acts in the way that Ezekiel did, as being all of a piece with their heathen contemporaries. To do this, however, blurs the distinctiveness of the religion of Israel and ignores the frequent explicit condemnations of sorcery and witchcraft which are to be found in the writings of the prophets (*cf.* Is. 8:19; 28:15; 47:9–13; Ezk. 13:17–23). Such practices were regarded as contravening Yahweh's law because they relied on attempts to coerce psychic forces (and therefore evil spirits) into doing man's will. They were thus a rejection of Yahweh's power and were to be condemned. Now it could be argued that the prophets were effecting good things by this means through the power of God's Spirit, but in practice the distinction would be too subtle for the by-stander to grasp and we must therefore reject it as being contradictory to the prophets' normal teaching. We are left therefore with the much more likely explanation that these actions were signs of what God intended to do and not attempts to bend God's will to what the action symbolized. In Ezekiel's case this kind of procedure was virtually forced upon him by the ritual silence he had to observe.

Examples of other prophets who used symbolical actions to accompany or illustrate their pronouncements are Ahijah (1 Ki. 11:30); Zedekiah (1 Ki. 22:11); Elisha (2 Ki. 13:17); Isaiah (Is. 20:2–4); Jeremiah (Je. 13:1–14; 19:1–10); Agabus (Acts 21:10ff.).

ii. The days of the punishment of Israel and Judah (4:4–8).

It looks very much as if the model of the siege of Jerusalem was set up as a semi-permanent visual aid, which remained while Ezekiel carried on these further actions. Whereas, in the first, the prophet occupied the role of Yahweh with his face set against Jerusalem, in the second he plays the part of his own people and acts as the bearer of the punishment for their sins. This is not to be taken in any way as a vicarious act, as if he could suffer on behalf of his people. It is purely descriptive, and its aim is to show the duration of the punishment of the two nations, and also that Judah as well as Israel will be sharing in it. The sufferings of Israel were apparent : ever since her capital city, Samaria, had been destroyed in 722/1 BC by Sargon II of Assyria, after a three-year siege by Shalmaneser V, Israel had been de-populated and her people scattered throughout the Assyrian Empire. Ezekiel's action now showed that Judah was to suffer similarly, though for a much shorter time.

4. It is not necessary to amend the MT to read with RSV, *I will lay the punishment of the house of Israel upon you.* The emen-dation has no MS support and it does not make the meaning any simpler. As it stands the verse seems to imply that just as the prophet rests the burden of his weight upon his left side, so this is a symbol of the weight of punishment which is being borne by Israel for her sins (so AV, RSV mg.). The symbolism of *upon your left side* was probably helped out by the prophet's lying on the ground in an east–west direction, with his head towards Jerusalem, and facing northwards as if towards Israel while on his left side and southwards towards Judah while on his right.

5, 6. The number of years represented by the 390 days for Israel and the 40 days for Judah presents problems both of the text and of its interpretation. That it is reckoned on the basis of *a day for each year* is straightforward and needs little comment. The same symbolism is found in Numbers 14:34; Daniel 9:24ff. The 40 years assigned to Judah's punishment is a round number and need not be taken too literally. It is clearly reminiscent of the wilderness wanderings. The actual duration of the exile was 59 years, reckoning from Ezekiel's captivity in 597 BC, or 49 years from the fall of Jerusalem. Jeremiah's figure of 70 years (Je. 25:12 ; 29:10) refers not to the period of actual exile but to the period of Babylonian supremacy, *i.e.* from 605 BC, the battle of Carchemish, to 539 BC. (See especially Je. 25:11, 'these nations shall serve the king of Babylon seventy years'.)

But where does the figure 390 come from? The following

points need to be borne in mind : (*a*) In both cases the period of time referred to means the period of suffering for sins previously committed. (*b*) Restoration will not take place until these periods of atonement for past sins have been endured. Only then can it be said, 'Speak tenderly to Jerusalem, and cry to her that her time of service is ended, that her iniquity is pardoned, that she has received from the Lord's hand double for all her sins' (Is. 40:2, RSV and mg.). (*c*) Restoration *will* come eventually (*cf.* 37:16ff.) and it will be simultaneous for Judah and Israel. These considerations lead to the conclusion that the two periods are to be taken as ending concurrently, and the time of Israel's punishment amounts to 350 years alone and 40 years with Judah. Against this it can be argued that Ezekiel's action in lying down on his left side for 390 days, and afterwards (*when you have completed these*) lying for a further 40 days on his right side, hardly fits in with an interpretation which makes the periods concurrent. But we must beware of confusing the symbolical actions with our interpretation of what they represent. They represent total periods : a total of 390 years for Israel's punishment and a total of 40 years for Judah's punishment. Once that has been made clear, as Ezekiel's actions did make it clear, it still remains for us to interpret the historical application of the message to the nations involved. So we must not necessarily insist that the prophet ought to have spent the last forty of his days lying on *both* sides to represent both Israel and Judah suffering at the same time. On chronological grounds, however, this turns out to be more likely. Ellison has pointed out that the difference in time between the dates mentioned in 1:2 and 8:1 is a year and two months. On the basis of a lunar year of 354 days (six months of 30 days alternating with six months of 29 days), this allows only a total of 413 days for the performance of this action. Even allowing that it may have been a leap year, the total can be extended no further than 442 days. This would just, but only just, permit Ezekiel to take 430 days for his actions, bearing in mind that allowance must also be made for the seven days of 3:15 and any other extra days that were needed for his preparations. While thus admitting that it is possible to take the consecutive view of these periods, Ellison in fact opts for the concurrent view in the light of the 390 days mentioned in 4:9. It seems to be the best way out of a difficult situation.

It may be, of course, that we are being unnecessarily literal in our treatment of these verses. Ezekiel's passion for the symbolical can easily encourage the reader to gloss over the realities of the situation and to care little for what, if anything, actually happened. But if he did in fact use symbolical actions to convey his messages, it is important that we try to understand what he actually did and how he did it. This clearly mattered to him, and it mattered to his observers that they saw it accurately and interpreted correctly what he was wanting to say. If we are to do the same, we must cast ourselves in the role of his fellow-exiles, and sit where they sat, and watch his every movement as closely as we may.

Before leaving this section, reference must be made to the reading of the LXX, which has 190 instead of 390 in verses 5 and 9, with a figure of 150 also inserted in verse 4. This clearly presupposes taking the numbers concurrently. Many commentators follow this reading (*e.g.* Toy, Davidson, Skinner, Stalker), arguing that it is both more reasonable and more in keeping with history. Presumably it is calculated from the fall of Samaria, but from there to the beginning of Judah's sufferings in 587 BC is only 134 years, not 150. The figure is nearer if it is taken to the end of the Judean exile at the fall of Babylon in 539 BC: this would give 182 years for the total period. However, the greater accuracy of the second calculation suggests the likelihood that the LXX figure was inserted after the event as a more reasonable correction of a very difficult Hebrew original. The 390 years of the MT are probably intended to go back beyond the siege of Samaria to the very foundation of the separated state of Israel under Jeroboam, the son of Nebat, who caused Israel to sin, *i.e.* to *c.* 931 BC. Whether this whole period of Israel's sin could be regarded as the period of the punishment for her iniquity is a matter of dispute. Neither textual reading is without its problems, and most commentators decide which they prefer according to criteria of probability and interpretation. Let it merely be said that the MT can be interpreted satisfactorily on the lines we have indicated, and that this is probably a case where the principle has to be applied of the more difficult reading being preferable.

7, 8. It would not be possible for Ezekiel to carry out all the instructions given in 4:9 – 5:4 if his hands were permanently tied, as is suggested in 4:8. Either this is to be taken metaphorically or, more likely, he spent a part of every day lying facing the requisite direction with his face towards the model of the besieged city, his arm bared, signifying readiness for drastic action (*cf*. Is. 52:10), and his body trussed with cords. Once he had performed this daily demonstration, he could release himself and do some of the other symbolical acts associated with the siege. Then, presumably, when no spectators were around, he could revert to a more normal manner of conduct within his house.

iii. The famine of Jerusalem (4:9–17). For the whole of the 390 days of Ezekiel's demonstration, he was to limit himself to a stringent diet. Two lessons are here combined : first, that Israel and Judah are to live on famine rations, and secondly, that their diet is to be unclean. There is some confusion in applying these points, because it is not quite clear whether they represent siege conditions within beleaguered Jerusalem or the defilement, as well as the enforced economies, of living under conditions of exile. Wellhausen[1] took the whole section as referring to the siege, which Ezekiel thought would last for 390 days (verse 9). He also regarded the 390 days of verse 5 as an error carried over from verse 9 by mistake, so that what was intended in verse 9 to refer to the days of the siege became in verse 5 the years of the Israelite exile. Verse 13 was then to be treated as a gloss, brought about by this confusion. Cornill reconstructed the text of the whole chapter even more drastically in order to group together the sections which referred to the siege and the exile

---

[1] *History of Israel*, Eng. tr. 1885, p. 273, note.

respectively. The result was that verses 4–6, 8, 9, 12–15 were assigned to a message about the uncleanness of the exile, and verses 1–3, 10, 11, 16, 17 to a message about the scarcities of a siege. Verse 7 suffered the inevitable fate of being deleted as a gloss. As the text stands, however, we must conclude somewhat diffidently that there is no clear-cut answer to this apparent confusion : the poor living conditions of the Israelite exiles in Assyrian territory is intermingled with the horrors of siege starvation and with the defilement of living in exile in Babylon. Perhaps those who watched Ezekiel weighing out his food, measuring his daily ration of water and doing his cooking were just as much at variance in their interpretation of its significance as commentators are today.

9–11. The diet imposed on Ezekiel consisted of a daily meal of *twenty shekels* of bread, made from a mixture of all kinds of grain, the normal *wheat and barley* being eked out by the addition of *beans and lentils, millet and spelt* – anything in fact that would satisfy hunger. The AV *fitches* is based on the Vulgate *viciam*, 'vetches': the Hebrew word is translated *spelt* in RSV (*cf.* Ex. 9:32 ; Is. 28:25) and this was apparently sown and cropped for making into an inferior kind of flour. There was no ritual defilement in the mixing of these grains, so far as we can tell from Leviticus 19:19 ; Deuteronomy 22:9 ; and the Mishnah. With a *shekel* calculated at about 11.4 grammes, this would amount to almost exactly 8 ounces of bread per day. The water measurement of one-sixth of a *hin* would be equal to a fraction over a pint, or 0.61 litres. This is not far short of starvation rations on any reckoning, and it seems incredible that Ezekiel could have lasted on it for over a year. On the other hand, it would not be out of harmony with our interpretation of this passage if we argued that this diet related only to his public demonstrative acts and if we at least allowed the possibility that he augmented it with other foods when nobody was looking!

10. *Once a day* (RSV). The literal translation, followed by AV, RV, is *from time to time*, but this conveys the wrong impression. A similar phrase is found in 1 Chronicles 9:25, which makes it clear that it refers to a recurring action which was to take place at the same time each day. Cooke translates 'at stated times', but this is not sufficiently clear without his explanatory note, 'i.e. at a certain time on one day and at the corresponding time on the next'.

12–17. While the prophet could accept calmly the limitations imposed on his diet, his whole being revolted at the command to bake his bread over a fire of human excrement. This was intended to show the defilement which would come upon the exiles through their being compelled to live and eat in a heathen environment. They would not be able to ensure that the meat they bought or were given had been killed correctly according to levitical requirements, nor were they to know if it had been offered first at heathen sacrifices. (The same problem faced the early Christians in apostolic times; *cf.* 1 Cor. 8:1ff.; Rev. 2:14, 20.) To maintain ceremonial purity under such circumstances was almost an impossibility, and that combined with separation from Jerusalem caused the exiles to be classed *en bloc* as ritually unclean. Ezekiel showed his awareness of the significance of this symbol by expostulating that he, if no-one else, had kept himself pure, certainly as far as unclean meat was concerned (14). As a concession to his feelings, God changed the fuel to *cow's dung* (15), which was a perfectly normal form of firing in the East and remains so to this day. It was probably not regarded as unclean by the Israelites and may have been in regular use among them as well as among their neighbours.

The two kinds of unclean meat mentioned in verse 14, the animal which has *died of itself* and the flesh which has been *torn by wild beasts*, were prohibited because the blood could not have been drained away correctly (see Lv. 17:11ff.; Dt. 12:16). The regulations are to be found in Exodus 22:31; Leviticus 22:8; and Deuteronomy 14:21. The *foul flesh* (Heb. *piggûl*) refers in Leviticus to sacrificial flesh which has turned unclean through being kept uneaten for three days (Lv. 7:18; 19:7), but in Isaiah 65:4 it is used in parallel with pig's flesh, as something inherently unclean. Davidson suggests as its meaning, 'carrion'.

It seems strange that God should command a thing and

83

then just as quickly retract it or modify it. He certainly did not treat the apostle Peter in the same way when he saw the vision of the sheet containing unclean animals let down before him on the housetop in Joppa (Acts 10:14f.). Perhaps the original command was never intended to do anything more than illustrate the uncleanness of their diet, which would never have come over to Ezekiel or his watchers (*cf.* verse 12, *in their sight*; could this have been acted out?), if the cow's dung had been used from the start. At all events, it is gratifying to note the concession that God graciously made to His servant's priestly scrupulousness on this occasion.

iv. The threefold fate of the people of Jerusalem (5:1-17).

Each of the four actions described in 4:1 – 5:4 dealt with a different aspect of the disaster that would shortly befall Jerusalem. First came the fact of the siege (4:1–3), then the duration of the punishment of Israel and Judah (4:4–8), and then the famine conditions of the siege and of the exile (4:9–17). Last of all came the enacted oracle of the fate of the inhabitants of Jerusalem (5:1–4).

1–4. The action which Ezekiel is commanded to perform is divisible into two stages. The first stage is described in verses 1 and 2, and consists of the weighing out of the prophet's shorn hair into three equal parts. When these have been disposed of in the three different ways described in verse 2, the prophet is told, almost as an afterthought, to retrieve a few hairs from the third portion and to treat these according to further distinctive instructions (3, 4). There is no need to conclude from this that Ezekiel's original prophecy consisted of only verses 1 and 2, the rest being secondary material, for all of it is necessary to an understanding of the prophet's message. The symbolism is obvious : a third of the inhabitants of Jerusalem would be destroyed within the city, a third would be killed by the sword in fighting around the city, and a third would be scattered among the nations and would continue to be harried by hostile forces. From among these survivors would emerge the handful of those who would be preserved.

The Hebrew word for the *sharp knife* (1, AV) is the common word for a *sword* (so RV, RSV), but it needed a sharp blade for the two uses to which it was to be put. First, it had to be used *as a barber's razor* (RV, RSV; not a separate implement, as AV implies) for cutting the prophet's hair and beard. Shaving the head was a mark of mourning (Is. 15:2; Je. 48:37) or of disgrace (2 Sa. 10:4), and maybe both nuances are incorporated in the symbolism here. Secondly, it was to be used to chop up the portion of hair *round about the city* (2, RSV) and it was to be brandished after the hair that was scattered to the wind. It takes little imagination to see Ezekiel in action. First, whetting the sword-blade to a sharp cutting-edge while the crowd gathered to see what new act was going to be performed. Then the horrified gasp from the bystanders as he went to work with his crude razor, followed by the meticulous weighing of the hair in the balances. Finally when all the hair was burnt or chopped up small or thrown to the winds, he would put down his sword and go looking on the sand for a few remaining hairs to tuck into the fold of his garment, and even some of these would be thrown into the fire that was burning beside the brick that represented Jerusalem.

The skirts of your robe (3, RSV; more literally, *in thy skirts*, AV, RV) are the lower extremities of the long, ankle-length tunic (Heb. *kuttōnet*), which could be gathered up and tucked into the girdle to form a pouch for carrying things (*cf.* Hg. 2:12). The meaning of verse 4a is that some of those who escape the fall of the city will nevertheless perish with it, though not necessarily in it, *i.e.* they will share the same fate as those destroyed in the city's overthrow. The added sentence, *from there a fire will come forth into all the house of Israel* (4b), must in the context refer to further devastation flaming forth from Jerusalem, possibly a reference to the debased remnant who were left in the vicinity of the destroyed city and who had to be purged out after the return from exile (see Ezr. 4:1-4).[1]

---

[1] Keil, however (pp. 85f.), argues plausibly for Kliefoth's view that the fire was a fire of purification and not of judgment. He compares the tenor

5-17. These verses contain an explanation of the symbols that have been acted out and a justification for God's stern dealing with His people. The phrase, *This is Jerusalem* (5), takes us back to 4:1 and the symbol of the engraved tile. Her situation *in the centre of the nations* reflects not only the actual layout of the siege and the armies that surrounded her, but also her place theologically as the centrepiece of God's favour in the world and the object of His covenant-love. From this idea there sprang up the concept of Jerusalem as 'the navel of the earth' (38:12, RV mg.), a belief popular in rabbinical writings and carried over into the early Fathers and into medieval cartography.[1]

6-10. The crime of the people of Jerusalem was that in spite of all God's favours they had been rebellious against His *ordinances* and *statutes*. These are words which Ezekiel frequently uses, in common with Leviticus and Deuteronomy, and they refer to an established corpus of law, obedience to which was integral to the covenant. Worse than that, the people had exceeded the nations in wickedness and had not even *acted according to the ordinances of the nations* that were round about them (7). RSV omits the negative here, but with only slight justification. For all these crimes the judgment is clear : *I, even I, am against you* (8). Unparalleled sin demands unparalleled punishment (9). The cannibalism which is not unknown in desperate siege conditions (*cf.* 2 Ki. 6:28f. ; Je. 19:9 ; La. 4:10) is described as a judgment executed by God (10), and it will all be done *in the sight of the nations* (8) so as to vindicate God's holiness and to make a public example of His disobedient people.

11. On top of disobedience and rebellion came the defilement of God's sanctuary with *detestable things* and *abominations*. This is the first reference in Ezekiel to the corrupt practices which were being carried on in the Temple between the

---

of 6:8-10, announcing the conversion of the remnant of the dispersed Israelites, and also quotes Luke 12:49. This could be the true meaning if the phrase is interpreted as a later gloss, but it does not naturally fit the context to give two such differing meanings to the word *fire*.

[1] *Cf. Jubilees* 8:12, 19; TB, *Yoma* 54b; *Sanhedrin* 37a; and the map of the world by Richard of Haldingham in Hereford Cathedral (*c.* 1280).

captivity of Jehoiachin and the final destruction of the city in 587 BC. Chapter 8 describes this in horrifying detail. For all this God says, *I will cut you down* (RSV). This is a variant reading on the MT, which has *I will diminish* (AV, RV) or *withdraw* (RSV mg.; *sc.* my eye?), and is to be preferred; but neither reading is very satisfactory.

12. The key to the symbolism of verse 2 is now given and we notice that the burning with fire is interpreted as death by pestilence and famine, *i.e.* during the siege and not in the flames that engulfed the city on its capture. In the event Ezekiel's acted prophecy was fulfilled, as many died during the siege and hundreds more were put to death when Zedekiah staged an attempted break-out from the beleaguered city. The biblical narrative may be read in 2 Kings 25:1-21; 2 Chronicles 36:17-21; Jeremiah 39:1-18.

13-17. In this concluding paragraph the judgments which God promised in verse 8 are described more fully. Words similar to those used in Isaiah 1:24 of the Lord's wrath against His enemies are now used against His own people (13). *I will vent my fury* (RSV) is literally 'I will quieten my fury' in the sense of 'appease' or 'assuage' (as in Zc. 6:8); and the phrase *I will be comforted* (AV, RV) similarly implies the relief that comes after the unburdening of powerful emotions, such as grief or anger. *Satisfy myself* (RSV) is a most misleading rendering of the Hebrew word *hinneḥamtî*.

The object of the punishment is to make Judah and Jerusalem a warning to *the nations round about you* (15). This amounts to a reversal of the intention of the covenant, which was originally that Israel should be a witness to the nations of God's truth and mercy: in Israel all the nations of the earth would be blessed (Gn. 22:18). But the result of her sins was that she became *a reproach and a taunt, a warning and a horror* (15). The words are piled on top of each other to express the accumulation of ridicule which will come upon the stricken city of Jerusalem. Their fulfilment is to be found in Lamentations 2:15, 16.

The punishments are to consist of *deadly arrows of famine* (16, RSV), the word translated *evil* in AV, RV having its regular meaning of 'baneful', 'hurtful' rather than 'wicked' in the moral sense. The punishment of famine, which is the theme of verse 16, becomes only one of four great evils mentioned in verse 17. Famine, pestilence and sword are three which often appear in apocalyptic writings, and wild beasts are sometimes added (*cf.* Dt. 32:23–25; Rev. 6:8). A similar quartet is found in Jeremiah 15:2. *Pestilence and blood* (17) are an alliterative pair of words and should be taken together as a unity. All these disasters are to prove to Israel and to the nations that *I, the Lord, have spoken* (13, 15, 17). The more indifferent men are to God's laws, the louder He has to speak. Verse 13 adds the phrase *in my zeal* (AV, RV), or *in my jealousy* (RSV). The Hebrew word *qin'â* suggests 'ardour', 'passionate feeling' (the root meaning is 'to grow purple in the face'), and therefore covers both zeal and jealousy, as well as resentment and indignation at an insult done to the honour of oneself or of another. In this last sense it is frequently attributed to God, not in any sinful or sub-Christian sense (as our word 'jealousy' usually implies) but with the idea of God being roused to deep feelings of concern on behalf of holiness and righteousness. A Christian need never feel ashamed when his emotions are similarly stirred. Such passion is all too rare in twentieth-century religion.

II. ORACLES OF JUDGMENT (6:1 – 7:27)

a. Prophecy against the mountains of Israel (6:1–14)

From this dramatized condemnation of Jerusalem and its people Ezekiel turns now to address the whole land of Judah, and particularly the mountains, which he singles out not only because they typified Judah's rugged terrain but because they were the sites for the high places which defiled the land. Many prophets before him had attacked the high places, and with good reason. Although worship was carried on at them nominally in the name of Yahweh, most of them had been originally Canaanite shrines which the Israelites had taken over for their own purposes. The idea may have been good in essence but in practice it blurred the distinctiveness of Israel's religion and led to all kinds of local corruptions of Yahweh worship. The prophets to a man deplored this policy and fought to remove the high places for ever, but they had little success. The kings of Judah who were Yahweh worshippers removed many idolatrous shrines and symbols, but most of them balked at wholesale destruction of the high places. The two notable exceptions were Hezekiah (*c.* 716–687 BC) and Josiah (*c.* 640–609 BC), but Hezekiah's reformation was immediately reversed by his successor, Manasseh (2 Ki. 21:3), and it does not seem as if Josiah's efforts were much more successful. In contrast with this chapter, it is worth reading 36:1–15, where the mountains of Israel are again addressed in a context of promised restoration.

1, 2. The formula, *The word of the Lord came to me* (lit. 'and a word of Yahweh was unto me saying'), implies that a new section is beginning, with no necessary chronological link with what has gone before. It occurs very frequently in Ezekiel as an introduction to his oracles. *Set your face toward* (2) is a phrase which can be used either of direction (Gn. 31:21), or of purpose (1 Ki. 2:15, AV, RV), or of opposition. Ezekiel uses the words mainly in this last sense (as in 13:17; 21:2; 25:2; 28:21; 38:2), though it is not impossible that while he uttered his prophecy he turned to face westwards in the direction of Judah. If the practice of turning to Jerusalem for prayer was already catching on among the exiles (*cf.* Dn. 6:10), there would be particular irony in his doing this in an act of condemnation.

3–7. The *high places* which God says that He will destroy with *a sword*, the symbol of destruction, are the Hebrew *bāmôṯ*, the sanctuaries or shrines situated usually, though not necessarily, on hill-tops, where the people of the locality worshipped under the leadership of the local priests. In the days before the establishment of the Temple at Jerusalem, they were regarded as innocuous. Samuel ministered at one high place (1 Sa. 9:14), probably in Ramah, and there was a famous high place at Gibeon where Solomon sacrificed (1 Ki. 3:4). This was gently frowned upon by the author of

Kings, but excused 'because no house had yet been built for the name of the Lord' (1 Ki. 3:2). However, once the Temple was built, formal worship anywhere else was officially prohibited, and after the division of the kingdom Jeroboam I of Israel had to set up the altars at Dan and Bethel to rival Jerusalem as the cult-centres of the north. Because no effective control could be exercised over high places they were wide open to the influence of Canaanite fertility practices, ancestor-worship and idolatry of various kinds. Each high place would have its altar for sacrifice, and perhaps a pillar (Heb. *maṣṣēḇâ*), which may well have been regarded as a phallic symbol, and an image of the Canaanite goddesses, Asherah or Ashtoreth. The *images* (AV; RV calls them *sun-images*) referred to in verse 4 are probably 'incense-stands' or *incense altars* (so RSV).[1] All these idolatrous features will be desecrated by contact with *the dead bodies of the people of Israel* and with human *bones* (5; *cf.* Nu. 19:16). The wording of verse 5 echoes Leviticus 26:30, and is a reminder of Josiah's practice of burning bones upon the altars of high places as an effective way of closing them down (2 Ki. 23:20). To the psalmist the ultimate punishment of the wicked is expressed in the words, 'God will scatter the bones of the ungodly' (Ps. 53:5) and 'As a rock which one cleaves and shatters on the land, so shall their bones be strewn at the mouth of Sheol' (Ps. 141:7). For a contemporary parallel, see Jeremiah 8:1f.

8–10. In these verses the prospect is held out of a remnant of the exiles who will remember the Lord and be ashamed of the evils which they have committed. God's mercy is never far behind His judgment : *Yet I will leave some of you alive* (8, RSV). The same idea is expressed in 12:16 and in 14:22, and in each case it is made clear that God's purpose in sparing them is so that they may learn through the severity of their punishments and that they may confess their sins and acknowledge the justice of their sufferings. RSV is probably right to follow the Versions which read *I have broken* (9), instead of the passive of AV, RV, but it is odd to find *eyes* as a second object of such a verb : RSV gratuitously inserts another verb,

[1] For a fuller discussion of these, see *ARI*, p. 215, note 58.

blinded, to fill out the meaning, but it has no place in the original Hebrew. The word for *idols* (Heb. *gillûlîm*) is a favourite with Ezekiel, occurring no less than thirty-eight times, as against nine times in the rest of the Old Testament. Its derivation is uncertain but it is quite likely that it is a home-made word consisting of the vowels of Hebrew *šiqqûṣ*, for which the dictionaries give the polite translation of 'detested thing', and the consonants of a noun meaning 'a pellet of dung'.[1] The final combination carries about as much disdain and revulsion as any word could do.

11–14. A fresh oracle is introduced with the formula, *Thus says the Lord God*. It is a kind of triumph-song at the vindication of God's honour in judgment. Clapping the hand and stamping the foot were gestures of scornful delight more suited to the Ammonites of Ezekiel's time (*cf.* 25:6) than to the Christian reader of today. The taunt-song was, however, a literary device in Hebrew poetry which could even be put into the mouth of God without any sense of inappropriateness. So we should perhaps interpret it for what it said about a particular situation and recognize that poetical zeal for God would probably be expressed somewhat differently in the cold light of prose. In keeping with the style of the triumph-song the phrase *Say, Alas!* should properly be rendered 'Say, Hurrah!' The anomaly of the words that follow it may be explained by understanding that it is the judgment on *the evil abominations* which is welcomed, not the abominations themselves. For the phrase, *He that is far off . . . and he that is near* (12), *cf.* 22:5 ; Jeremiah 25:26 ; Daniel 9:7. It is a typically Hebrew comprehensive term, like 'he that goes out and he that comes in', meaning all without distinction. *He that is left* refers to any who escape the judgments of *pestilence* and *the sword*. By these judgments defilement will come to every place where there is an altar, not only on the *high hills* and *mountain tops*, but also *under every leafy oak* where sacrifices are offered. The fact that burials also took place under oak-trees (Gn. 35:8 ; 1 Ch. 10:12) suggests the existence of shrines for

---

[1] There may be a connection here with a Palmyrene *gᵉlālā*, 'a stone stela'; *cf.* Akk. *galālu*, a stone slab treated in some special way.

ancestor-worship at these sites. All these would be desecrated with dead bodies and the land of Judah would become *desolate and waste* (14; Heb. *šemāmâ û-mešammâ* – a delightful alliteration for a devastating judgment). *From the wilderness to Riblah* (RSV) depends upon a slight variation of the text, but Hebrew 'd' and 'r' are frequently confused and there is some MS evidence for *Riblah*. Riblah, or Riblath, was in the extreme north on the river Orontes in the district of Hamath. Compare the phrase 'from the entrance of Hamath to the Brook of the Arabah' (Am. 6:14) which also means 'from one end of the country to the other'.

The aim of God's judgment is described four times in this chapter : *Then they will know that I am the Lord* (7, 10, 13, 14). The words typify Ezekiel's message and longing, that Yahweh may be known by all men, Israelite and non-Israelite, for what He is – the one true God, the God of the world, the God of history, the God who speaks and does not speak *in vain* (10).

b. 'The end has come' (7:1–27)

A new collection of pronouncements is introduced with the same formula as began chapter 6. Verses 2–13 consist of three short oracles, all in similar vein, linked together by the common phrase 'the end has come', 'your doom has come', 'the time has come'. The fact that the message needed so much reiteration can only be understood against the background of popular belief in the inviolability of Jerusalem. Its destruction was inconceivable to the Israelite mind. As long as God was God, God's Temple and God's city would stand. This had been the message of Isaiah when kings of Judah had feared for the city's safety and were toying with the idea of turning to heathen armies for assistance. But now the situation was different. Isaiah's confidence could no longer be justified after 150 years of increasing apostasy. The people were living in the past, but God was judging the present. His verdict was that the end was imminent.

1–4. Ezekiel was not the first to use the refrain *the end has* *come.* Amos had used it (8:2) when he made his famous pun on the basket of summer fruit.[1] From there it became part of the common language of eschatology and was associated with the day of the Lord's judgment on all men. For Ezekiel, the destruction of Jerusalem was an act of almost apocalyptic intensity; it was a tragic, but necessary, culmination of centuries of human sin and divine long-suffering. The pattern could not go on for ever : if God was to be consistent, He must at some time call a halt. Times without number He had relented and spared His people. Now at last He says, *My eye will not spare you, nor will I have pity* (4). The end had come.

5-9. It is impossible to catch the staccato style of the Hebrew in any translation, but an indication of it is to be found in the repetition of words, especially of the word *come* which occurs six times in verses 5-7. Coupled with this is a play on words, reminiscent of Amos, which links *end* with *watcheth* (6, AV; RV *awaketh*). RSV tries to catch the assonance by translating *awakened*. The Hebrew words are *qēṣ*, 'end'; *haqqēṣ*, 'the end'; *hēqîṣ*, 'awakened'.

Your doom (7, 10, RSV) presents an unsolved problem. The word (Heb. *ṣᵉp̄îrâ*) occurs elsewhere only in Isaiah 28:5, where it means 'diadem' or 'chaplet'. A similar word in Aramaic means *morning*, and this is followed by AV; but this would normally suggest blessing and not calamity. Others think of 'a turn of events' and so 'misfortune', and this is how the word *doom* came to be used. It cannot, however, be described as anything more than a good guess that fits the context.[2] The description of God as *I am the Lord, who smite* (9) cries out for emendation by those who fail to see the grim irony in so much prophetic writing. To hearers and readers who were used to names of God like 'Jehovah-jireh' and 'Jehovah-nissi' (Gn. 22:14; Ex. 17:15), it must have come home with tremendous force to have Him described as 'Jehovah-makkeh'. The Lord who had provided and protected was about to strike.

---

[1] See RSV mg. on Am. 8:2.
[2] Akk. *ṣabāru*, used of a wall 'buckling' before it falls, may provide an etymological explanation for this word.

10–13. The imminence of the day is likened to a *rod* (10, AV, RV; RSV *injustice* is a weak emendation) that has put forth blossom and, like Aaron's rod, it is meant to act as 'a sign for the rebels' (Nu. 17:10). For the rod is typical of, and parallel to, *pride* which *has budded* (10) and *violence* which has grown (11). But none of the things in which pride takes satisfaction shall remain: *abundance, wealth, pre-eminence* (11, RSV), all shall go. Once this doom falls commercial transactions will be of no consequence, and the smile of the buyer who thinks he has made a good bargain and the long face of the seller who pretends he has been worsted will be a thing of the past (12). And as for restitution in the year of jubilee, that is quite unthinkable (13; *cf.* Lv. 25:10, 13f.). Once again the oracle is a hotch-potch of irony and word-play; at one stage *wrath* (Heb. *ḥārôn*) *is upon all their multitude* (12), at the next *the vision* (Heb. *ḥāzôn*) *is upon all their multitude* (13, RSV mg., without the correction). The seller *shall not return* and the vision *shall not turn back* (13: same word).

14–22. Even though the people prepare themselves to resist the impending disaster and *have blown the trumpet and made all ready* (14), defence is useless. In the face of what is coming *knees* will be *weak as water* (17). The only thing the defenders can do is to put on sackcloth and throw their money out into the streets (18, 19): *their silver and gold* will for once be powerless to do them good. No amount of money can buy food when the food is not there. So the very things which the backsliding Israelites had valued and which had been the cause of their downfall would become *an unclean thing* (19, 20) in the day of God's wrath. This word, *niddâ*, belongs to the language of female impurity and expresses the revulsion that will be felt not only towards their wealth, but also towards *their beautiful ornament* (20, RSV), *i.e.* their expensively decked idols. Far more horrifying will be that God's *precious place* (22, RSV; lit. 'treasured') will be allowed to suffer profanation by foreigners. This is a clear reference to the Temple, which is described in similarly endearing terms in 24:21, 25. The emotive words used are a healthy reminder to the reader that when God acts in judgment He Himself suffers pain and grief as well as those whom His holiness has condemned.

23–27. *Make the chain* (RV, RSV mg.), to carry the exiles into captivity, cries the prophet. But the Hebrew is difficult and RSV follows LXX in joining the words to the previous verse and translating *and make a desolation*. As so often the variant shows us little more than the translator's look of despair, a despair matched by that of the afflicted Israelites who in the midst of their sufferings *will seek peace* (25), but it will be too late. Then the recognized channels of God's guidance will be blocked. *Prophet, priest* and *elders* will have nothing to say (26) : king, prince and people will be helpless with despair (27). A similar threat had been spoken by Micah (Mi. 3:5–7), and the words may well be a deliberate riposte to the arrogance of Jeremiah's contemporaries who thought that 'the law shall not perish from the priest, nor counsel from the wise, nor the word from the prophet' (Je. 18:18). Notice that there is no suggestion of a conflict between prophet and priest : both are accepted spokesmen in Israelite religious life. The prophet received oracles through religious experience (*vision*) ; the priest gave instruction (*law*; Heb. *tôrâ*) based on known judgments, either codified as law or handed down by tradition ; the elders gave advice to the king in affairs of state. Ezekiel normally avoids the word for *king* (Heb. *meleḵ*), preferring the term *nāśî'*, *prince*, so it may be that in 27a we have a doublet which expresses only one idea in two phrases. This possibility is strengthened by the LXX, which omits the phrase *the king mourns*.

III. VISION OF THE PUNISHMENT OF JERUSALEM (8:1 – 11:25)

a. The idolatries being practised in the Temple (8:1–18)

Exactly fourteen months after his first vision, Ezekiel had another similar experience. In those intervening weeks he had clearly become recognized and respected as a prophet, and the elders of the exiled Judeans came to him in his house for consultation. On the particular occasion described in 8:1, it is more than likely that the elders, having come to question him about a matter, even perhaps about the state of affairs in Jerusalem, were sitting with him awaiting his reply. This could be a long time coming, for a true prophet like Ezekiel would never give an answer on the spur of the moment, as some less worthy prophets were inclined to do, but would await a word from God through a visionary experience or after a period of prolonged spiritual gestation. When eventually the message did come or the vision was given (and of course there was no guarantee that it would), there was never a doubt in the mind of the spokesman or of the hearers that it had come from God. If there ever was any doubt, the final proof of the prophet's genuineness lay in the fulfilment of his words (*cf.* Dt. 18:21f.).

It was at a time like this that Ezekiel was caught up in the trance which is described from 8:2 to 11:24. It begins with his feeling himself spirited away to Jerusalem where the link-up with his former vision is sealed as he sees there the same vision of God's chariot-throne which he had seen by the river Chebar. Then in four separate movements he is shown four of the 'abominations' which are supposedly taking place within the Temple precincts (8:5–18).

It is often debated whether Ezekiel was describing the actual state of affairs in Jerusalem, or was only speaking symbolically. How, for instance, was he to know what was going on hundreds of miles away? Had he secret sources of information, human or supernatural? Even allowing that communication between Jerusalem and Babylon was possible,[1] is it conceivable that the practices described in this chapter could possibly have been countenanced by the Temple authorities? In view of the problems which such questions pose, it seems preferable to regard the four abominations as symbolical, or rather typical, of the religious deviations of different sections of the Jerusalem community. The first (the image of jealousy; probably this was an actual fact) related to king and people; the second (animal worship)

[1] See Introduction, p. 24.

96

related to the elders of Israel; the third (weeping for Tammuz) absorbed the interest of the women; and the fourth (sun worship) was restricted to the inner court, where only priests and Levites could go. If however all these things were going on as Ezekiel described, it would mean that a complete disintegration of the national religion had taken place; and that would be by no means impossible.

8:1–4. Transported to Jerusalem. For the chronology, see the Introduction, pp. 36f. Once again the trance-like experience is described in the words *the hand of the Lord God fell there upon me* (*cf.* 1:3; 3:14, 22). The angelic being who immediately confronts him is very much like the description of the one who was seated on the chariot-throne (1:26f.). What Davidson calls the 'reverential vagueness' of the description (note the repetition of the word 'appear/appearance'), convinces us that this must be a meeting with the Lord. *He put forth* not His hand (that would be too anthropomorphic) but *the form of a hand*, and Ezekiel was lifted up by the Spirit and taken to Jerusalem, where he was set down at *the entrance of the gateway of the inner court that faces north* (3). The northern gateway was one of three which gave access from the outer court of the Temple to the inner court (the other two facing east and south respectively). The entrance of the gateway would be on the outer court side. A glance at the plan on p. 257 (though this does not of course represent the shape of Solomon's Temple) will show that Ezekiel was set down in the outer court just by this gateway, not many yards from where *the image of jealousy* had been erected. An explanatory note at the end of verse 3 shows that it was called *the image of jealousy* because it *provokes to jealousy*, *i.e.* it was an insult both to God and to His Temple and to His people.

It is remarkable that, despite all the corruptions that existed, Ezekiel should say that *the glory of the God of Israel was there* (4). It was as if he wanted to throw into sharp relief the difference between the God who belonged there and the deviations which were practised there, so making the crimes all the more heinous. Perhaps he was also trying to say that

God would stay with His people until the very last moment of their rejection of Him.

8:5, 6. The image of jealousy. Manasseh had put a wooden image of Asherah, the Canaanite goddess, in the house of the Lord (2 Ki. 21:7), and although 2 Chronicles 33:15 tells how he subsequently removed it, it must have reappeared, because Josiah later had it taken out and burnt at the brook Kidron (2 Ki. 23:6). From Ezekiel's words it looks as if one of Josiah's successors had made another and set it up by the northern gate.[1] This was the most honourable of the three gateways because, the royal palace being on the north side of the Temple, the king would have used it whenever he went in to worship. It is called the *altar gate* (5), because the sacrificial victims were slaughtered 'on the north side of the altar before the Lord' (Lv. 1:11).

8:7–13. Animal worship. The exact location of this cannot be identified, nor does it seem necessary that it should be. Essentially it is something done in secret, and the prophet is told how to gain secret access to this chamber of horrors and to surprise the elders in the very act. Engraved upon the walls (*portrayed*, 10, EVV, is inadequate for a word meaning 'incised' or 'carved in relief') were *all kinds of creeping things, loathsome beasts*, and *idols. Creeping things* (Heb. *remeś*) are specifically mentioned as part of God's good creation (Gn. 1:24); they are not by definition all unclean, as the AV of Leviticus 11:41 would suggest, for the word translated 'creeping things' in that context is the Hebrew *šereṣ*. They do, however, include many reptiles and small verminous creatures that scurry and slither over the ground, from snakes to scorpions, and these certainly were unclean. The serpent-deities known from Egyptian, Canaanite and Baby-

---

[1] Albright (*ARI*, pp. 165f.) describes chapter 8 as 'a valuable description of Syro-Mesopotamian syncretism in the priestly and noble circles of Jerusalem'. He interprets the *image* (Heb. *semel*) as a 'figured slab' engraved with cultic and mythological scenes, and compares similar finds from Gozan and Carchemish. On this chapter see also T. H. Gaster in *JBL*, LX, 1941, pp. 289–310.

lonian religions give grounds for supposing that this incident reflects the widespread influence of foreign cults on Israelite worship, cultivated no doubt from political, more than purely religious, motives.

Seventy men of the elders . . . of Israel (10) : these were not an official assembly, like the later Sanhedrin, but a round number of Israel's leaders. The size of the group, however, implies that it was the majority who reverenced foreign deities. The naming of *Jaazaniah the son of Shaphan* suggests a direct indictment by Ezekiel of a man whose family had been prominent in Jerusalem's public life. *Shaphan* is probably to be identified with Josiah's secretary-of-state (2 Ki. 22:3), and Ahikam, another of Shaphan's sons, was an influential supporter of Jeremiah (Je. 26:24). Clearly Jaazaniah was the black sheep of a worthy family.

As the elders performed their secret mysteries, burning incense to their borrowed gods, Ezekiel's divine guide points out that this vision is typical of what they are all doing individually, *every man in his chambers of imagery* (12, RV ; RSV *in his room of pictures*). The difficult phrase suggests that each elder had a room at home where he surreptitiously indulged his idolatrous inclinations, confident that there was no Yahweh around either to see or to care (12).

8:14, 15. Nature worship. Probably right outside the sacred precincts, at *the entrance of the north gate* into the outer court of the Temple, Ezekiel saw the women *weeping for Tammuz*. Tammuz was a Sumerian god of vegetation who in popular mythology died and became the god of the underworld. The cult associated with him was partly a mourning ritual, but also incorporated fertility rites. It became extremely popular in the Ancient Near East and in the Eastern Mediterranean, where it wore Greek dress and was linked with the names of Adonis and Aphrodite.[1] Indications of its influence in Old Testament times are few, but one such may be found in Isaiah 17:10f., the planting of 'Tammuz-gardens'.

[1] See art. 'Tammuz' in *NBD*, p. 1238; also E. Yamauchi, 'Tammuz and the Bible', *JBL*, LXXXIV, 1965, pp. 283–290.

8:16–18. Sun worship. The crowning abomination was
to take place at the very *door of the temple of the Lord* (16).
There, in the place where they ought to have been weeping
and calling upon God to spare His people (Joel 2:17), the
priests were deliberately turning their backs on Him. By its
east–west orientation, the Temple lent itself to solar worship,
and the fact that Josiah in his reformation had to destroy
'horses dedicated to the sun' and 'the chariots of the sun'
(2 Ki. 23:11) indicates that some kings of Judah had exploited the possibilities.[1] The number given, *about twenty-five
men*, suggests that not a large number of the priests had
succumbed to this particular form of worship. Nevertheless,
they were senior men (9:6 calls them 'elders') and they were
publicly misusing the Temple for a practice which was an
outright denial of the holy purpose for which it was dedicated.
And, as if that was not enough, *they have filled the land with
violence, and have returned to provoke me to anger* (17, AV). When
church leadership becomes corrupted there is no end to the
chaos that is caused to the life of the nation.

Lo, they put the branch to their nose (17). This is described by
Muilenburg as 'some obscure rite, probably connected with
practices of the Adonis cult'.[2] But the Hebrew is doubtful.
Their nose, 'appām, is traditionally held to be a scribal correction for 'my nose', 'appî : an understandable desire to
avoid such a crude reference to God. The word for *put* really
means 'send forth'. Early Jewish commentators translated
zᵉmôrâ (*branch*) as 'stench'. The result, 'they put forth a
stench before my nose', is still somewhat obscure, but now it
falls more appropriately in the category of obscenity rather
than of Tammuz-worship, which is not required at this stage.
To say that anything 'stinks in God's nostrils' is not a pretty
phrase to use, but then these forms of idolatry were not
pretty either.[3]

---

[1] See further H. G. May, 'Some Aspects of Solar Worship in Jerusalem',
ZAW, LV, 1937, pp. 269–281.
[2] In Peake, p. 574.
[3] A very different interpretation has been suggested on the basis of
pictorial designs on some Assyrian reliefs. These show people holding
branches to their noses in an attitude of reverence and worship. See *Iraq*,

b. The seven executioners : punishment by slaughter (9:1–11)

The punishment, pronounced in 8:18 upon the people of Jerusalem, is now in vision executed. First, in chapter 9, comes the slaying of individual unbelievers by the angelic executioners of God's judgment. When that is done, it is time for the city to be showered with the burning coals of destruction (10:1f.). There are many similarities here with later apocalyptic descriptions of final judgment, so we may regard these verses as in some sense archetypal.[1] The ideas are not however completely original, as a glance at Amos 9:1 ; Isaiah 6:6, and the Passover narrative will show.[2] But if there is any truth at all in the description of Ezekiel as the 'father of apocalyptic', it is to these chapters that one turns for the earliest evidence.

1, 2. The *executioners of the city* (RSV; from a verb meaning 'to visit', *i.e.* with punishment) are called up by the Lord, who is also acting as Ezekiel's guide, and they are clearly to be understood as angels, though they are described as *men* (2). They appear *from the direction of the upper gate, which faces north*, *i.e.* either from the place where the 'image of jealousy' had been (8:3) or from where the women had been weeping for Tammuz (8:14). Six of them had each a *destroying weapon in his hand* (1), also described as a *slaughter weapon* (2, AV, RV), and this is almost identical with the word for a 'war-club' used in Jeremiah 51:20. Beside them was *a man clothed in linen*, a mark of dignity, as befitted a priest (Ex. 28:42 ; 1 Sa. 2:18 ; 22:18) or a messenger of God (Dn. 10:5). At his side was *a writing case* (RSV ; AV, RV *inkhorn*) : the word is peculiar to this chapter and may be a loan-word from Egyptian, where it refers to the scribe's writing equipment, incorporating pen, ink-horn and wax writing-tablet. Together the seven solemn

---

XX, 1958, p. 16. A full discussion is to be found in H. W. F. Saggs's article, 'The Branch to the Nose', *JTS*, New Series XI, 1960, pp. 318–329.

[1] *Cf.*, for instance, the seven angels of Tobit 12:15 and Revelation 8:2ff.; the marking of the faithful in Revelation 7:3; and the recording angels of Enoch 89:59ff. See also TB, *Shabbath* 55a.

[2] Ex. 12:22ff. *Cf.* also 2 Sa. 24:16.

figures entered the inner court and stood waiting *beside the bronze altar* (*cf.* 2 Ki. 16:14).

3-7. There is some confusion about the actual movements of *the glory of the God of Israel* in this section, because at one moment He is represented by the heavenly figure on the chariot-throne, while at the next He is Ezekiel's personal guide. But too much accuracy is not to be expected in what was after all a visionary experience and we must not press for detailed explanations. There is, however, significance in the description of the glory moving *from the cherubim* (3), the place in the holy of holies where God was thought to reside,[1] to *the threshold of the house* (*cf.* 10:4, where the words are repeated), for this was the preliminary move before the final departure of the Lord from His Temple (11:23). From this new vantage-point He gives His instructions, first to the recording angel (4) and then to the six (5, 6).

The *mark* which is to be put on men's foreheads is the *tāw*, the final letter of the Hebrew alphabet. Early Christian commentators were quick to notice that in the oldest Hebrew script the letter was written as X, a cross. To the Hebrew reader this meant nothing more than a mark used for a signature (as in Jb. 31:35) or an asterisk in the margin of a book (as the Qumran scribes annotated some Messianic passages in one of their Isaiah scrolls).[2] But many Christians would echo Ellison's verdict that 'this is one of the many examples where the Hebrew prophets spoke better than they knew'.[3]

It is worth noting that the procedure for inflicting God's punishment was selective, in keeping with the principle of 18:4, 'the soul that sins shall die'. The basis for exemption from the slaughter was the individual's deep concern (*who sigh and groan*, 4) over the city's apostasy. This was what Amos had looked for among the luxury-loving revellers of

---

[1] But see below, pp. 104f.
[2] This, however, is an important plank in Dr. J. L. Teicher's argument, aimed at identifying the Qumran sect with a Judeo-Christian group; *cf.* his article, 'The Christian Interpretation of the Sign X in the Isaiah Scroll', *VT*, V, 1955, pp. 189ff.
[3] Ellison, p. 44.

Jerusalem and Samaria whom he castigated with his tongue. Their most guilty sin was that they 'did not grieve over the ruin of Joseph' (Am. 6:6). In both cases the criterion that was needed was not strictly a religious quality, like faith, or an outward act, like sacrifice, but an affair of the heart – a passionate concern for God and for His people. Failing that, there was no mark, and judgment followed just as surely as it had done for the households that lacked the blood on the doorposts on the night of the first Passover. There was no other exemption : age and sex did not enter into it (6) : only the mark would save.

The judgment began, as it always must (*cf.* 1 Pet. 4:17), with the household of God. The first to be slain by the six executioners were *the elders who were before the house*, probably the twenty-five priestly sun-worshippers of 8:16. Their slaughter meant defilement of the holy place (7), but that was a small price to pay for the vindication of God's name.

8–11. Distressed at the appalling thoroughness of the slaughter, the prophet appeals to God not to destroy *all the residue of Israel* (8, AV, RV). God's people had been steadily whittled away. First, the northern tribes had gone, with the depopulation of Samaria ; then the people of Judah had been decimated by invasion and exile. If God's punishment was to be as severe as this vision suggested, there would be scarcely a remnant left at all. But the appeal is no use : Israel's sin has gone too far for any intercession. Compare with this Abraham's plea for Sodom (Gn. 18:22ff.), and Amos's attempts to intercede for Israel (Am. 7:1–6). For all Ezekiel's outward appearance of severity, beneath the hard shell there was a heart that felt deeply for and with his people. He did not relish the message of judgment that he had to give, still less the reality that followed when the message was rejected. This was one of the secrets of his greatness. Though his forehead was made as hard as adamant (3:9), his heart was always a heart of flesh (36:26).

c. The Lord's chariot-throne : punishment by fire (10:1–22)

The six executioners disappear from the scene and are replaced by a further detailed description of the Lord's chariot-throne, which adds little to our knowledge from 1:13–25. The connecting link is the man clothed in linen, who from being the agent of deliverance in the previous scene becomes now the agent of fiery judgment. He is a strangely anonymous character, and his appearance of anonymity is only increased by the fact that we are never allowed to see him at work. We only know that his first task was completed because of the laconic report in 9:11, and of the second all that is explicitly stated is that he took the burning coals from the hands of a cherub *and went out* (7). Later writers would certainly have wanted to give him a name and make him a Gabriel or a Raphael, but in Ezekiel's day angels had no names!

The important feature about the chariot-throne which this chapter incorporates is the identification of the 'living creatures' of 1:5ff. with *cherubim* (15). Why it has taken so long for this identification to be made is baffling, but it may be that Ezekiel is saying that only when he saw the cherubim in the Temple did he realize that these were the very creatures which he had seen in his vision by the river Chebar. This is a reasonable explanation, because Ezekiel had not yet qualified as a priest before he went into exile and so he would never in person have seen the cherub-figures carved on the inside walls of the Temple (1 Ki. 6:29) and on the double-doors (1 Ki. 6:35) and on the Temple furnishings (1 Ki. 7:29, 36), where only priests could see them clearly. But there is no need to press the point too much, for he could hardly have been brought up in a priestly family without this kind of knowledge. It is just that for reasons of literary artifice he deliberately withholds the identification until this stage, and in so doing he cleverly fills in the moment of suspense which follows the angel's departure from the presence of the Lord to carry out his destructive task.

In the Old Testament the *cherubim* had a variety of roles.

Little can be gained from the etymology of the word, which has links in cognate languages meaning 'to bless', 'to intercede' and 'to be mighty'.[1] A better assessment comes from its Hebrew context and usage. Their first responsibility was to act as attendants and protectors of a sacred shrine, as in the case of Solomon's Temple and as carried over into Ezekiel's ideal temple of the future (41:18–20). Protection was also their role in the Garden of Eden, where they wielded the flaming sword to keep the way to the tree of life (Gn. 3:24). Their function as the two figures on the lid of the ark in the Most Holy Place is probably meant to involve worship as well as protection. According to Exodus 25:18–20 they stand with their heads bowed and their faces looking down towards the mercy-seat as if in never-ending, silent adoration. A further suggestion, which would apply in some cases, is that the cherubim were in fact represented as throne-animals on which the Deity sat. The idea comes from a group of references which describe the Lord as 'enthroned on (or above) the cherubim',[2] or from Psalm 18:10, where 'He rode on a cherub, and flew; he came swiftly upon the wings of the wind'. This is not far removed from the role occupied by the cherubim in Ezekiel's vision, where they bear up the throne of God on their extended wings and provide the motive-power for the whole complicated structure.

In appearance they varied considerably. Ezekiel describes quite differently the four-faced creatures of 1:5–8, with wings, hooves and hands, and the two-faced decorative figures on the panelling of his ideal temple in 41:18–20; but both are called cherubim. For further suggestions about their appearance, consult the article in *NBD*, pp. 208f. and especially figs. 56, 167 and 205.

1. This verse interrupts the natural flow of the episode

---

[1] Heb. *kᵉrûḇ* : *cf.* Akk. *karābu*, 'to pray'; *karibu*, 'intercessor'. According to Cooke (p. 112) the word was used to describe the winged, human-headed bulls which flanked the entrances to temples and palaces; they were thought to intercede with the greater gods on behalf of men. Others attribute to the noun more the idea of 'protector' or 'guardian' against evil influences.

[2] 1 Sa. 4:4; 2 Sa. 6:2; 2 Ki. 19:15; 1 Ch. 13:6; Pss. 80:1; 99:1.

which runs from 9:11 to 10:2, and is similar to what has already been described in 1:26. It does, however, introduce the reader once again to the vision of the first chapter, which now occupies the centre of the picture, and it cannot simply be deleted as a repetitive gloss. It describes only the throne, as if to imply that it was empty, awaiting the moment when the Lord would remount (10:18). We are forced to ask ourselves where this had been throughout the vision. 8:4 simply stated that 'the glory of the God of Israel was there'. Where? There are two possibilities. One is that the glory was in (or over) the Most Holy Place in the Temple, *i.e.* where the Lord belonged. From there it arose and moved to the threshold of the Temple, as described in 9:3, where the executive commands of judgment were pronounced. Alternatively, the reference to 'the cherubim' in 9:3 is an anticipation of the chariot-throne of the following chapter, and we are then to imagine that 8:4 simply meant that the Lord, seated on His chariot-throne, was there in the Temple court. Subsequently He dismounted from his cherub-chariot (9:3) and stood upon the threshold. While this second suggestion leaves unexplained the sudden reference to 'the cherubim' in 9:3, it does have the advantage of leaving us at the beginning of chapter 10 with an empty throne (verse 1) and the Lord still standing on the threshold to give His instructions to the man clothed in linen and to receive reports from him. Either way, 10:4 presents a difficulty, but it is best to understand that as a pluperfect, harking back to what was described in 9:3.

2. For the *burning coals*, *cf.* 1:13. In Isaiah 6:6 a burning coal was used for the purging of the prophet's sin, and not as a symbol of judgment. In Ezekiel's mind, Jerusalem was going to be treated in the same way as Sodom and Gomorrah (Gn. 19:24).

7. In an unusual touch of realism, based perhaps on Isaiah 6:6, Ezekiel describes how *a cherub* (lit. 'the cherub', *i.e.* the one nearest to the man as he approached the chariot-throne) handed him the coals which were to be scattered over the city. Possibly it was meant to show that even an angelic messenger like the man clothed in linen had to keep his distance from the aweful throne of God.

9–17. Of these verses, 9–12 are almost identical with 1:15–18, with the substitution of *cherubim* for 'living creatures'. Read RSV in verse 12. Verse 14 unusually substitutes *cherub* where we would have expected 'ox', on the basis of 1:10. It is probably due to a scribal error.[1]

18–22. At last *the glory of the Lord* came out from the Temple doorway (by which we must assume that the destroying angel had reported back once again), and *stood over the cherubim*. This was the signal for the chariot-throne to rise up and move off in the direction of the *east gate* (19), en route for the mountain east of Jerusalem (11:23) and thence away. But as if to delay the final departing, the episode described in 11:1–21 is inserted at this point.

d. The death of Pelatiah (11:1–13)

Before the glory of the Lord finally departs from Jerusalem, Ezekiel has two messages to pass on, one relating to the prospects of the people in Jerusalem (11:1–13) and the other to those already in exile with him (11:14–21). The first of these is addressed to a political group who are accused of advocating policies harmful to Jerusalem (2). What their policy actually was is dependent upon the translation given to verse 3, which will be discussed below, but they were either a militant war-party who were calling for every effort to repel the Babylonian armies, or they were disregarding Ezekiel's warnings of judgment to come and were serenely confident that all would be well. To these the prophet foretold death by the sword outside the protective walls of the city (10f.).

Despite hesitations that have been expressed by many commentators, it seems best to understand the whole of this chapter as being a part of the vision which began in 8:2 and ends in 11:24. This means that Ezekiel prophesied in the context of his vision and that, still only in vision, one of his

---

[1] Cooke quotes TB, *Hagîga* 13b, on the omission of the ox : 'Resh Lakish said, Ezekiel besought the Merciful One with regard to it, and He changed it into a cherub.'

hearers named Pelatiah dropped down dead. Any other interpretation demands some dislocation or emendation of the text as we have it, and it is clearly our duty first to try to understand what has been given before ever we venture to improve on it. A discussion of the various suggestions that have been made will be given in the commentary on verse 13, and in so far as this whole subject relates to the location of Ezekiel's ministry, in Babylon or in Jerusalem, reference must also be made to the Introduction.[1]

1–4. Ezekiel is transported to the *door of the gateway* on the east side of the Temple, that is to say, outside the sacred area, and there, in what was traditionally a place for public assembly (*cf.* Je. 26:10), he sees a group of *twenty-five men*. These men are nothing to do with the twenty-five sun-worshipping priests of 8:16, but are a political pressure-group led by *princes of the people, i.e.* members of the nobility of Israel.[2] Among them were *Jaazaniah the son of Azzur*, who is not to be confused with his three contemporaries of the same name, viz. the son of Shaphan (8:11), the son of Jeremiah the Rechabite (Je. 35:3), and the son of the Maacathite (2 Ki. 25:23; Je. 40:8; 42:1);[3] and also *Pelatiah the son of Benaiah*, who is otherwise unknown to us.

The *wicked counsel* of which these men are accused is summarized by the cryptic slogan attributed to them: *The time is not near to build houses; this city is the cauldron, and we are the flesh* (3, RSV). The possible interpretations of these words are as follows: (*a*) AV translates, *It is not near* (*i.e.* the threatened judgment); *let us build houses*. This sentiment expresses confidence that all will be well and, if building houses is taken as a symbol of peaceful activity (*cf.* 28:26), it advocates a policy of ignoring the threat of a further Babylonian invasion. A variant of this is to interpret *houses* as 'fortifications', but

[1] See pp. 23ff.

[2] Most of the leading citizens, however, had been deported with Ezekiel in 597 BC, so those who were left in Jerusalem were probably not of high quality.

[3] The 'Jaazaniah, servant of the king', whose seal was discovered in 1932 at Tell en-Nasbeh (biblical Mizpah), may well have been 'the son of the Maacathite', Gedaliah's army-commander at Mizpah. See *DOTT*, p. 222; *NBD*, p. 592.

this is not warranted by the ordinary Hebrew word *bāttîm*, though it would fit a context of warlike preparations. A more serious weakness of this interpretation is the linguistic one. The Hebrew reads *lō' beqārôḇ benôṯ bāttîm*, lit. 'not at hand to build houses'. The infinitive 'to build' can hardly become the hortative 'let us build', and the word 'at hand' must be complementary to the idea of 'house-building'. (*b*) On the basis of Jeremiah 29:5, Keil took 'house-building' as a reference to living in exile and this slogan as a deliberate attempt to ridicule Jeremiah's policy. The meaning would thus be 'the house-building in exile is still a long way off; it will not come to this, that Jerusalem should fall . . . into the hands of the king of Babylon'.[1] This ingenious suggestion presupposes, however, that reader as well as hearer would automatically recognize the allusion to Jeremiah's teaching, and this must be considered very doubtful. (*c*) RV mg. and RSV mg. put the phrase as a question, *Is not the time near to build houses?* That is to say, 'We are quite safe : let us carry on our normal peace-time occupations.' This is not impossible, and LXX also translates interrogatively 'Have not the houses been recently rebuilt?'; but it is not easy to see why the advocates of such peaceful policies should be condemned by Ezekiel as devising iniquity and giving wicked counsel. (*d*) There is much to be said, therefore, linguistically and in the context, for the RV, RSV rendering, namely that it is inappropriate to be building for peace when danger threatens. The only right policy is to prepare for war in the firm assurance that the city defences will be impregnable : the defenders will be as safe from the fires of war as meat is in the cauldron that protects it from the flames. Such an attitude would readily be seen by Ezekiel to be sheer folly and deserving of the sternest condemnation. It not only ignored the explicit warnings of Jeremiah that resistance to Babylon would bring greater disaster than sub-mission (*cf.* Je. 21:8–10), but it also reeked of the sublime self-confidence which was to be Jerusalem's undoing.

5–12. In contrast with this party's view that they were *the flesh* (3), the worthy part of the nation, as against the offal

[1] Keil, pp. 144f.

who had gone into exile, Ezekiel retorts that the real men of worth in Jerusalem were the many innocent men who had been slain (6), either by political purges or more likely in the fighting which was the result of these evil policies. He was virtually saying: 'The only good Jerusalemite is a dead Jerusalemite.' But as for the war-mongers (note the repetition of the emphatic *you* in verses 7-12), they shall be taken out of the cauldron (7, 9) and will die far away *at the border of Israel* (10, 11), a reference to what was to take place at Riblah after the siege (see 2 Ki. 25:18-21).

13. *Pelatiah . . . died.* The text does not insist on it, but it seems reasonable to suppose that Pelatiah was a known figure in Jerusalem and that his death, which was seen in the vision, actually took place far away in Jerusalem at that very moment. Subsequent reports of the incident reaching the exiles would have confirmed the authenticity of the vision and of Ezekiel's supernatural powers. Similar instances may be found in the events relating to the siege and fall of Jerusalem (*cf.* 24:2, 16, 27). The incident so frightened Ezekiel, as another such occurrence did the early church (Acts 5:5), that he again pleaded with God for his people (*cf.* 9:8). It is this intercession which leads into the second of his messages in this chapter, relating to a hopeful future for the despised exiles.

e. A new heart for God's people in exile (11:14-25)

It is early to be finding at this stage a prophecy of hope for the exiled community. In the main this was kept for the period after the fall of Jerusalem, *i.e.* in chapters 33 onwards. But other passages in these opening oracles indicate that God had plans to restore a remnant of His people (*e.g.* 5:3; 6:8, 9; 12:16; 16:60, *etc.*), and these would return to their native land to become the heirs of all their nation's heritage and not least to enjoy a new covenant-relationship with their God. In this Ezekiel was aligning himself with the hopeful outlook of his older contemporary, Jeremiah (*cf.* Je. 24:7; 31:33; 32:39f.).

15. The voice of orthodoxy spoke clearly and logically.

The exiles had departed from the holy city; they were on foreign soil; they were unclean and God-forsaken. Those who remained in Jerusalem were the righteous ones and were the recipients of all God's favours. Ezekiel saw differently. God showed him that his *fellow exiles* (reading with LXX, 'men of your exile', *gālûtekâ*, for the MT 'men of your kindred, or redemption', *ge'ullātekâ*) now represented *the whole house of Israel*, adding *all of them* as if to complete the identification. Far from being the outcasts of Israel, the exiles had become the true Israel. The scornful *Get you far from the Lord* (AV, RV) is reminiscent of David's lament in 1 Samuel 26:19, 'They have driven me out this day that I should have no share in the heritage of the Lord, saying, "Go, serve other gods."'

16-18. The proof that the exiles were God's people is drawn both from what God has done for them (16) and from what He promises them (17ff.). Even while they were *scattered among the countries*, God had been to them *in small measure* (RSV mg.) *a sanctuary*, making up to them for the lack of a temple and sacrifices by being their protection and their source of strength. This encouraging retrospect is coupled with the promise of the gift of *the land of Israel* (17). Such words have a Mosaic ring about them, as if the promised land of Canaan is being held out to the wilderness wanderers once again. The desert experience would not last for ever : one day they would possess the land – not by arrogant claim (as in verse 15), but by a gracious gift of God – and their worship would be purified of all the foreign, corrupting influences that had beset the Israelites since Joshua's day.

19-21. More than that, in a supreme act of grace, there would be given to them *a new heart* and *a new spirit*. If MT is followed, with EVV, the gift is of *one heart*, implying the re-union of the old northern and southern kingdoms, as in 37:15-22, but this is less likely than the variants *new* (some Heb. MSS, Syr.) or 'another' (LXX), especially in the light of the promise to replace their *stony heart* with a *heart of flesh* (19). The classic biblical character who received this gift was Saul (1 Sa. 10:9), but it is a recurrent feature of both Jeremiah's and Ezekiel's prophecy (Je. 32:39, LXX; Ezk. 18:31; 36:26; *cf*. Ps. 51:10). How it is to come is not explained, but the wording suggests a radical transplantation quite different from what had been generally known and experienced before this time. It was to result in an almost spontaneous obedience to God's commandments, which can only be fully understood in the light of the gift of the Holy Spirit to the church at Pentecost.

There seems to be in this verse a deliberate echo of verse 18 in the repetition of the verb 'to remove' or 'take away'. This is lost in RSV, which has *remove* in verse 18 and *take* in verse 19. But Cooke[1] notices it and comments, 'If the home-coming Jews *put away* the external obstacles (v. 18), Jahveh will *put away* the internal.' The preparation for God's work in man was to be man's willingness to repent and to take practical steps to demonstrate his repentance. This does not mean that human beings have to clean up their lives in readiness for God to enter them, but it does mean that God can do nothing for the man who will not recognize his sins and turn from them.

As always, the covenant-promise of blessing and union with God as His peculiar people (20) is set alongside the solemn consequences that will come upon the heads of those *whose heart goes after* all the corrupt practices from which they are to keep themselves free (*cf*. 18). It is worth remembering that God's blessings always have a reverse, as well as an obverse, side. They are never to be thought of as a superlative collection of benefits available for all those who wish to take advantage of them. Moses set before the people 'a blessing and a curse' (Dt. 11:26); Christ spoke of two ways, one leading to life and the other to destruction (Mt. 7:13f.). The infinite gain of heaven is always matched in Scripture by the irreparable loss of hell.

22–25. The glory of the Lord then rose up from its position just eastwards of the Temple (11:1), and moved away to the Mount of Olives, *the mountain which is on the east side of the city*. There it paused, as if loth to go any further. No further

[1] Cooke, pp. 125f.

movement is described, as if the prophet is saying that though the Lord has left His Temple and the holy city He is still standing by in case there should be a repentance on the part of the people. Alternatively, it may be that we are intended to infer that the glory of the Lord did move on from the Mount of Olives and that He transferred His presence to the exiles' encampment in Babylon. The eastward direction of the departure lends support to this view, but it can be nothing more than a supposition. When eventually the glory returned to the Temple, as described in 43:1–4, it was from the east that it came. Keil[1] suggests that the Lord was waiting on the Mount of Olives to execute the promised judgment on the city, and he compares Zechariah 14:4; Luke 19:41, and even Luke 24:50, regarding Christ's ascension as an act of judgment upon the Jews.

The Spirit which returned Ezekiel from his vision back to the reality of facing the exiles in his own house was the same divine energy which had carried him to Jerusalem by a lock of his hair (*cf.* 8:3). For the phrase *the vision . . . went up from me*, *cf.* Genesis 17:22; 35:13. It was the only appropriate way of describing the prophet's return to his natural senses. The elders who had been waiting all this long time, while Ezekiel was with them but at the same time miles away from them, now had a lot to listen to (25).

IV. ORACLES ABOUT THE SINS OF ISRAEL AND JERUSALEM (12:1 – 24:27)

The argument of the book so far has consisted mainly of the iteration of Ezekiel's message that Jerusalem is doomed. He has demonstrated this by symbolic action, in vision and by spoken oracle. He has given adequate justification for such a fate by describing the iniquities, religious and moral, which have brought it on. Now a new series of actions and oracles attempts to deal with objections that people raise to this horrifying prospect. The section could, in today's idiom, be

[1] Keil, p. 154.

entitled 'Objections to Judgment', as long as it is understood that the objections are raised only to be demolished. They are the objections of those who say, 'We have heard all these threats before, but nothing has ever come of them.' Or of the false prophets who claim equal authority for oracles which promise peace and safety. Or of those who think that it is impossible for the Lord to cast away His people : they *must* be delivered, either for the sake of the righteousness of the few, or on the ground of God's covenant-mercies in time past. However, before he deals with all these varying viewpoints, the prophet has some more symbolical acts to perform. Note in passing the parallelism between the acted prophecies of chapters 4 and 5, following directly after the first account of his vision, and those of chapter 12, which follow the second account.

a. Two more enacted messages (12:1–20)

i. Going into exile (12:1–16). The essence of this action is that it is to be done in full view of Ezekiel's inquisitive compatriots. As earlier they gathered round to watch the daily ritual of lying on the ground with hands tied (4:4ff.) and the weighing out of the prophet's meagre rations (4:10f.), so now he is commanded to play the part of an exile for all to see. No doubt Ezekiel's strange doings were becoming a common talking-point among the exiles, and there was never a shortage of spectators to watch and to gossip about every detail of what he did. In this way he soon developed as good a system of communication as any in Tel Abib.

The action consisted of two parts : by day he collected up the bare essentials for the long journey of going into exile ; then as evening drew on he dug through the wall of his house, as though making a surreptitious getaway, and went out into the night carrying his bundle on his shoulder. As he did this he was to cover his eyes, according to verse 6, though this is omitted from the description in the following verse.

2, 3. It is attractive to suppose that the *rebellious house, who have eyes to see, but see not, who have ears to hear, but hear not* is an allusion to the acted messages already given but probably not yet heeded by the exiles. God now speaks to Ezekiel and expresses the hope, *perhaps they will understand*. There is certainly an echo here of 2:3–7, as also of Isaiah 6:9f. and Jeremiah 5:21. Jesus' use of the parabolic method of teaching is further indication of the principle that in God's service the preacher's knowledge that his words will be ignored is never to be used as an excuse for not uttering the words (*cf.* Mt. 13:13–15; Mk. 8:18; Jn. 12:37–41). Ezekiel, like Jeremiah, had to be reminded that it was always possible that some would understand, and in this he may be regarded as the exemplar for all Christian workers in seemingly impossible situations or in singularly unfruitful spheres of service. There must always be the element of *perhaps they will* in such a ministry. And even though the result may still be negative, the obligation to speak is still there, if only to justify the hearer's condemnation.

5–7. The *wall* referred to is that of a house (Heb. *qîr*; as distinct from *ḥômâ*, which means a city-wall) and is an indication of the settled manner of life of the exiles who must have lived in typical Babylonian dwellings built of sun-dried bricks (*cf.* also 8:1; Je. 29:5). These bricks could have been removed by hand (7), though not without effort, and this would indicate both the difficulties of escape from Jerusalem and more particularly the attempt that was made by Zedekiah to breach the walls and evacuate the besieged city, as described in 2 Kings 25:4; Jeremiah 39:4. Tel Abib would probably have had no city walls for Ezekiel to demonstrate his message more accurately.

8–16. The meaning of the symbolic act. The action which was first commanded (2–6), and then obeyed (7), is *in the morning* explained (9–16). The impression is given that not even Ezekiel was fully aware of the meaning of his actions on the day that he performed them, except in so far as they signified generally the prospect of further exile for the people of Jerusalem. These verses not only confirm this symbolical meaning but also indicate that his actions were prophetic of what was to happen to King Zedekiah, *the prince in Jerusalem*

(10).[1] He would flee the city unceremoniously at dead of night. The phrase *he shall cover his face* (12) may refer to his being disguised, in which case Ezekiel would probably have worn some head-covering to represent it, or it may be a forward look to his being blinded by his captors at Riblah (referred to clearly in verse 13, *yet he shall not see it*), which could have been represented by the prophet either by a blindfold or by holding his hand over his eyes. The LXX follows the former interpretation by rendering verse 12 : 'he shall cover his face, so that he may not *be seen* by eye.'

13. Zedekiah was to find not only the armies of Nebuchadrezzar against him, but also the arm of the Lord. The failure of his escape-plan and his capture by the Babylonians were God's doing. For the picture of God as a hunter (*my net . . . my snare*), cf. Hosea 7:12. See also Lamentations 1:13; Ezekiel 19:8.

14–16. The language of verse 14 is reminiscent of 5:2, as all the armies and *helpers* (lit. 'help', the abstract being used for the personal plural) of the prince are scattered with the sword. Their experiences will teach them what otherwise they would never have learnt, namely *that I am the Lord* (15). What men fail to appreciate in prosperity, they will occasionally learn through adversity. As in 6:9f. ; 7:16 ; 14:22, God *will let a few of them escape* so that they can testify to His truth and vindicate His honour (16). Only as they confess their people's sins among the nations will it be seen that Israel's God is both holy and powerful : without such admissions He would simply be regarded as incapable of protecting His own people against the enemy. Ezekiel here shows his passion for Yahweh's vindication in circumstances which, without his message, would have brought nothing but disgrace in heathen eyes upon His name.

ii. The terror of the inhabitants of Jerusalem (12:17–20). The second action is very brief and can scarcely be compared with the first. It simply involves the manner

---

[1] Note again the use of the term *prince* and not 'king'; cf. Introduction, p. 32.

in which the prophet is to eat the economy rations, which were allotted to him in 4:9-17. He is to put on a show of fearfulness and terror and to explain it as being symbolic of the frightening violence and destruction which are to come upon *the people of the land* (19). This phrase (Heb. *ʿam hāʾāreṣ*) is used consistently to refer to the peasant population of Judah, as distinct from the ruling classes, and particularly to those left there during the exile.[1] Here the words are augmented by the explanatory phrase, *the inhabitants of Jerusalem in the land of Israel*. All this will come about *on account of the violence of all those who dwell in it*, *i.e.* in the land. The sufferings that the population will have to undergo are attributed directly to the sufferings which they have inflicted on others. Violence breeds violence. If anyone dares to question his fate, the answer will be found within himself. Human perversity often imagines that, given reasonable luck, it is possible to sin with impunity. Ezekiel declares that in this instance at least oppression will get its due reward. In so doing God will show Himself righteous, and the sinner will at last realize *that I am the Lord* (20).

b. Two popular sayings corrected (12:21-28)

There now follows a group of oracles, extending from 12:21 to 14:11, which all relate to the problem of true and false prophecy. This must have been an acute problem for all the prophets of Old Testament times and especially for men like Jeremiah and Ezekiel, whose message did not naturally commend itself to their hearers. The struggle between Jeremiah and Hananiah (Je. 28) illustrates the issue clearly. Here were two men speaking contradictory words, ostensibly from the Lord. The bystanders were helpless to know which was true. The simple rule of thumb given in Deuteronomy 18:22, the fulfilment of the word spoken, was too far distant to be an immediate guide, and the test of orthodoxy given in Deuteronomy 13:1ff. was not relevant to the issue. In the event the verbal contest escalated until Jeremiah pronounced

[1] For a full discussion of this phrase, see de Vaux, pp. 70ff.

a death-prophecy, which did take effect and was his vindication. But this could hardly happen every time.

The same problem dogged the apostolic church, where prophecy was a charismatic feature and where the spurious could so easily mislead. Again a number of warnings and simple rules were thrown out for the guidance of believers (*cf.* 1 Thes. 5:21f.; 2 Thes. 2:1-3; 1 Jn. 2:18-23; 4:1-3). But ultimately the criterion was to be found within the hearer ('he who is of God hears the words of God', Jn. 8:47), and in the life of the prophet ('you will know them by their fruits', Mt. 7:16).

Ezekiel, like his contemporary, Jeremiah, had an unacceptable message to deliver: it was threatening and unhopeful. Inevitably his hearers were prejudiced against him, and it was easy for them to react by ignoring his words because they saw no immediate fulfilment. They could almost claim Deuteronomy 18:22 to support them if they wished. Or, if it was going too far to say that Ezekiel's prophecies were false, they could always salve their consciences by consigning the fulfilment of his words to the distant future with no relevance to the present day. These two attitudes Ezekiel now deals with.

22. What began as an opinion had taken the form of a clever, pithy saying (*proverb*; Heb. *māšāl*) and had been canonized. Moffatt's 'Time passes, but no vision ever comes to anything' gets the sense better than EVV, but still lacks the four-worded pungency of the Hebrew which literally says, 'They-lengthen the-days (subj.) and-it-dies every-vision.' A memorable slogan can wield tremendous influence, for good as well as for evil.

23-25. God's reply also comes in slogan form: 'They-draw-near the-days (subj.) and-the-word-of every-vision.' The Hebrew 'word' is used in the sense of *fulfilment* (RSV); *effect* (AV, RV) also implies the effective accomplishment of the message in the vision. This was the nature of the word of God: it would not return empty (Is. 55:11), because it was a living word that went forth with all the vitality and authority of the God who uttered it. Fulfilment would be the death of false slogans, however catchy, and also of false prophecy which produced 'smooth' or *flattering* messages by doubtful means. *Divination* (24) suggests that the false prophets used mechanical means of obtaining their oracles, either by the use of lots or by throwing arrows into the air and studying the way they fell, or by other methods of augury. The term clearly carries overtones of opprobrium. All this will be done away and there will be no more delay in bringing God's words to fruition. The long build-up of threats will soon turn into deeds, and it will be *in your days, O rebellious house* (25) that the word spoken will be performed.

26–28. The second attitude is slightly different, though the answer to it is identical. It is less sceptical than the first, but it is mistaken in that it classifies all Ezekiel's threatenings with distant 'day of the Lord' sayings. Again the Lord responds to it with a promise of no more delay.

The appropriateness of this section to current views on the second coming of our Lord is remarkable. Some who hear the Christian assertions that Christ will return to this earth react by saying that more than 1,900 years have passed without anything happening and so the doctrine may be safely ignored. Others consider that it is such a futuristic concept that it need have no relevance to the world in which they presently live. Both views are dangerous, because both ignore the immediacy of prophecy. Whether fulfilment is a long time coming or is near at hand, the church which receives such prophecy has a duty to live in the light of its fulfilment. For the similar problem in apostolic days, see 2 Peter 3:3–13.

c. Prophecy against the prophets and prophetesses of Israel (13:1–23)

After dealing in chapter 12 with the mistaken views of the people, Ezekiel addresses himself to the false prophets who have misled them. While not denying them their title of prophets, he denounces them scathingly for the deleterious effect their empty-headed pronouncements are having and have had upon Israelite life. They have undermined the stability of the nation at a time when it needed to be built up (5), and they have given their blessing to the crumbling edifice of the state when it should have been condemned and reconstructed afresh (10).

13:1-7. The charge of undermining the nation. The heart of this denunciation is the phrase *like foxes among ruins* (4, RSV; AV *deserts*, only in the sense of deserted habitations), a picture which suggests that the prophets have no real concern for the people among whom they live. They burrow among the foundations without any regard for the welfare of the place, intent only on making dens for themselves or, to change the metaphor, on feathering their own nests. Such action is not only foolish and irresponsible, but morally reprehensible, and Ezekiel uses the strongest word to describe their folly. *Foolish* (3) is the Hebrew *nāḇāl*, which covers much more than mere stupidity. The fool was spiritually and morally insensitive; he was inclined to blasphemy (Ps. 74:18) and to atheism (Ps. 14:1); he was churlish and arrogant, like his namesake Nabal of Carmel (1 Sa. 25); he was capable of gross immorality (2 Sa. 13:13). He was in fact the very antithesis of all that the wise man stood for in terms of spiritual perception, self-discipline, restraint, godly fear and humility. For prophets to be described thus was strong language indeed, but when we remember that Jeremiah had accused two of them of committing adultery with their neighbours' wives (23:14; 29:23), we can see that it was fully justified. The whole of Jeremiah 29 really needs to be read in conjunction with Ezekiel's denunciations in order to appreciate the complexity of the problem with which these two men of God were faced.

The condemnation of the prophets is based, however, not upon any immorality or villainy of which they may be guilty, but on the way in which they compose their pronouncements. This throws a great deal of light incidentally on the genuine prophetic consciousness in Israel. These foolish prophets *prophesy out of their own minds* (2, RSV; lit. *out of their heart*, but in Hebrew the heart, *lēḇ*, was the organ of thought and will as well as being the seat of the emotions). The parallel phrase, *who follow their own spirit* (3), suggests a conflict between the human spirit and the Spirit of God. The truly inspired prophet was to be so dominated by the Spirit of God that his own spirit was in subjection to its influence. There was in prophecy the sense of divine invasion which produced a message that had a quality of supernatural 'otherness' about it. It was not simply the product of a human mind. This does not mean that ordinary thought-processes were despised by the prophets : the artifice and skill of their compositions bear witness to that. It does mean, however, that human thought had to be ignited and raised to a higher degree of intensity by the Spirit before a prophet could be sure he was truly a spokesman for the Lord. Though some tried to work this up by self-inflicted means, like the prophets of Baal on Mount Carmel, the true prophet knew that it was not his own doing. 'The Lord God has spoken ; who can but prophesy?' (Am. 3:8).

Far from being undermined, what Israel needed was to be buttressed in her hour of crisis. The language of these verses does not indicate whether Ezekiel is thinking more of life in Jerusalem or of the life of Israel in exile : there were prophets, good and bad, in both communities. But the needs were similar in Jerusalem and in Tel Abib. What was broken down needed defending and restoring, and the false prophets had failed right there (5).

5. *The day of the Lord* in Ezekiel refers to the day of judgment which the Lord has decreed upon His people and particularly upon Jerusalem. It is to be identified here with the sack of Jerusalem in 587 BC, a day in which the storm of judgment eventually broke. But the actual occurrence of an act of judgment does not exhaust the meaning of the phrase : the day of the Lord can never be said to have taken place. It is always future and consists of the next successive culminating act of God in judgment, or sometimes in vindication.

13:8–16. The charge of encouraging false security.
The first two verses of this section give the condemnation
which the false prophets are to suffer. Basically, it is that they
merit the implacable opposition of God, *I am against you* (8).
They have therefore no hope of ultimate success or recognition
for their ministry, and their expectation that the Lord will
ulfil their word (6) will be rudely shattered. Their punishment
is to be threefold (9). First, they will lose the place of honour
which they have long enjoyed among the leading citizens of
Israel : the *assembly* (AV ; *council*, RV, RSV) means the kinnj
circle of the community. Secondly, they will be struec off
from the civil register of full citizens, so losing one of the most
cherished rights of any adult Israelite male. And thirdly, they
would never return to the land of Israel and so would be
deprived of the one hopeful prospect which made xiler
endurable.

10. The *wall* which the people build is a flimsy party-wall
(Heb. *ḥayiṣ*, a word found only here and described by Kimchi
as 'an inferior partition'). It stands for the empty hopes which
they are erecting for themselves and which the false prophets
are blandly endorsing. *Whitewash* (RSV correctly ; *untempered
mortar*, AV, RV, is based on an incorrect identification with a
word meaning 'unseasoned') is closely akin to a root meaning
'to plaster over', used in Job 13:4 ; Psalm 119:69, of smearing
a person with lies. So the people's futile hopes are encouraged
by the prophets' lying lullabies of peace. It is a common
failing for preachers to want to speak pleasing and appeasing
words to their people, but if they are to be true to their
calling they must be sure to receive and to impart nothing
but God's clear word, irrespective of the consequences.
When church leaders encourage their people in sub-Christian
standards or unbiblical ways they make themselves doubly
guilty.

11. *There shall be an overflowing shower; and ye, O great
hailstones, shall fall* (AV, RV). There is a double meaning
concealed in the first of these phrases. The word for 'overflowing' means both 'flooding' as of a raging torrent (well
expressed by RSV *a deluge of rain*) and also 'rinsing off', as if

the effect of the downpour is to wash away the whitewash and leave the flimsy wall naked and exposed to the destructive hailstones. Most commentators find the address to *ye great hailstones* unnatural, and prefer to repoint to give the sense 'and I will cause great hailstones to fall'. This is preferable to RSV which solves the problem by omitting altogether the word 'and you'.

12. The effect of God's judgment is to make the work of the false prophets appear contemptible, as their failure is held in derision : *Where is the daubing . . .?* This, however, will be only the prelude, for soon the wall itself will fall (14) and the false prophets of peace will perish with it (15, 16). At this stage the figure of the wall, which began by representing popular optimism, comes to be identified with the city of Jerusalem, on whose impregnability their empty hopes had centred. The strongest condemnation, however, goes not to the people but to those who led them into error. 'Woe to the man by whom the temptation comes !' (Mt. 18:7).

13:17-23. The charge against the prophetesses. There are only a handful of passages in the Old Testament which are critical of a class of women, and this section keeps company with Isaiah 3:16 – 4:1 ; 32:9-13 and Amos 4:1-3. The only female prophets that are known to us are women like Deborah (Jdg. 4:4ff.) and Huldah (2 Ki. 22:14), though Moses' sister, Miriam, merited the title (Ex. 15:20) and Nehemiah refers to 'the prophetess Noadiah' among his intimidators (Ne. 6:14).[1] While recognizing therefore that prophecy was open to women as well as to men, there do not appear to have been many such women and it is probably a mistake to think of a class or order of prophetesses. Indeed, Ezekiel's language suggests that these were more like witches or sorceresses who practised strange magic arts (*cf.* 1 Sa. 28:7). In times of national decay or crisis such quacks are often thrown up and they prey upon credulous and anxious minds. It is not surprising that at this time Israel had her share of them. No doubt the successful encroachment of

[1] In the New Testament, see Lk. 2:36ff. and Acts 21:9.

Babylonian influence, where divination and necromancy abounded, added further encouragement to their work.

18. It is not very clear what these women were doing. AV has *that sew pillows to all armholes*, but the Hebrew reads 'who sew amulets(?) upon all joints of the hands'. The 'joints of the hands' are interpreted as *elbows* by RV, and *wrists* by RSV. Both are possible and the choice must be determined on the grounds of sense. The word for *pillows* or *magic bands* (RSV) occurs only here and in verse 20. It is a common word in modern Hebrew for cushions or pillows, and this is how the LXX translated it, but some ancient writers thought in terms of amulets or even phylacteries.[1] Babylonian practices suggest, however, that this may have been a magical binding of the wrists of the inquirer to symbolize the binding power of the spell or incantation that accompanied it. Along with this the women made *kerchiefs* (AV, RV) or, better, *veils* (RSV), the word meaning a long drape which reached to the ground, shrouding the whole body, and these apparently came in all sizes *for the heads of persons of every stature*! This then was their equipment in their *hunt for souls*. It is not possible that the word for soul (Heb. *nepeš*) could have the meaning of a disembodied spirit : this is a totally unhebraic concept. It means the total person, the self, not just a part of him. By their sorceries these women were trying to possess and dominate those who came under their influence, and like so many witch-doctors they held the power of life and death over them.

How they used their occult powers is not clear. Cooke holds that the inquirer had his wrists bound and the sorceress covered her head with the veil, but he has to emend the text slightly to get this meaning. Despite the arguments he brings forward,[2] it seems more in keeping with the Hebrew text to understand both the binding and the veiling as being applied by the sorceress to her client. By means of a variety of spells and incantations she captivated him and claimed the power

---

[1] So Ephrem Syrus, whose comment is quoted in Cooke, p. 145, and the Hebrew column of Origen's *Hexapla*.
[2] See Cooke, p. 146.

to keep him alive on payment of certain sums. Hence the accusation that *you . . . keep other souls alive for your profit.*

19. The *handfuls of barley* and *pieces of bread*, which used to be regarded as the payments in kind which the women received, were in fact used in divination, either as accompanying sacrificial offerings or more likely as auguries to be examined to see whether a sick client would live or die.[1]

20. *To make them fly* (AV, RV) : read with RV mg., *like birds*. The text is probably confused and RSV follows Cornill's emendation to read *I will let the souls that you hunt go free like birds*. The sense, if not the Hebrew text, is clear.

22, 23. In contrast to the condemnation of the prophets (8f., 13ff.) the prophetesses appear to be treated quite lightly. Their power is broken and their *delusive visions* will be seen no more, but apparently they will not suffer more than the loss of their influence and livelihood (23). Their fault is no more than that they have *disheartened the righteous* and *encouraged the wicked* (22). They have in fact caused damage to the people's morale and abused the influence which the uncertain times thrust into their hands. They have been moral bloodsuckers at a time when the people needed as never before to lean upon the one holy God who treats them all as individuals with the strictest fairness and impartiality. They offered the promise of a spurious salvation, when true safety was available to all who would turn from their wicked ways. Mild as it was, they certainly earned their condemnation.[2]

d. Condemnation of those who are set on idolatry (14:1–11)

These words were addressed to a particular group of elders who were sitting at Ezekiel's feet (*cf.* 8:1 ; 20:1). They had come presumably in the hope of hearing some oracle about

---

[1] It is valuable to read the Hittite rituals against impotence and against domestic quarrel, quoted in *ANET*, pp. 349–351, in order to appreciate the detailed procedure which such sorceries involved.

[2] A full study of this passage has been made by W. H. Brownlee, 'Exorcising the Souls from Ezekiel xiii, 17–23', *JBL*, LXIX, 1950, pp. 367–373.

the length of their exile or giving news of affairs at home in Jerusalem. The oracle was given, but it was not what they expected.

3. Note the contemptible *these men*. The charge against them is that they have been infected by their Babylonian environment and the attractions of its idolatrous religion. Nothing had changed outwardly in their allegiance to the Lord, but they had taken *idols into their hearts* and in so doing they had put in front of their own faces the stumbling-block which would cause them to fall into iniquity. The phrase, *the stumbling block of their iniquity*, is peculiar to Ezekiel (7:19; 14:3, 4, 7; 18:30; 44:12) and usually refers to idols which the prophet recognized as being supremely 'the occasion of sin' for his people. The Lord demands an exclusive allegiance, inwardly as well as outwardly, from His people, and those who consult Him or pray to Him when they cherish other gods in their hearts will not be heard (*cf.* Ps. 66:18).

4. In place of a reply, God gives the prophet an oracle of judgment which sets out in general terms (*any man of the house of Israel who . . .*) what will happen when the man of divided allegiance inquires of a true prophet. No oracle will be given, but *I the Lord will answer him myself*, in actions and not in words. The words have a sinister ring about them and verse 8 enlarges on their meaning, but the ultimate aim is put positively in verses 5 and 11. The Lord intends to capture the hearts of His estranged people so that they may become His people in reality.

6. The way to this right relationship is by repentance (lit. 'return') and rejection (lit. 'cause to return') of their idolatry. The usual term for repentance, from the Hebrew root *nāḥam*, is basically an emotional word meaning 'to be sorry', 'to grieve'. Ezekiel however chooses the more practical word 'to turn back' (Heb. *šûḇ*) and he uses it twice in slightly different forms to produce the effect which only RV retains: *Return ye, and turn yourselves*.

7. The introduction of the sojourner (Heb. *gēr*), the resident alien with limited rights and obligations, suggests that Ezekiel's oracle is of wider application than simply to the elders in exile of verse 1. LXX interprets them as 'prose-lytes'.

9. If a prophet does give a response to an inquirer of this sort, it is clear indication that the man is a false prophet. He is *deceived* and it is the Lord who has deceived him. Cooke comments : 'Such a statement is only intelligible when we remember that ancient habits of thought overlooked secon-dary causes, and attributed events directly to the action of God.'[1] He also compares Amos 3:6 and Isaiah 45:7. This does not mean that the prophet who acts wrongly is not a free agent and bears no responsibility. He is deceived because he has lost his spiritual perception. He fails to detect the in-sincerity of his inquirer and he works up some answer, as the false prophets of chapter 13 did, without a true divine in-spiration. A comparable case is the contest between Micaiah and the lying prophets of Ahab (1 Ki. 22:18–23). On the face of it, the lying prophets were producing words that they knew would please : they were prophesying 'out of their own minds'. But in the deepest sense, it was the Lord who was responsible for the chain reaction which showed itself in such behaviour. They had succumbed to spiritual blindness and so the lies they uttered were all part of God's judgment upon them.

10. So, quite rightly, *they shall bear their punishment*, false prophet and idolatrous inquirer alike, for their responsibility is shared.

e. The righteous few will not avert the judgment (14:12–23)

These verses are an answer to the objections of those who say that God will not be as ruthless in His judgment as prophets like Jeremiah and Ezekiel were saying He would be, because He cannot afford to ignore the righteousness of some of His godly people. To do so, they claim, would make God unjust. God would surely spare His people out of respect for the prayers and the piety of the minority of faithful men who

---

[1] Cooke, p. 151.

staked their all upon Him. This attitude is nothing less than using the saints as an insurance policy to cover the sinners. It has been a human failing in every generation. A community is a trifle embarrassed to have a saint among its number, but it derives a sense of security from his presence, rather like the possession of a religious lucky charm. A family with no pretensions to spirituality is often glad to have a minister of religion in one of its branches, however far removed. Ezekiel's message is that there are no party tickets to deliverance. The righteous man saves no-one but himself.

The message is worked out in two stages. First, in verses 12–20, the general principle is stated that if and when God sends one of His four judgments (famine, evil beasts, the sword and pestilence) upon a land, not even the presence of three super-saints like Noah, Daniel and Job will save anyone but themselves. Then this principle is applied, in verses 21–23, to Jerusalem. Much less will the righteous be able to save the wicked when God's judgment falls upon the holy city. But if a handful of survivors are spared, it will not be that they are righteous and have saved themselves. They will be allowed to go away into exile so that those already there may see *their ways and their doings* (22) and realize how utterly justified God was in His judgments.

It may be argued that there was justification for believing that the righteous remnant would save the whole city on the grounds of Abraham's intercession for Sodom (Gn. 18:23ff.). Clearly the attitude of mind which Ezekiel was trying to correct sprang from a knowledge of this ancient tradition. But his point is that though Sodom may have been offered security if a sufficient number of righteous men were to be found within her walls, Jerusalem's sin was so great that no such mercy applied in her case. This is the doctrine of personal responsibility taken to its logical conclusion. There is no way round it; judgment must fall on the sinner, as it justly fell on Sodom (16:46–49).

13. *Committing a trespass* (RV) is far too mild a translation for a strong Hebrew verb with its cognate accusative following it. The root meaning is of 'acting treacherously' and so breaking a solemn covenant. It is used of the sin of Achan in relation to the devoted thing (the *ḥerem*, Jos. 7:1) and of a wife's adulterous act (Nu. 5:12), both of which incurred the death penalty. The meaning here is similarly of a land which by its unfaithfulness deserves the ultimate in punishment.

14. Almost certainly these men represent the ancient exemplars of piety in Hebrew tradition. Not only was the Flood story known to Ezekiel's readers, but also the character of its hero as 'a righteous man, blameless in his generation', who walked with God (Gn. 6:9). Job, too, was known as the man who was 'blameless and upright, one who feared God, and turned away from evil' (Jb. 1:1). Daniel alone is unknown from the Bible. He can hardly be Ezekiel's contemporary in exile : in any case the word used here is 'Dani'el' and not 'Daniyye'l' as in the book of that name. The likelihood is that this is the 'Dan'el' of the ancient Canaanite epic discovered in 1930 at Ras Shamra, the ancient Ugarit, on the north Syrian coast, and dating from about 1400 BC.[1] He appears there mainly as the dispenser of fertility, but also as the upright one, judging the cause of the widow and of the fatherless. We must suppose either that this early Semitic literature was known to later Hebrew generations or, more likely, that ancient Hebrew traditions which have not survived incorporated material centred around a character of the same name and similar character to the Ugaritic Dan'el.

16. Noah was able to save his closest relatives in the ark, but Job's righteousness did not avail to save his seven sons and three daughters (Jb. 1:18f.). It is the pattern of Job which is to be followed in the case of Jerusalem.

21. For the four classic means of divine judgment, *sword, famine, evil beasts, and pestilence* (there is no significance in the variation of order from verses 13–19), see note on 5:17. Muilenburg notes that in the Babylonian Gilgamesh Epic, which contains the famous parallel version of the Flood, after the waters had subsided and Utnapishtim had offered sacrifices to the gods, the mother-goddess Ea taunted the god Enlil who had sent the flood and asked him why he had not

[1] The Tale of Aqhat : see *DOTT*, pp. 124–128; *ANET*, pp. 149–155.

sent the lion, the wolf, a famine or a pestilence.[1] This suggests that these four judgments corresponded to disasters which were universally feared throughout the Ancient Near East.

22. Three possible interpretations have been put forward for the phrase *their ways and their doings*. Hitzig took it to mean the 'righteous acts' of the survivors which had merited the deliverance, and which would thus console the exiles with thoughts of the justice of God. Others have seen in the phrase a reference to the 'fate and sufferings' of the survivors, who would thus prove to be a living testimony to the exiles of the severity of God's judgment. But most recent commentators recognize that the context demands that these words refer to 'unrighteous doings' for which due punishment has been meted out, and Cooke points out that in Ezekiel *doings* always has a bad sense. So the remnant of the fugitives would be wicked men; they would *lead out sons and daughters* in a way that not even the three righteous heroes would have been allowed to do (16, 18, 20); and it would all take place in order to convince the exiles of God's justice, that He had not brought about the destruction of Jerusalem *without cause* (23).

23. At first sight it is hard to imagine how the sight of evil men suffering punishment *will console you* (AV *comfort*). The word is an unusual one. At its heart, the Hebrew root *nāḥam* means 'to breathe a deep breath'.[2] In the form in which it is used here, traditionally translated by the words 'comfort' and 'console', it means to soothe, to calm down, to cause someone to breathe slowly and deeply. Such comfort is imparted by bringing good news (as in Is. 40:1) or by giving adequate reasons to explain what would otherwise be disturbing (as here). As Snaith has pointed out, the word in Hebrew means not to comfort *in* sorrow, but to comfort *out of* sorrow, *i.e.* to bring new facts to bear upon a situation so that the hearer's attitude of mind is changed.[3] It is with this very

---

[1] In Peake, p. 577. The reference may be found in *DOTT*, p. 23 or in *ANET*, p. 95.

[2] See D. Winton Thomas, 'A Note on the Hebrew Root נחם', *ET*, XLIV, 1933, pp. 191f.

[3] N. H. Snaith, 'The Meaning of the Paraclete', *ET*, LVII, 1945, pp. 47–50.

purpose in view that the unrighteous survivors of Jerusalem's overthrow were to be allowed to escape. Only then would the embittered exiles see the justice of it all.

f. The parable of the vine (15:1-8)

In this poem Ezekiel likens Israel to a vine, a comparison which has a long history in Hebrew tradition going back at least as far as the blessing of Jacob (Gn. 49:22). Usually the force of the simile is to be found in the fruit-bearing properties of the vine which make it so highly esteemed among men, but which are all too rarely evident in the life of Israel as a nation (*cf.* Dt. 32:32 ; Is. 5:1-7 ; Je. 2:21 ; Ho. 10:1). Ezekiel, however, ignores the fruit, as if to imply that there is no question of Israel producing anything good, and instead draws a picture of a wild vine of the forest whose only point of comparison is the quality of its wood. This is notoriously useless, not being firm enough even for making a peg to hang a pot from, and it is of even less value when it has been charred in a fire. The figure used here is of the wood having been thrown on to the fire as fuel, being subsequently snatched from the burning – but for what purpose? The application is then made to Jerusalem : insignificant and not worthy to be compared with the nations and cities round about ; then charred in the fires of enemy invasion in the days of Jehoiachin ; spared from total destruction in 597 BC, but fit for nothing more than to be thrown back into the fire to be utterly consumed.

Implicit in the parable is the prophet's response to those who imagined that Israel, as the vine of the Lord's planting, was indestructible. Cut down she might be, they thought, but it was only a temporary setback : before long the stock would shoot again and Israel would flourish as she had done in days gone by. Such naive optimism was the object of Ezekiel's incessant condemnation. Israel and Jerusalem were finished.

2. The phrase, *the vine branch which is among the trees of the forest* (RV, RSV), is in apposition to *the vine* of the first half of the verse, but in view of the comparison it is almost impossible to translate it idiomatically. The sense is clear : How much better is the wood of the vine than any other wood? Answer, it is no better. How much better is the branch of the vine (than any other branch) among the trees of the forest? Answer, not at all. The word *vine branch* (the same as is found in 8:17) is a twig that is trimmed off at pruning-time, and its use by Ezekiel serves to underline Israel's relative insignificance as a nation.

3. The *pin* (Heb. *yāṯēḏ*) is the common word for a tent-peg, but it can also be used as here for a wooden *peg* fixed in a wall. It developed the meaning of someone who could be relied upon, as in Isaiah 22:23ff.; Zechariah 10:4; *cf.* also Ezra 9:8. Israel was neither useful nor dependable.

4. No part of Israel is unaffected by the searing experiences she has gone through.

6–8. Only at this stage does Ezekiel begin the application of what hitherto has been an unrelated parable (*cf.* the similar pattern in Is. 5:1–7). EVV are wrong to translate the second verb *so will I give*, when they have put the identical word in the perfect tense in the preceding stichos. The sense as well as the grammar demands that we follow RV mg., *so have I given*, for the inhabitants of Jerusalem were according to the analogy consigned to the fire when the Babylonians first assaulted their city. It was a past event which the temporary relief of Zedekiah's puppet reign had not affected. So verse 7 follows on (and again only RV mg. gets the tenses right), *they have gone forth from the fire, but the fire shall* still *devour them*. On the phrase *acted faithlessly*, see note above on 14:13.

g. Jerusalem the faithless (16:1–63)

It had been the genius of Hosea to understand the relationship between the Lord and His people in terms of the covenant of marriage, and he had drawn on the experiences of his own wife's unfaithfulness to demonstrate Israel's spiritual adultery. Hosea had stressed by contrast the faithful covenant-love that God still showed to His wayward bride (Ho. 2:14–20). Ezekiel drew on this analogy of the marriage-bond but couched it in terms which might well have been borrowed from a popular oriental tale of a foundling child being rescued by a passing traveller and eventually wedded by him. The idea of the 'rags-to-riches' plot has endeared itself to every generation and every culture that likes listening to good stories. As told by Ezekiel, however, the story is no longer endearing. It has great pathos in its conception, but only a tragic crudity in its telling. The Christian reader may, not surprisingly, feel nauseated at the indelicate realism of Ezekiel's language, but Ezekiel meant it that way. He was telling of ugly sins and he made the parable fit the facts.

Instead of dealing with a particular objection, voiced or implied, against his message of judgment on Jerusalem, Ezekiel in this chapter gives a survey of Israel's spiritual history from her earliest origins up to his own day. This in itself should be enough to justify the Lord in His decisive action against Jerusalem. At the same time, Ezekiel sees beyond the immediate catastrophe of judgment to God's ultimate purpose of restoration and forgiveness (53–63), but this may have been incorporated by him after the destruction of Jerusalem had taken place (see notes below).

16:1-7. The unwanted foundling. Although the city of *Jerusalem* is specifically addressed (2, 3), the parable applies to the whole nation and its history, and interesting observations are made on the Hebrews' physical ancestry. Their *origin* and *birth are of the land of the Canaanites* (3), an allusion to the fact that Jerusalem was a Canaanite city (so Davidson, *in loc.*), or more probably because it was in Canaan that Israel first became an established nation. The statement is heavy with sarcasm, however, for the term 'Canaanite' was a by-word for moral decadence. Nor must we take the accusation of mixed parentage out of its satirical context, for Hebrew tradition looked back to pure Aramaean stock (Dt. 26:5) through the patriarchs. The element of truth in Ezekiel's words is to be found in the undoubted fact that Israel assimilated many foreign influences from her Canaanite environment as well as from non-Semitic sources. The Amorites were one of the

peoples who populated Canaan, according to the lists of
nations in Exodus 13:5 ; 23:23, *etc.* They were a west-Semitic
people whose existence in the Near East is attested from as
early a period as the third millennium BC. From being a
desert people they infiltrated Babylonia and established the
powerful kingdom which Hammurabi made famous, as well
as other city-states like the celebrated Mari, excavated from
1933 to 1960 by André Parrot. At the time of the conquest of
Canaan they held most of Transjordan and the defeat of their
kings, Sihon and Og, was the prelude to Joshua's successful
invasion. They are frequently found linked with the Hittites
in the Old Testament, but the latter were originally an
Indo-European nation centred on Asia Minor. The Hittites of
Canaan were a small immigrant group who had moved far
away from their original home.[1]

4. The exposure of female infants is not unknown in the
East even at the present day. On the obstetrics of the verse
Cooke quotes Dr. Masterman describing present-day customs
among Arabs : 'As soon as the navel is cut the midwife rubs
the child all over with salt, water, and oil, and tightly swathes
it in clothes for seven days ; at the end of that time she removes
the dirty clothes, washes the child and anoints it, and then
wraps it up again for seven days – and so on till the fortieth
day.'[2] The salt appears to have had an antiseptic rather than
a ceremonial quality. The suggestion that it was a ritual act
of dedication, comparable to the covenant of salt (Lv. 2:13 ;
Nu. 18:19 ; 2 Ch. 13:5), has little to commend it.

The word for *to supple thee* (AV ; Heb. *lemišʿî*) is unknown
elsewhere. The Targum has 'for cleansing', based probably
on a kindred Arabic root meaning 'to wash'. Vulgate's *in
salutem* links it with the root *yāšaʿ*, 'to save'. LXX and many
commentators omit the word altogether. RV, RSV follow the
Targum tradition, which gives the required sense, but the
word still remains a philological mystery.[3]

---

[1] See further H. A. Hoffner's Tyndale Biblical Archaeology lecture for
1968 on 'Some Contributions of Hittitology to Old Testament Study',
Tyndale Bulletin, XX, 1969, pp. 27ff.

[2] Cooke, p. 162 ; quoting from *PEFQ*, 1918, pp. 118f.

[3] Akk. has two words from a cognate root, *mašaʿu*; one meaning 'to anoint'
(*cf.* Heb. *m-š-ḥ*), the other meaning 'to take away'.

6. RSV has the support of several MSS as well as the Versions for omitting the repetition of the phrase *I said to you in your blood, Live.* Several commentators, with RV, want to divide the words differently and to render *In thy blood live,* but they cannot agree about the meaning of the preposition : 'In spite of thy blood, live !' (Davidson) ; 'with thy blood upon thee continue in life' (Cooke) ; 'Although lying in thy blood, in which thou wouldst inevitably bleed to death, thou shalt live' (Keil). RSV has the virtue of expressing simply God's act of salvation : finding the exposed infant struggling and kicking (*weltering,* RV, RSV ; not *polluted,* AV) in its own blood, He ordained it to life in the state in which He found it.

7. The opening words are almost certainly confused. It is best to join the opening word to verse 6 and amend with LXX to read, 'Live and grow up ; like a plant of the field I have made you.' *Thou art come to excellent ornaments* (AV) makes as little sense in English as in Hebrew ; a slight alteration of the text makes the more appropriate 'Thou didst come to the time of menstruation', which lies behind RSV *and arrived at full maidenhood.*

16:8–14. Marriage and adornment. The second time the traveller passes by he finds that his rescued waif has come of marriageable age. He uses the customary symbolic act of spreading his *skirt, i.e.* the lower part of his long-flowing tunic, over her (*cf.* Ru. 3:9), thus claiming her in marriage. He then proceeds to clean and purify her, because her outward state had not improved with the passing of time : she was still naked and blood-stained. But with her benefactor's attentions and his gifts of clothing and jewellery she became a queen among the nations and her beauty was renowned far and wide.

The reference in verse 8 to entering *into a covenant with you,* while being a legitimate expression for the marriage contract (*cf.* Pr. 2:17 ; Mal. 2:14), hints at the historical reality of which this story is but the allegory. It seems therefore quite permissible to historicize the description of this courtship and to see the covenant of marriage as a reference to the Sinai covenant, the time at which Israel in the purpose of God had come of age as a nation. The first time that the Lord passed by would then be either in patriarchal times (so Davidson) or when Israel was in Egypt (Keil). Skinner[1] doubts whether Ezekiel would ever have presented the patriarchal period in quite such a poor light and feels that the betrothal and adornment of Israel fit better with the age of David and Solomon than the rugged wilderness days. Certainly the period of nakedness and pollution corresponds well with the Egyptian period where Israel grew up into a large nation, but it is less easy to determine precisely whether patriarchal times were allowed for in this allegory or not. Probably the command to live (6) represents God's will to save Israel through Joseph at a time when the tribe could so easily have been lost through famine (*cf.* Ps. 105:17ff.). This was followed by the period of growth until eventually Sinai established the marriage-covenant. There was still, however, much for God to do for His partner before she attained to the reputation for wealth and nobility which Skinner is right to identify with the united monarchy. Having said that, we must be on our guard against over-pressing a parable like this in order to insist that every feature has its historical counterpart. The broad picture is discernible but there will inevitably be omissions and inconsistencies.

10. The *badgers' skin* (AV) is the same as the material used in the covering of the Tabernacle (Nu. 4:6ff.). The various translations give *sealskin* (RV), *porpoiseskin* (RV mg.), *leather* (RSV). 'Badger' is certainly not right, because the skin had to be both suitable for shoes and also large enough for one of them to cover the ark. The likeliest candidate is the dugong, a seal-like animal of the order Siremia, which is found in the Red Sea; its skin is used by the bedouin for making sandals. There may well be a connection between the Arabic for this creature (*tuḥas*) and the Hebrew word used here (*taḥaš*).[2]

11, 12. This is the bridal jewellery (*cf.* Gn. 24:22) which the bridegroom was expected to supply. The *jewel on thy forehead* (AV) should be *a ring on your nose* (RSV). It would have

---

[1] Skinner, p. 130. [2] See *IDB*, vol. 2, p. 252.

been clipped on to the outer part of the nostril (see also Gn. 24:47 ; Is. 3:21 ; Ho. 2:13).

13. For the rich fare, reminiscent of God's bounty to Israel, see Deuteronomy 32:13f. ; Hosea 2:8.

14. This verse brings the climax of God's gracious and lavish generosity to undeserving Israel. Her life, her married status, her wealth, her beauty, are all entirely due to the Lord who chose to do this for her. She contributed no merit or worthiness of her own : it was all of grace. The same truth is expressed by Old Testament writers in Deuteronomy 7:7f. ; 9:4ff. ; 32:10 ; Jeremiah 2:2 ; Hosea 9:10. It is also carried over into New Testament thought, as it represents perfectly the love and initiative of God in finding, saving and entering into covenant with people who would otherwise be doomed to die. Then, having made them His, He pours upon them every gift and blessing that earth or heaven affords (*cf.* Rom. 8:32 ; Eph. 2:3–8).

16:15–34. The bride's harlotries. The very things which God had given Israel became the means of her downfall : her beauty (15), garments (16, 18), jewellery (17) and food (19). Even the children of her union with the Lord were used as offerings for pagan sacrifice (20f.). She had forgotten the warning of Deuteronomy 6:10–12 : 'And when the Lord your God brings you into the land which he swore to your fathers . . . to give you, with great and goodly cities, which you did not build, and houses full of all good things, which you did not fill, . . . then take heed lest you forget the Lord, who brought you out of the land of Egypt, out of the house of bondage.'

15. For the indiscriminate prostitution, *cf.* Genesis 38:14ff.; Jeremiah 3:2.

16. The *gaily decked shrines* (RSV) indicate the colourful hangings of the tents that were set up at the high places (see note on 6:3), which were seen by Ezekiel to be places for feasting, fornication, idolatry and child-sacrifice. In 2 Kings 23:7, the women wove tents or hangings for Asherah in the Temple precincts, until Josiah put an end to them.

20, 21. Putting children through the fire to Molech (a

phrase found in Lv. 18:21; 2 Ki. 23:10; and Je. 32:35) is here explained as involving first slaying the child and then burning its body as a sacrifice to the god. Ahaz was guilty of this (2 Ki. 16:3) and so was Manasseh (2 Ki. 21:6). It was abhorrent to the true religion of Israel, for whom the ancient tradition of God's thwarting of the sacrifice of Isaac on Mount Moriah must have been a permanent reminder that such behaviour was not required (Gn. 22:13). Though it was by some mistakenly regarded as being the ultimate in religious devotion, Micah taught that something far deeper and more demanding was asked by Yahweh of His worshippers (Mi. 6:6-8).

23-25. From the sin of idolatry at high places, Ezekiel turns to the practice of heathen cults in the city of Jerusalem. The language suggests that shrines were set up at street-corners, but in view of the use of terms like *eminent place* (24; RSV *vaulted chamber*) and *high* (*lofty*) *place* (24, 25), it may be that these were roof-top shrines which were situated at strategic and commanding positions at the intersections of the city streets. They would be used for fertility rites in connection with Canaanite religion, rather than simply as places for commercial prostitution. The phrase, *opened thy feet*, is a euphemism for self-exposure; RSV *offering yourself*.

26-29. Specific harlotries with *Egyptians* (26), *Philistines* (27), *Assyrians* (28) and Babylonians (29) refer not only to religious infidelity but to political intrigue and alliances. These were repeatedly attacked by the prophets, notably Isaiah (Is. 20:5, 6; 30:1-5; 31:1) and Hosea (Ho. 7:11; 12:1), but the temptation for the small state of Judah to turn to their more powerful neighbours was always great, even though it never seemed to do them any good when they succumbed to the temptation. Ezekiel tells of an appeal to Egypt by Zedekiah (17:13-17), but it only provided temporary relief (*cf.* Je. 37:3-5). The hostility of the prophets to such political affiliations was only partly because they regarded them as showing a lack of trust in the protecting power of Yahweh. The main reason was that in any such alliance between a lesser and a greater power, it was normal for the weaker party to take into its religious system the gods and the worship of the stronger as a sign that they were accepting his patronage. So here the religious and the political are closely intertwined in the interpretation of the allegory. Ezekiel points out incidentally the consequences of Israel's prostitution of herself. God's reaction was that He was provoked to anger (26), for which His appointed punishment was to diminish her *allotted portion* (27), which refers to loss of territory by enemy annexation. We know from the Taylor Prism that Sennacherib did just that in 701 BC.[1] Her paramours, while taking advantage of her licentiousness, were in fact disgusted and ashamed because of it (27). And she herself found no satisfaction in what she did, but craved insatiably for more (28, 29). Quite apart from the allegorical interpretation of these verses, they stand as a shrewd observation for any generation on the effects of prostitution on the three parties most closely involved.

30-34. The perversion which marked Israel's behaviour is that, whereas the common prostitute plied her trade for hire, Israel *scorned hire* (31). Indeed Ezekiel goes so far as to say that no-one solicited her, but that she did the soliciting and actually bribed men to come to her (33, 34). Ellison well comments : 'The adulteress may by some be excused by the strength of passion and blind love, but for a harlot there is no excuse except that of stark necessity. But for Israel there is not even this excuse. She has not been paid by her lovers, but has paid those that have taken their pleasure of her'[2] (*cf.* Ho. 8:9).

16:35-43. Israel's punishment. Because Israel had courted the favours of heathen kingdoms and bribed them for support in times of national emergency, and because she was sold on every kind of pagan practice and willingly absorbed foreign cults as the whim took her, God pronounces his unmistakable word of judgment upon her. Maintaining the

---

[1] 'His (Hezekiah's) towns which I had despoiled I cut off from his land, giving them to Mitinti, king of Ashdod, Padi, king of Ekron, and Sillibel, king of Gaza, and so reduced his land' (*DOTT*, p. 67).

[2] Ellison, p. 63.

language of the allegory, He promises that Israel's own lovers will be the agents of her devastation. They will surround her and expose her publicly (37) and inflict upon her the punishment due to adulteresses and infanticides (38). This applies well to the ravages of the Babylonian armies under Nebuchadrezzar, but Ezekiel 25 castigates the Ammonites, the Moabites, the Edomites and the Philistines also for their part in the total overthrow, so the words *all your lovers* (37) are truer than would at first appear. For the punishment of exposure, *cf.* Hosea 2:10, and for the treachery of Israel's friends, *cf.* Lamentations 1:2. The fact that these nations are both the agents of God's judgment on Israel and also the objects of His wrath for so doing (*cf.* Ezk. 25) is not to be wondered at. Isaiah spoke of Assyria both as the rod of God's anger and also as guilty of the sin of arrogance in fulfilling His purpose (Is. 10:5, 12). The determinative will of God is based on foreknowledge of men's minds and gives no exemption to human responsibility.

Only when all this has been done for all to see (41), and Israel has been rendered incapable of playing the harlot any more, will God's fury be assuaged and He *will be no more angry* (42). Such references to fury, jealousy and wrath are readily misunderstood by readers of the Old Testament (though the New Testament is not without such language), who think of these as essentially human and sinful qualities. Certainly the expressions are vigorously anthropomorphic, but then any language about a personal God must be. They need to be understood not in the light of human emotions of vindictiveness and malice, but in the context of God's righteousness, holiness and consistent purity. Tasker sums it up well by saying: 'Just as human love is deficient if the element of anger is entirely lacking . . . so too is anger an essential element of divine love. God's love is inseparably connected with His holiness and His justice. He must therefore manifest anger when confronted with sin and evil.'[1]

16:44–58. Samaria and Sodom. At this stage Ezekiel

[1] R. V. G. Tasker, *The Biblical Doctrine of the Wrath of God*, 1951, p. v.

takes up a completely new allegory, but links it on to the
first by the reference to Israel's mixed parentage so as to make
it appear an expansion of what has gone before. Two sisters,
Samaria the elder and Sodom the younger, are invented for
the sinful Judah, but the prophet says that even though they
were in their day a byword for complacent prosperity and
pride (Sodom, 49, 50), and religious abominations of every
kind (Samaria, 51), Judah's sins have outstripped theirs both
in number and in intensity (52). In so doing Judah is said to
have *justified* her sisters (52; AV, RV), or better, *made your
sisters appear righteous* (RSV). There will, however, be a day of
restoration for Sodom, Samaria and Jerusalem, but this will
bring nothing but a heightened sense of shame and further
humiliation for the harlot city.

45. It is easy to see how Samaria and Sodom *loathed their
husbands and their children* : the husband was Yahweh (*cf*. Ho.
2:16), whom they had rejected by their proud and idolatrous
ways, and the children were those whom they had sacrificed
at heathen altars. It is less easy to see the logic of the Hittite
mother loathing her husband, unless we understand it also as
a reference to Yahweh, whom even the heathen were expected
to serve.[1] Cornill resolved the difficulty by deleting both
sentences ; Cooke supposed that they were there simply 'to
fill out the figure'. Perhaps we must not press the details too
closely when Ezekiel is saying no more than that there was a
family tendency to rejection of the Lord and His standards by
virtue of their mixed, Canaanitish ancestry.

49. The sin of Sodom as described here, very different
from the traditional interpretation, has much to say to the
affluent Western world of today.

51. Our Lord was using the same idea as Ezekiel when He
rebuked the city of Capernaum in Matthew 11:23f.

53. *Turn again their captivity* (RV) should be translated
throughout the Old Testament, with RSV, *restore their fortunes*.

56. Read as a question, *Was not your sister Sodom a byword . . .?*

---

[1] *Cf*. Theodoret's comment : 'He shows by this, that He is not the God
of the Jews only, but of Gentiles also; for God once gave oracles to them,
before they chose the abomination of idolatry' (quoted by Keil, p. 222n.).

(RSV). The word *š^emû'â* means a 'report', a 'news item'. Before her own sins came to light Jerusalem could conceitedly gossip about Sodom, but not when she herself had begun to fill the same role for the tattling women of *Edom* (not *Aram*, Syria) and Philistia (57).

16:59–63. The everlasting covenant. These concluding verses presuppose the fall of Jerusalem, which in any case Ezekiel regarded as a certainty, and look beyond it to a new relationship based on forgiveness, which would last for ever. The message is on the same lines as Jeremiah's promise that God would write His laws on the people's hearts (Je. 31:31–34) and is similar to Ezekiel's later oracle of the new heart and new spirit (36:25–32). It can be argued, as Ellison does, that this section was written later than 587 BC, and would fit better into the latter half of his book, on the ground that it would be inconsistent with the gloom of his oracles at this stage to give such a word of hope. This may be true, but we have already seen that many early oracles of doom contained a clear ray of hope and there is surely no inconsistency in allowing a similar gleam here.

61. *Not by thy covenant*, *i.e.* the privilege of being given responsibility for Samaria and Sodom once again was not due to Judah's old covenant, because she had broken it. It would be 'an act of God's goodness in no way depending on former relations' (Davidson, *in loc.*).

63. When God forgives our sins, He also forgets them (Is. 43:25). But the sinner can never completely forget : Paul remembered that he had persecuted the church (1 Cor. 15:9 ; 1 Tim. 1:13) ; John Newton remembered his slave-trading days. The value of such memory is that it keeps a man back from pride. Not even the justified sinner should forget that he has a past of which he is right to be ashamed.

h. The parable of the two eagles (17:1–24)

The theme of this chapter is the treachery of Zedekiah, the puppet-king appointed by Nebuchadrezzar to replace the captive Jehoiachin. It was as a result of this treachery that Nebuchadrezzar eventually marched on Jerusalem to besiege and destroy it (587 BC), but as this is foretold by Ezekiel in verse 20 it is clear that the utterance of this parable is to be dated a year or two before then, say about 590 BC. This accords well with the position of this oracle in the book, because the last preceding date (8:1) was 592 BC and the following date (20:1) is eleven months later.

The chapter divides into three sections: (*a*) the parable (1–10); (*b*) its meaning (11–21); (*c*) a promise of great days to come (22–24).

17:1–10. The two eagles. The poem which Ezekiel recites is both a *riddle* (2, EVV; Heb. *ḥîḍâ*), which means anything put enigmatically and requiring explanation, and an *allegory* (RSV; *parable*, AV, RV; Heb. *māšāl*), which is the same as the word translated 'proverb' in 12:22. The *māšāl* was an extensive literary type, covering everything from a pithy epigram to a lengthy allegory or a psalm. Its root meaning is the verb 'to be like', 'to compare', but this does not restrict its use to similes or parables. The essence of Hebrew poetry is parallelism, the repetition of one idea in slightly different terms, as in a verse like

'My eye wastes away because of grief,
  it grows weak because of all my foes' (Ps. 6:7).

In the book of Proverbs this parallelism usually draws out an antithesis, as in

'A bad messenger plunges men into trouble,
  but a faithful envoy brings healing' (Pr. 13:17).

In both examples, however, the parallelism amounts to a form of 'comparison', and so the Hebrew *māšāl* can be applied to it. The denominative verb *māšal* can, in fact, be rendered 'to speak in poetical sentences'.

In this chapter of Ezekiel the allegory is worked out in detail.[1] The first *great eagle* is Nebuchadrezzar who, with his

---

[1] See also R. S. Foster, 'A Note on Ezekiel xvii 1–10 and 22–24', *VT*, VIII, 1958, pp. 374–379.

massive military array, comes to Judah (represented by *Lebanon*), snatches away its nobility (*the top of the cedar*, 3, RV, RSV) and removes them to Babylon. Knox translates : 'he . . . carried it off to Merchant-land, set it down in Traffic City.' He then takes *of the seed of the land, i.e.* a member of the royal family, namely Jehoiachin's uncle, Zedekiah (*cf.* 2 Ki. 24:17) and plants him *like a willow twig*[1] in a fertile seed-bed (5 ; lit. 'a field of seed'), which can be no other than his native Jerusalem, where he duly flourishes. However, he is never anything more than a *low spreading vine* (6), with limited powers and influence, always dependent on his Babylonian master and with his *branches turned* in subservience *toward him*. The second eagle (7) is Egypt, to whom this vine turns for sustenance, but the prophet sees no future in this move. The vine will wither away and be uprooted by the king of Babylon with the greatest ease (9, 10).

Verse 8 presents a problem of interpretation. AV, RV seem to imply the happy state of Zedekiah under Nebuchadrezzar's authority. The words are virtually a repeat of verse 5, as if to show how unnecessary and unwise it was of him to be courting Egypt. RSV, translating *From the bed where it was planted he transplanted it*, or better, with mg., *it was transplanted*, suggests that Zedekiah's appeal to Egypt was like a further transplanting of the tender young vine which would render it weaker and more vulnerable. This is an attractive and legitimate rendering of the MT, but it confuses the picture. Before, Zedekiah's planting had been in the watered fertile lands of Palestine, the 'land of brooks of water' (Dt. 8:7 ; 11:11), where he was able to grow up in dependence upon Babylon. A change of direction in the vine's growth is a very different thing from being transplanted to another situation altogether. This would mean that Zedekiah was moving his court from Jerusalem to Egypt, and nothing so drastic was ever envisaged, so far as we know. The only way that RSV's interpretation can be logically defended is by explaining verse 5 as the planting of the seed royal (Jehoiachin or Zedekiah ?)

---

[1] Heb. *ṣaḇṣāḇâ*; RSV rendering of this rare word is confirmed by G. R. Driver's note in *Biblica*, XXXV, 1954, p. 152.

in the watered land of Babylon, *i.e.* in the sphere of his allegiance. This is how Howie, for instance, interprets it, but he further complicates the issue by taking the first twig as Jehoiachin thriving in captivity and the vine of verse 7 as Zedekiah, whose allegiance is transplanted to Egypt.[1] On the whole the AV, RV interpretation is more consistent with the parable being told.

17:11–21. The parable explained. The most notable feature of the prophet's explanation is the way it shows how the dependent relationship imposed by Nebuchadrezzar on Zedekiah is regarded as amounting to a solemn covenant which the vassal breaks at his peril. Whatever may be thought of the standards of heathen nations, and Nebuchadrezzar's policy was undoubtedly to make his neighbours weak and to keep them weak (14), Zedekiah had no option but to submit to his overlord. By sending ambassadors to Egypt, he *despised the oath* and *broke the covenant* (18), and, says Yahweh, this was *my oath* and *my covenant* (19). Such rebellion would bring not only the displeasure of Babylon, but the punishment of God – though in practice the one was identical with the other (20).

The implications of this attitude are far-reaching. It indicates that agreements entered into and obligations incurred by worshippers of God are as binding as if they had been made with God in person. What applied in the elemental code of international politics among the small states of the Middle East in the sixth century BC, must surely apply with equal force to international agreements in today's more enlightened (?) world. And what applies to nations must presumably be binding for social and personal relationships as well. The breaking of a treaty, a contract, a promise or any other kind of covenant involves God as well as the person who is thus aggrieved.

The historical situation outlined in these verses is illuminated by the narrative in Jeremiah 37, which shows that an Egyptian force was apparently sent in the direction of Jerusalem, probably in the summer of 588 BC, in response to

[1] Howie, pp. 44f.

Zedekiah's overtures and that the approach of this army caused a temporary lifting of the siege of Jerusalem which a Babylonian punitive force had already begun in January of the same year (2 Ki. 25:1 ; Je. 52:4). We know nothing of the fate of the Egyptians but we can presume that their efforts were unsuccessful, and possibly only half-hearted as well, because the siege was soon renewed for a further year until Jerusalem finally fell in July 587 BC. An interesting cross-reference is to be found in the Lachish letters, a collection of twenty-one ostraca found in the excavated ruins of Lachish (modern Tell ed-Duweir) and including reports sent in to the military governor there from one of his outlying commanders about the progress of the campaign against the Babylonian armies. One of these, datable about 590 BC, supplies the information that 'Coniah, the son of Elnathan, commander of the army, has gone down on his way to Egypt'.[1] We are left to surmise the object of his departure, but it may well have been to obtain assistance from Pharaoh Psammetichus II (593–588).

17:22-24. Another parable of the cedar tree. This time it is the Lord God who takes action. After the failure of the two great eagles to make a success of establishing the state of Israel under their extensive and powerful patronage, God says, *I myself* (emphatic) *will plant it* upon a high mountain where it will grow and be conspicuous and attract the birds of the air to shelter under its protection. The *sprig from the lofty top of the cedar* (22, RSV) refers to a member of the Davidic dynasty, though Ezekiel could hardly have known how this was going to be fulfilled. The kingly line would, however, flourish, contrary to all appearances, and other nations would be incorporated under its secure and wide-spreading dominion. In so doing, the Lord would reverse the expected order of things, so that powerful nations like Babylon and Egypt (*the high tree, the green tree*) would wither and fade, while the low and the dry would by His word be made to flourish (24 ; *cf.* 1 Sa. 2:4–8 ; Lk. 1:51–53).

[1] *DOTT*, p. 214.

i. The law of individual responsibility (18:1–32)

The objection with which Ezekiel deals in this chapter is expressed in the words of the well-worn saying, 'The fathers have eaten sour grapes, and the children's teeth are set on edge' (2). That this was a common proverb in ancient Israel around this time is evidenced by Jeremiah's reference to it (Je. 31:29), though he used it in a slightly different context from Ezekiel.[1] The meaning is common to both references, however, for the proverb is saying that the sufferings of one generation are due to the misdeeds of their forbears. Both Jeremiah and Ezekiel saw this as a pernicious doctrine, because it inevitably led to a spirit of fatalism and irresponsibility. If the fault could really be laid at the door of a previous generation, those on whom the judgment was falling could reasonably shrug off any sense of sin and accuse God of injustice ('The way of the Lord is not just', verse 25).

Before we side with Ezekiel in deploring this attitude, let us first note two factors which made the proverb eminently reasonable and doubtless accounted for its widespread appeal. First, the concept of continuing responsibility for ancestral sins is a deeply-rooted belief inherited from the Ten Commandments at Sinai. 'I the Lord your God am a jealous God, visiting the iniquity of the fathers upon the children to the third and the fourth generation of those who hate me' (Ex. 20:5). Secondly, it had been the basis of much of Ezekiel's own teaching, namely that the sufferings of the exile could be traced back to the persistent rebellion, idolatry and unfaithfulness to the covenant of previous generations of Israelites. The exile was, in effect, merely the due consequence of these accumulating acts of disobedience. Furthermore there was the element of apparent injustice in the way in which God's judgment fell indiscriminately upon the nation, upon both the bad and the good.

To this Ezekiel replies by asserting, without however

---

[1] The setting in Jeremiah is eschatological (note the phrases, 'in those days', 'the days are coming' in Je. 31:27, 29, 31). The cessation of the use of this proverb is a feature associated by Jeremiah with the coming days of the new covenant which God will make with Judah and Israel.

arguing the point, that in God's eyes people are individuals and He treats them as such. Every man is a matter of concern to Him. 'All souls are mine' (4). The righteous man will live; the wicked will die. Everyone will be responsible to God for his own conduct. To this Ezekiel would surely add that, so far from their having cause to blame their sinful forbears for their present sufferings, the exiles were *more* guilty than their fathers because they had sinned more and their idolatries were greater (*cf.* chapter 8). It could not all be blamed on Manasseh and his reign of wickedness.

As if to reinforce his assertion about the freedom of the individual, Ezekiel proceeds in verses 21ff. to hold out the possibility of a changed life. Individual judgment is never so final that it cannot be reversed by a change of heart and of conduct. The wicked man can repent and do righteously and live, and conversely the righteous man can revert to sinful ways and incur the judgment of death. In a word, the judgment will fall upon each man as it finds him.

This classic statement of individual responsibility must not, however, be taken in complete isolation. It is not a flat contradiction of the traditional view of corporate responsibility. It is rather a counterpoise to it. The corporate unity of the family or tribal group was of the *esse* of Hebrew psychology. It was bound up with the idea of the continuance of the family line by direct sonship, as well as with the covenant relationship that existed between the God of Israel and the community of Israel. To have denied all this would have needed more than a bare assertion. The whole attitude to life would have had to be radically rewritten and dogmatically reformulated by Ezekiel. Communal solidarity and corporate responsibility were facts, to which experience bore witness. Ezekiel's aim is to show that they are not the only facts. God's redeemed community is a nation of righteous or repentant individuals. And in the situation with which the prophet was immediately concerned, it was dangerous for the exiles to be concealing themselves behind an unbalanced view of their national responsibility in order to avoid the prophetic demand for repentance and a new way of life.

2. The attitude is well expressed in Lamentations 5:7 : 'Our fathers sinned, and are no more ; and we bear their iniquities.'

3. Jeremiah looked forward to the day when this proverb would no longer be used (Je. 31:29) ; but Ezekiel insists that it should cease forthwith.

4. As in 13:20, the word *souls* must not be understood in terms of disembodied spirits. The Hebrew soul (*nep̄eš*) represented the totality of the person or the life-force within him. No one English word can translate the various nuances which the four uses of *nep̄eš* in this verse carry. Possibly the nearest rendering, to avoid the ambiguous word 'soul', would be 'All *lives* are mine ; the *life* of the father . . . the *life* of the son . . . the *person* that sins shall die.'

18:5–20. Three cases to illustrate the principle. The examples given are of a righteous man doing right (5–9) ; a wicked son of a righteous father (10–13) ; and a righteous son of a wicked father (14–18). Described in terms of three generations of one family they may well suggest the lives of the three great kings of the seventh century : Hezekiah, Manasseh his son, and Josiah the grandson of Manasseh.

6. The list consists mainly of moral qualities, though the first two are religious offences. Eating *upon the mountains* means taking part in sacrificial meals at high places, which is fittingly coupled with lifting up the eyes, presumably in prayer or some kind of subservience, to *idols* (for the Heb. *gillûlîm*, see on 6:9). The offence of adultery, expressly forbidden in the Decalogue, is linked with a ceremonial defilement referred to in Leviticus 15:24 ; 18:19. Although the second of these is not repeated in the lists in verses 11 and 15, that is no argument for deleting it here as an addition ; both offences occur again in 22:10f.

7. Oppression was the high-handed action of the powerful landowner or merchant against the poor man who was in debt or against the weak man who did not know, or could not make use of, his citizen-rights. The fatherless and the widow and the resident-alien ('sojourner') were easy targets for the unscrupulous (*cf.* Am. 2:6f. ; Mal. 3:5). Restoring *to the* *debtor his pledge* refers to the duty of returning to a debtor any article taken in pledge which was necessary to him for his existence or well-being, *e.g.* his cloak at night (*cf.* Ex. 22:26; Dt. 24:6; Am. 2:8).

8. The embargo on usury, found here and in similar lists of ethical demands (*e.g.* Ps. 15:5), refers to charitable loans to people in distress. Deuteronomy 23:19f. permitted interest on loans to foreigners but not to fellow-Israelites. The practice destroyed the spirit of true charity, opened the way to extortion by means of high interest-rates and inevitably led to the enslavement of the debtor who could not repay when required to. This is a very different thing from modern money-lending practices for commercial purposes. But in both cases the principle of *true justice between man and man* is called for.

9. The concluding requirements, as it were summing up the religious and moral demands which have been laid down, are plainly religious. In the mind of Ezekiel, as with all the Old Testament writers, morality was the expression of a man's religion. There could be no divorce between the two.

13. *He shall not live . . . he shall surely die.* The latter phrase is the common legal formula for condemnation. What does it signify here? Probably the alternative fates of life and death refer to what will take place in the judgment which is imminent. But Muilenburg is right to suggest that 'there is more than an implication that the righteous experience life and the unrighteous experience death here and now'.[1] The Hebrew concepts of life and death represent not two distinct states, but the two poles on the one graduated scale of existence. At its lower end are death, suffering, illness and even weariness; at its higher end are varying degrees of prosperity, with happiness and the divine blessing as the *summum bonum*. This is, in fact, not far short of the 'life abundant' or 'eternal life' of the New Testament, namely a life lived in the presence and under the blessing of God.

19. The three cases just described lead back to the problem of the sour grapes. If the son is thought of as a part of his father, a continuation of his personality in a succeeding

[1] Peake, *in loc.*

generation, why should he not suffer along with his father and share in his father's punishment? Ezekiel's categorical denial states that iniquity is not necessarily inherited, any more than righteousness is. The individual's righteousness or wickedness *shall be upon himself* (20).

18:21–32. The case of a changed life. The logical development of his previous argument is for Ezekiel to go on to say that an individual need not live under the shadow of his former sins. If he can turn from his father's sins, he can presumably turn from his own.

23. This, however, is not bare logic. The reason behind the assertion is the preference (if that is not too weak a word) that God has for men to repent and live. It is the Lord's longing and will and purpose that men should be saved. Such a longing should be shared by every preacher who ventures to speak about the judgment of God. *Cf.* 2 Peter 3:9.

24. The converse is also unhappily true: an upright beginning can be blighted by a fall into sin. The reference is not to a temporary lapse, but to a persistent choice of evil which changes the course of a man's life.

The charge of injustice which is levelled against the Lord (25, 29) is turned back upon the accusers. It is they whose ways are not *just* (RSV; *equal*, AV, RV). The law of individual responsibility which Ezekiel has been expounding is supremely fair, for every man has his own personal choice and the chance to live. God will judge *every one according to his ways* (30). It is the combination of this fact and the knowledge that God has *no pleasure in the death of any one* (32) that leads Ezekiel to appeal to the people in God's name to repent and turn to Him. As a people they may be rebellious and idolatrous, but as individuals they can be appealed to and, through their repentance, can be saved.

31. *Get yourselves a new heart and a new spirit!* The language is that of human exhortation. It would be unfair to Ezekiel to suggest that he regarded these as being anything other than gifts of God. He himself says so in 36:26, 'A new heart I will give you, and a new spirit I will put within you.' Individual effort and activity are needed, however, at the human level in order to effect repentance and enable the spiritual reformation to take place. Fatalism results in inactivity and is deadly to the soul. To live by the proverb of verse 2 is to capitulate and die. *Why will you die, O house of Israel?*

j. A lament over the kings of Israel (19:1–14)

This poem is the first example Ezekiel has given us of the *qînâ*, variously translated 'dirge', 'elegy' or 'lamentation'. It consists of a composition written in the distinctive mournful tones of the *qînâ* rhythm, in which the two members of the couplet are of unequal length in the pattern of 3:2. Only rarely can this rhythm be caught in an English translation, because in Hebrew the beats are usually one to a word and when translated a single Hebrew word often needs several English words to express its meaning. Verse 2b illustrates the metre best :

1   2   3

In-the-midst of-lions she-couched,

1   2

rearing her-whelps.

Other examples of the same metre in Ezekiel are found in 26:17f.; 27:3–9; 28:12–19; 32:2–8. It occurs frequently elsewhere in the Old Testament, especially in the Psalms (where even Psalm 23 uses it) and in prophetic laments, and of course it is typical of much of Lamentations.

The subjects of Ezekiel's lament were Jehoahaz, son of Josiah, who was taken captive to Egypt in 609 BC (4); Jehoiachin, son of Jehoiakim, who was exiled to Babylon in 597 BC (9); and Zedekiah, also a son of Josiah, who was the last of the Davidic line of rulers and virtually ended the dynasty (14). If the poem is to be dated with the rest of the section it accompanies, between 592 and 591 BC, the first part is a historical retrospect but Zedekiah had not yet rebelled and succumbed to Babylonian might. Some would therefore regard verses 10–14 as a later addition, and this may be true, but there is no need to deny them to Ezekiel whose style they follow closely. Alternatively, the reference to Zedekiah's disastrous end could be prophetic, and the poem could then be regarded as a unity. The theme applied to all three of these kings is that of human greatness brought to nought. For all their prowess and renown these men fell victims to the judgment of God on their lives. That is not to say that Ezekiel would have described them all as thoroughly corrupt, though he had little good to say for Zedekiah. It is probable that he would have shared the assessment of the writer of 2 Kings that they 'did what was evil in the sight of the Lord' (2 Ki. 23:32 ; 24:9, 19). His zeal for the Davidic covenant, however, did not allow him to see three of its inheritors disappear into exile without profound sorrow and emotion. This was no taunt-song. The judgment of the Lord could be very grievous, and Ezekiel felt it keenly.

1. Note again the avoidance of the word *melek*, 'king', in favour of the more general *nāśî*', 'prince'. Cf. 7:27 ; 12:12.

2-4. The fate of Jehoahaz. The *lioness* is to be understood, not as Hamutal, wife of Josiah and mother of Jehoahaz and Zedekiah, but as the nation who mothered these kings. Lions, incidentally, were common in Palestine until shortly after the Crusades, and Hebrew had five different words to describe them (all of which occur in Jb. 4:10f., and three of which are found here in verse 2). For the lion as a part of the national, Davidic imagery, *cf.* Genesis 49:9 ; Micah 5:8 ; and possibly 1 Kings 10:19f. Muilenburg refers to the royal lion on the seal of Shema found at Megiddo.[1]

Jehoahaz reigned for only three months, so the description of his renown must be regarded as a poetic transference to express the glory of the Davidic line which Jehoahaz represented. He was carried off to Egypt by Pharaoh Necho (2 Ki. 23:33) and eventually died there, as Jeremiah had foretold (Je. 22:10-12 ; Shallum was another name for the same man).

19:5-9. The fate of Jehoiachin. Jehoahaz was succeeded by his brother Jehoiakim, but Ezekiel passes over him and

---

[1] In Peake, p. 579a; the seal is illustrated in *ANEP*, No. 276, or in A. Reifenberg, *Ancient Hebrew Seals* (1950), fig. 1.

moves straight on to the latter's son, Jehoiachin. He also reigned for only three months before becoming the victim of his father's misdemeanours. Jerusalem was already under attack, because of Jehoiakim's refusal to pay tribute to Nebuchadrezzar, when the eighteen-year-old prince came to the throne. His reign was brief and pathetic, and his exile in Babylon long and wearisome. See 2 Kings 24:8–15 ; 25:27–30.[1]

5. *Baffled* (RSV) is a guess, in an attempt to make sense of a rare Hebrew form (*waited*, AV, RV). A slight emendation, proposed by Cornill, gives 'she had acted foolishly', but the difficulty still remains.

7. The incredible RV mg. *and he knew their widows* may be understood as follows : the Hebrew for 'widows' and 'citadels' is very similar and was occasionally confused (*e.g.* Is. 13:22), and the root 'to know' almost certainly shared the same letters (*y-d-ʿ*) as a root meaning 'to humiliate' and this was a source of frequent confusion. RSV quite rightly renders *he ravaged their strongholds*, which makes for perfect parallelism with the phrase that follows it.

9. The word for *cage* (Heb. *sûḡar*) is a loan-word from Akk. *šigaru*, meaning either an animal's cage, or a neck-band with which lines of prisoners were roped together. The word in modern Hebrew means a 'dog-collar' !

19:10–14. The fate of Zedekiah. Although the picture has changed, the *mother* is still to be taken as the nation Israel. The symbol of the vine and the vineyard was a favourite with Ezekiel (15:1–6 ; 17:1–10) as well as with other writers (Is. 5:1–7 ; 27:2–6 ; Ps. 80:8–16 ; *cf.* Mt. 21:33–41 ; Jn. 15:1–8). It had an honourable ancestry from Genesis 49:9–12, where can be found the same imagery of lions, sceptres and vines as Ezekiel uses here. In this allegory the vine, planted in a well-watered land, flourishes and sends out sturdy shoots like so many royal sceptres, and these represented the nation's succession of rulers. When the vine was pulled up by its roots, however, its strong stem withered away and was burnt. The

[1] For a fuller survey of the historical background to this chapter, see Introduction, pp. 31f.

vine was transplanted to a desert land and at the same time fire came out of its chief branch and destroyed all its fruit and the rest of its foliage. This is clearly a reference to Zedekiah, the last ruler of Israel, who was regarded as the cause of the nation's ultimate collapse.

10. *In thy blood* (AV, RV) can hardly be right, and many emendations have been proposed. The likeliest presuppose a confusion of *dām*, 'blood', with either *dāmâ*, 'to be like' (so RV mg., *in thy likeness*), or *rāmâ*, 'height', 'loftiness'. RSV *vineyard* is weak.

14. The verse refers to Zedekiah's rebellion which brought in its wake the punitive Babylonian measures which virtually ended Israel's national identity, at least for many years, and certainly brought the Davidic line to an end. Thus the cause of its own destruction was found within itself, and it is worth noting that most institutions involving human beings end in much the same way.

k. A review of Israel's past history and of God's future plans for her (20:1–44)

Unlike the illustration of the foundling child (chapter 16) and the parable of Oholah and Oholibah (chapter 23), we have here a description of Israel's past history of continuing rebellion against the Lord, expressed in actual historical terms without the aid of metaphor and allegory. The chapter traces the main events of the past, beginning with Egypt and leading on to the Exodus, the wilderness experience, life in Canaan and eventual dispersion among the nations. There are a number of themes which recur : (*a*) the rebelliousness of Israel, despite God's merciful treatment of them in giving them numerous blessings and in repeatedly withholding His wrath from being poured out upon them. (*b*) The wilderness wanderings, as being more than simply an episode in Israel's history. They represented a state of mind and its consequences. So the final period of Israel's history, the dispersion in exile, is seen as a reversion to the wilderness life which had preceded the settlement in Canaan (verse 35 : 'I will bring you into the wilderness of the peoples'). (*c*) The motive of Yahweh's concern for His own name. This is a new feature in Ezekiel's writing and it appears later on in chapters 36 and 39, but it is not wholly absent anywhere from the prophet's thought. Its significance is that it represents a cessation by God of His covenant blessings towards Israel because they had so completely abandoned their own responsibilities under the covenant. All the covenant requirements, like the statutes and ordinances of Sinai, had been broken and the covenant sign, the sabbath, had been profaned : God was therefore justified in carrying out the sanctions of the covenant. He was still, however, a God of mercy ; but now His merciful acts were prompted primarily by concern for His own 'name' (*i.e.* glory, reputation), and with an eye to the conclusions which would be drawn by the watching nations of the world.

20:1–4. The enquiry of the elders. The date is given as the tenth day of the month *Ab* (July–August) in the year 591 BC.[1] No indication is given of the purpose of the elders' visit. It may have been that they had come to sit at Ezekiel's feet in the hope of hearing some news of the homeland or a word from God about the length of their exile, as in 14:1. They may have set Ezekiel a particular question which they wanted answering. Verse 32 has been taken by some to suggest that the elders were advocating a form of syncretism and were trying to gain Ezekiel's support for their policy. This would certainly accord with the decisive rejection in Ezekiel's reply, but the question remains entirely speculative. The reason given for the refusal to answer the elders' enquiry is cryptically given as *the abominations of their fathers* (4). To interpret this as an accusation against the elders on the grounds of their forefathers' sins would involve a denial of much that Ezekiel has been arguing in relation to individual responsibility. The point is that for some unexplained reason the enquiry is an impertinent one and needs only a rehearsal of Israel's past sins to show that history has answered the question for them. This explains the impatience of the repeated *Will you judge them* (4),

[1] See chronological notes in Introduction, p. 36.

156

a phrase which has the force of an imperative : 'set out the case against them'.

20:5–9. Israel in Egypt. The frequency of the strong word of asseveration, *I lifted up my hand* (RSV *I swore*), in verses 5, 6, 15, 23, 28 and 42, illustrates the abundance of God's grace in so binding Himself to His covenant mercies to Israel. This grace was first shown in the self-revelation of Yahweh to Moses (Ex. 6:2–8) in the words, *I am the Lord* (*i.e.* Yahweh) *your God*. It is regarded in this passage as the moment in time when the Lord *chose* Israel, the only occasion incidentally when this word is used in Ezekiel. Israel's history begins therefore, not with Abraham, but with Moses and the burning bush and the name of Yahweh, revealed as the definitive name of Israel's covenant God.

6. The first stage of Israel's history is marked by God's promise of a *land flowing with milk and honey*, a consciously extravagant description of a blessing of superlative worth (*cf.* Je. 3:19). The only stipulation made was the rejection of the *idols of Egypt* (7), a command which was totally ignored (8). There is no indication in the Pentateuch of the religious life of the Israelites in Egypt, but it is safe to assume that they were not very successful in maintaining this religious purity, if later history is anything to go by, and we can imagine the long and difficult task Moses had to educate his people to accept the Yahweh-revelation which had been made to him at the burning bush. The demand of the first of the Ten Commandments implies that Israel had to move out of a stage of the acceptance of other gods into an exclusive worship of Yahweh.

9. The *name* of Yahweh expresses His nature, His total personality as He has revealed Himself. It is parallel to His 'glory', *i.e.* His glorious majesty, and it can refer to His reputation in the eyes of men. If men think right thoughts about Him and recognize His attributes for what they are and so worship Him, they may be said to 'sanctify' Him ; and conversely, to misunderstand His nature and to regard Him less highly than He ought to be regarded is to *profane* His name. It is the duty of the new Israel, as it was of the old Israel, to see that God's name is not profaned through inadequate witness to His nature and His truth. The believer's sins and shortcomings inevitably result in such profanation. But God can and does frequently take special measures to counteract this and to ensure that faithful witness to Him and His power is not completely extinguished.

20:10–26. Israel in the wilderness. The pattern of grace, rebellion and wrath withheld, which is attributed to Israel's history in Egypt in verses 5–9, is now worked out in relation to the wilderness period. First, in verses 10–17, there is mention of the gracious deliverance of the Exodus, the gift of the Law and the ordaining of the sabbath as a sign of the covenant. It is worth noting that, despite New Testament strictures on the spiritual value of the law as an instrument of salvation (*e.g.* Jn. 1:17; Acts 13:39; Rom. 3:20; Gal. 3:19ff.), it is quite clearly regarded as a gracious gift of God through Moses to His people and it was ordained so that by the observance of it *man shall live*, *i.e.* 'prosper', both materially and spiritually (*cf.* Dt. 4:40; Jos. 1:7f.). In face of Israel's rejection of His grace, the Lord *thought* to destroy them utterly (13) and *swore* not to allow them into Canaan (15), but even these decisions were changed in the face of His overriding concern for His name. There is nothing inconsistent in the Deity changing His mind, or 'repenting', under such circumstances.

Secondly, in verses 18–26, God gives a similar chance to the second generation of Israelites in the wilderness, but the response is identical with that of their fathers. This time, although once again God refrains from pouring out His wrath, He does leave Israel with two unhappy legacies, namely the threat of dispersion from Canaan among foreign peoples (23, 24), and the harmful ordinance of the offering of the firstborn (25, 26). The latter presents an acute problem of interpretation. It seems to refer to the unlawful practice of 'passing children through the fire to Molech', a form of child-sacrifice so strongly and frequently condemned in the

Old Testament that it may well have happened far more than the occasional times it is mentioned (*e.g.* 2 Ki. 21:6; 2 Ch. 28:3; *cf.* 2 Ki. 17:17; 23:10, 13; Je. 7:31; 32:35). But this could never be described as an ordinance of God. It may be that the ordinance referred to is that of the offering of the first-born with its insistence that everything that opens the womb belongs to the Lord. This is modified by the law of redemption whereby a substitute or a ransom-price can be provided for first-born children (Ex. 22:29; Nu. 18:15ff.). But the occasional continuance of child-sacrifice was probably due to a misinterpretation of this law, and so Ezekiel could imply that God had ultimately made it so. The alternative is to understand these verses in the manner of Romans 1:24, which is saying that the consequence of spiritual perversity is that God 'gives men up' to grosser sins.

20:27–29. Israel in Canaan. The crowning rebellion of Israel's history was that when finally, in the mercy of God, they entered into the land of promise, they promptly took over the heathen Canaanite hill-top shrines as their own places of sacrifice, and offerings which should have proved acceptable to God were nothing less than an 'irritation' (28; EVV *provocation*) to Him. *Bamah* (29), 'high place', is introduced for the sake of the play on words with *mâ* ('what') and *bā'* ('go'). It is not to be taken as a serious attempt at etymology on Ezekiel's part. A possible English equivalent would be: '*Why* the *high altar* to which you *all turn*?'

20:30–39. The consequences of Israel's past. The word now comes to the present house of Israel who have been committing these idolatrous practices *to this day* (31). In particular, the elders who came to enquire of the Lord are addressed and told that there will be no word for them. The insidious attitude of assimilation to the idolatrous ways of the heathen will not be allowed to happen (32). God will intervene and with the same *mighty hand* and *outstretched arm* as saved Israel at the Exodus, He will become *king* over them and lead them in judgment into another wilderness experience (*cf.* Ho.

2:14f.; 12:9). This will serve as a purging for Israel; the unclean will not return and those who want their idolatry can practise it, but in isolation from the faithful Israelites so as not to profane God's name any more (39).

20:40–44. God's good purposes for Israel. A purified remnant will worship the Lord on His *holy mountain*, Mount Zion, the ordained centre for His worship and the place of His dwelling. The choicest offerings will be made, the people's worship will be accepted, and this will prove to be a manifestation to all the nations of Yahweh's *holiness* (41). AV, RV render this, *I will be sanctified in you*, which means 'I will be recognized as God among you', and this, more than any personal concern for His rebellious people, remains God's ultimate aim (see note above on verse 9). At the same time, the people will be overcome with shame for their past sins (43) and presumably their repentant spirit will also testify to the nature and holiness of God. It is precisely at this point, for their lack of a sense of shame and a spirit of repentance, that the elders are shown to be guilty and found unworthy to receive a word from a holy God.

l. Judgment by fire and by sword (20:45 – 21:32)[1]

20:45–49. A forest fire in the south. Ezekiel is commanded to address his words *toward the south* (46). Although the word appears three times in this verse in AV and RV, the Hebrew uses three different words (*têmānâ, dārôm* and *negeb*). Of these the first two are general poetic words to describe the southerly direction, whereas the third refers to a named geographical area, called in modern Israel the Negev, which lay to the south of the Judean hills. Today this is waterless desert, except where agricultural settlements have irrigated it into a state of cultivation, but we know that in Old Testament times there was greater afforestation throughout Palestine, and so a reference to *the forest of the Negeb* (RSV) does not have

---

[1] The unity of this section is made more plain in the Hebrew text, where chapter 21 begins at 20:45 (EVV) and goes on for 37 verses.

to be regarded as completely figurative. Ezekiel may have reinforced his words by facing southwards as he uttered his oracle, predicting that the Lord will cause a forest fire to sweep through the land from south to north. All will see it and no-one will be able to avoid its heat (47 ; *all faces . . . shall be scorched by it*). Men will realize that it has been sent by the Lord as an act of judgment. Verse 49 presupposes that Ezekiel has spoken his oracle and has been ridiculed by his hearers as a *speaker of parables* (RV), or, to retain the cognate form of the Hebrew, a 'riddler of riddles'. In view of what has gone before the complaint is not without its justification.

21:1-7. The parable explained. The phraseology of verses 2-5 is designed to match that of 20:46-48. The south becomes first *Jerusalem*, then *the sanctuaries*, and finally *the land of Israel*. The forest fire becomes a *sword*, which will slay *both righteous and wicked* ('the green tree and the dry tree'), and *all flesh* will recognize that it is the Lord who has done this (5). The theme of the sword of the Lord may be traced back to Joshua's vision, on the banks of the river Jordan, of the commander of the army of the Lord with his drawn sword in his hand (Jos. 5:13ff.). There He was fighting for His people to enable them to enter the promised land in victory. In other passages, especially in the prophets, God wields His sword against Israel's enemies (Dt. 32:41 ; Is. 31:8 ; 34:5-8 ; 66:16 ; Je. 25:31 ; 50:35ff. ; Zp. 2:12). The sword is thus His instrument of judgment and features prominently in apocalyptic battle-scenes in intertestamental writing. Ezekiel, however, is using it here of God's punishment upon Israel, though in other prophecies he implies that the sword of the Lord has been put into the hands of the king of Babylon so that God's judgment may be worked out through his armies upon the might of Pharaoh, king of Egypt (30:24 ; 32:11-15). In the collection of oracles that comprise this section, it seems as if the only unifying factor which has brought them together is the recurrence of this theme of the sword of the Lord (verses 3-5 ; 11-15 ; 19, 20, 28).

6, 7. Ezekiel's distress is yet another symbol of the overwhelming dismay that will come upon Israel in their moment of judgment. Just as his failure to mourn over the death of his wife is treated as symbolic of a grief too great for tears (24:23), so here he speaks his message with the symbolism, not of actions, but of emotions. *With the breaking of thy loins* (AV, RV), for which RSV gives *with breaking heart*, is a phrase expressing deep emotional distress. The loins were regarded as the seat of strength, and so this represents complete nervous and physical collapse (*cf.* 29:7; Ps. 69:23; Na. 2:10). The same sense of panic and emotional paralysis will afflict the people when they hear *the tidings*, or 'the news' : 'It's coming !'

21:8–17. The song of the sword. Some of this section is clearly in poetry, but it is not possible to discern the original poem from prose comments that are interspersed. The only recognizable part is the opening couplet which may be rendered

> A sword, a sword ! It is sharpened
>   and polished as well.
> Sharpened to slay and to slaughter,
>   polished like lightning.

This may be an adaptation of an older poem rather like the equally pithy Song of Lamech (Gn. 4:23f.), or it may even have been the words that went with a sword-dance. Howie thinks that Ezekiel could have accompanied these words with some such sword-brandishing. However he quickly breaks off to ask, *Or do we make mirth?* This and the sentence which follows are impossible to understand in MT. RSV emends the pointing slightly to give *You have despised the rod, my son, with everything of wood*. Taken this way, the prophet is rebuking his hearers for inattention ('do you think I am joking?'), and accusing them of scorning all former instruments of punishment. The *rod* suggests Isaiah's description of the Assyrians as 'the rod of my anger' (Is. 10:5). Now, however, wood will be replaced by steel, and it will not be simply a *testing* (13; follow RSV) ; it will be wholesale destruction *upon my people*. Smiting the thigh (12) was a gesture of grief and despair (Je. 31:19).

14. Although the identity of the slayer is not given in verse 11, it is evident that Ezekiel has a part in the slaughter, if only in providing the applause to go with it. This indicates that he did in all probability act out this warning of impending judgment and play the part of an exultant onlooker as the swordplay went on. The sighings and groans that came earlier from his lips are sufficient evidence that it was not his nature to exult over the destruction, but we must understand it as a necessary and graphic accompaniment of the oracle which, as God's spokesman, he had to fulfil. For in so doing he was demonstrating God's approval at what was taking place : *I also will clap my hands*, says the Lord (17).

21:18-27. The sword of the king of Babylon. The word which occurs most frequently in this section is the word *appoint* (AV ; 19, 20, 22 twice). The Hebrew word is the more modest *śûm* or *śîm*, which simply means 'to put' or 'to place'. It does however suggest once again that Ezekiel is intended to combine his message here with a symbolical performance of the advance of the Babylonian king along the road to Jerusalem, with suitable routes mapped out upon the ground. The first act is to mark out the road stemming from Babylon, or probably from the north, shaped like an inverted Y, with Jerusalem and Rabbath Ammon (suitably sign-posted) at the end of its two prongs. Then the various kinds of divination practised by the king as he stood at the parting of the ways are re-enacted. The alternatives were an assault on the Ammonite capital city (modern Amman) or a siege of Jerusalem.

21. Three methods of divination are described. The first is shaking the *arrows*, or belomancy (AV is misleading here). In this, arrows were marked with names of people or places, shaken up in a quiver, and one was drawn out, as in drawing lots. The second is consultation of the *teraphim* : these were small images of household or ancestral gods, the possession of which played an important part in matters of legal inheritance (*cf.* Gn. 31:19ff.). They were sometimes used idolatrously or for necromancy and were among the abominations removed

by Josiah (2 Ki. 23:24). What they looked like or how they
were consulted we do not know. But if they were figures of
ancestors they would presumably be used as mediums for
obtaining oracles from the departed.[1] The third is hepatoscopy,
examination of the *liver* or entrails of a sacrificed victim. This
was a common feature of Babylonian divination and it was
carried over into ancient Rome as well. The interpretation of
the markings on such organs was one of the skills in which
Ancient Near Eastern soothsayers were instructed, as numbers
of clay models unearthed by archaeologists appear to indicate.[2]

22. RSV is right to omit the first of the two phrases *to set
battering rams*, inserted by accidental repetition after *Jerusalem*
(see RSV mg.). In any case, *to appoint captains* (AV) is not the
right rendering of these words. On *mound* (*sōlᵉlâ*) and *fort*
(*dāyēq*), see note on 4:2.

23. It will be no use the people of Jerusalem shrugging off
these warnings and regarding them as *false divination* : Nebuchadrezzar will come and will bring their guilt home to them.
The phrase, *they have sworn solemn oaths*, is difficult and some
would omit it (with LXX). As it stands (lit. 'oaths of oaths to
them'), it may give the grounds of their iniquity, namely
Zedekiah's broken covenant with Babylon (17:16ff.) or his
amnesty of the slaves which was subsequently retracted (Je.
34:8ff.). Alternatively, by taking *šāḇûaʿ* as 'seven' and not as
'oath', a translation 'they have seven sevens'='seven weeks', or
'weeks of weeks', could imply that the people of Jerusalem
think they have all the time in the world to prepare against
the threatened siege.

25, 26. Zedekiah is addressed typically, not as king,
meleḵ, but as prince, *nāśîʾ*, a word without Messianic overtones.
The *mitre* (RV ; *diadem* in AV) is the *turban* (from a word meaning
'to wind', so RSV) worn by the high priest (Ex. 28:4, 37, 39 ;
29:6 ; 39:28, 31 ; Lv. 8:9 ; 16:4). It is used only here as a
symbol of royalty. There is no evidence that Zedekiah had
added to his crimes by usurping priestly functions.

27. The triple repetition of a word is the strongest superlative the Hebrew language can give (*cf.* 'Holy, holy, holy' in

[1] See *NBD*, art. 'Teraphim', p. 1253. [2] See *NBD*, fig. 135, p. 742.

Is. 6:3, or the formula of Je. 7:4). So Ezekiel spells out the *overthrow* of the kingly line, and he concludes with a cryptic reference back to Genesis 49:10 with its distant prospect of the one who had always been expected and to whom the right of kingship genuinely belonged. When he eventually appears, the crown and diadem will be given to him, for he will be the culmination of everything to which the Davidic house and the Messianic kingship in Israel have always pointed.[1]

21:28-32. The sword of Ammon. In a passage which is very obscure but has obvious affinities with earlier parts of the chapter, especially verses 9-17, the Ammonites are represented as wielding a sword against Israel. This may reflect the period during or after the siege of Jerusalem when the Ammonites joined with others in taking advantage of Judah's plight by attacking and plundering her lands. This apparently is done under the influence of false auguries and lying visions (29), but God stays their hand and calls upon them to *return it to its sheath* (30). Words of condemnation follow : in his own land Ammon will be judged and punished. He will suffer at the hands of *brutish men, skilful to destroy* (31), who are later designated as 'the people of the East' (25:4), *i.e.* the savage tribesmen of the desert. So the Ammonites' vindictive plans will rebound back upon themselves, as the further oracle on their fate makes clear (25:1-7). Their ultimate fate will be worse than Israel's and worse even than Egypt's, for they will be *no more remembered*. To the Semitic mind nothing could be more terrible : no prospect of restoration, no continuance in succeeding generations, no memorial, not even a memory. Oblivion.

m. Three oracles on the defilement of Jerusalem (22:1-31)

This chapter consists of three oracles, each beginning with the phrase, 'The word of the Lord came to me' (1, 17, 23). They may originally have been uttered on separate occasions,

[1] See *NBD*, art. 'Shiloh', p. 1177.

but they have been grouped together because they share the same theme of the indictment of Jerusalem for her sins. May describes the chapter in its present form as a three-point sermon by the final editor of Ezekiel, who is anxious that his contemporaries should take warning from the fate of Jerusalem. The first (2–16) condemns Jerusalem as the city of blood and catalogues the variety of sins, religious, sexual, social and judicial, which are found in her. The two most frequently used words are *blood* (2, 3, 4, 6, 9, 12, 13) and *in you* (6, 7, 9, 10, 11, 12, 16). The punishment for all this is to be dispersion among the nations, as if that will enable the Lord to consume away the city's defilement from her (15). The second oracle (17–22) uses the metaphor of the smelting of silver, and this points to the long and painful agonies of testing which Israel is about to undergo. All the elements in the nation will be gathered together in Jerusalem and will there experience the fires of the wrath of God. There is no mention of any refined silver resulting from this process, though silver may be reckoned among the elements which make up Israel; but see below for a discussion of the passage. The verdict on Israel is that they are all dross (19). The third oracle (23–31) makes detailed criticisms of the different classes of Israelite society – the princes, the priests, the prophets, the nobles and the people of the land. All of them have failed in their responsibilities; not a man has been found who will stand in the breach. So the Lord will pour out upon them the due recompense for their misdeeds. Their fate is sealed.

Many commentators follow Hölscher and Herntrich in seeing this third oracle as a later composition, interpreting verse 31 not as a prophetic perfect but as an actual past tense looking back to the fall of Jerusalem. Cross-reference is regularly made to Zephaniah 3:1–4, but the date and authorship of those verses are also matters of question[1] and the precise relationship between the two passages is not altogether clear. It could well be that the oracle was written up after

---

[1] For further discussion, see J. P. Hyatt, 'The Date and Background of Zephaniah', *JNES*, VII, 1948, pp. 25–29; L. P. Smith and E. R. Lacheman, 'The Authorship of the Book of Zephaniah', *JNES*, IX, 1950, pp. 137–142.

the event and therefore reflected this in its language, but it is equally permissible to see the verbs as prophetic perfects designed to stress the imminence and absolute finality of the judgment that was about to fall.

22:1–16. The bloody city. As in 20:4 and 23:36, the phrase *wilt thou judge* (or 'are you prepared to judge?', JB) means much more than simply acting as arbiter. It involves the prophet in the job which today is done partly by the prosecutor, and partly by the judge when he passes sentence on a man already pronounced guilty by a jury. So Ezekiel's 'judging' consists of showing to the guilty city of Jerusalem both the extent of her crimes and also the consequences that are about to be inflicted upon her. He is in a sense 'justifying' both the verdict and the punishment. The combination of bloodshed and idolatry in verse 3 is a reminder that the worship of idols did involve bloodshed in the form of child sacrifice ('making your sons to pass through the fire to Molech'; *cf.* 16:21; 20:26, 31; 23:37), but the accusation would also have covered judicial murder and oppression on the Naboth pattern (1 Ki. 21) as well as depriving citizens of their liberty and livelihood or committing any act of violence which incurred blood-guiltiness.

For the catalogue of sins enumerated here, compare 18:15–17. Some relate to the Ten Commandments, but most to Levitical laws in the so-called Holiness Code (Lv. 17–26). On contempt for parents (7), *cf.* Exodus 20:12; on the *stranger* (Heb. *gēr*) and the *fatherless* and *widow*, *cf.* Exodus 22:21f. But see also Leviticus 19:3; 20:9; and 19:33, where similar concerns are expressed. Other comparisons may usefully be made, as follows: with verse 9, *cf.* Leviticus 19:16; with verse 10, *cf.* Leviticus 18:7, 19; with verse 11, *cf.* Leviticus 18:20; 20:10, 12, 17. Bribery (12) is condemned in Exodus 23:8; as well as in Isaiah 1:23; Amos 5:12; Micah 3:11. Rapacity has been such an all-absorbing occupation that there has been no time left to think of God. 'Social morality depends upon the remembrance of God' (Cooke). God responds to these sins with a gesture of scorn, a snap of the fingers (13). When He

acts in judgment, their courage will melt away[1] : they will be
scattered among the nations and they will *be profaned* in the
sight of the heathen (16, RV; not *take thine inheritance*, as AV).
RSV emends to *I shall be profaned through you*, but this does not
make sense beside the avowed intention that Israel may *know
that I am the Lord,* and RV is to be preferred. The over-all
picture of extortion, bloodshed, immorality, incest and
irreligion is a terrifying description of any nation whose
appointed time is drawing near. Political commentators please
note.

22:17–22. The furnace of affliction. The figure of the
refining of precious metal is frequently employed by Old
Testament writers (*cf.* Is. 1:22, 25; 48:10; Je. 6:27–30; 9:7;
Zc. 13:9; Mal. 3:2–4), but whereas the purpose is usually to
produce the refined product, Ezekiel here uses the figure to
show that Israel is nothing but worthless dross. For this
reason they are to be gathered together again and put into
the furnace to endure the burning heat of God's judgment.
No good will come out of this except that they will know that
it is the Lord's fury which is being poured out upon them (22).
On the basis of verse 20, which includes silver among all the
constituent elements of the ore that is put into the furnace,
RSV inserts *silver* in verse 18 at the beginning of the list of
metals, presuming that it had accidentally slipped to the end
of the sentence. This seems a quite unnecessary intrusion into
the text where the writer is being significantly silent. Verse 20
describes the actual process on which the metaphor is based,
but verse 18 seems to be saying that the whole operation is in
fact a waste of effort. Israel has no silver in her : she is utterly
worthless, all dross. If anything it is better to regard *silver* in
verse 18 as a gloss.

22:23–31. The sins of all classes of society. The land
is described in this oracle as deprived of the blessings of rain.
Most commentators prefer to follow LXX in verse 24, which
translates not 'cleansed' but 'rained upon' : thus, 'a land

[1] Verse 14 could be interpreted as 'Will you be able to brazen it out . . .?'

without rain and without shower'. Similarly, LXX seems to have preserved a better reading in verse 25, 'whose princes' (*'ašer neśî'ēhā*), for the MT 'a conspiracy of her prophets' (*qešer nebî'ēhā*). This word for 'prince' (*nāśî'*) is different from that used in verse 27, where the word is *śārîm*, 'nobles'. The former refers to members of the royal house; the latter is used for leaders or chiefs of the people.

The indictment of the royal house in Israel is based on their practice of exacting wealth from their people, almost certainly to the accompaniment of violence and murder. Clearly, Naboth's fate was not an isolated incident. Passages like 11:6 suggest that some of the more unscrupulous kings of Judah may well have liquidated foes for the sake either of material gain or political advantage. For the phrase, *they have made many widows* (25), cf. Jeremiah 15:8. Such kingship ran counter to the principles enunciated by God in the Davidic covenant, in which obedience to His commandments and statutes was a primary condition. David's line had therefore failed quite notoriously in their responsibilities. The priests too were guilty. Entrusted with Yahweh's law (*tôrâ*), they had done violence to it and to the holiness which they were intended to preserve. All had been reduced to a common level of uncleanness, whether it was the holiness of worship or of foods or of times and seasons (26). Their failure to maintain the distinctive quality of the things of God meant that God too was disregarded and treated with contempt. The nobles shared some of the accusations for extortion and cruelty laid against their royal masters (*cf.* 27 with 25). The prophets supported them by acting as religious tranquillizers (following RSV, *daubed for them*) and by whitewashing their crimes with correct, but empty, formulae (27). On *whitewash*, see the notes on 13:10f.

Finally, *the people of the land* (29) follow the patterns of behaviour set by their leaders. The *'am hā'āreṣ* were the common people; not obviously the poorest of the peasantry, but all those who possessed full citizen rights. They were thus able to find some people less privileged than themselves whom they could tyrannize.

With this degree of universal corruption, God looks in vain for just one man who will try to interpose himself to stop the national ruin. But there was no-one with the moral courage to stem the tide : the leaders were ungodly and those who should have been godly had compromised their position. Presumably Jeremiah was an exception to Ezekiel's general condemnation, but he had no kingly status and few listened to his words. Any nation which lacks godly leadership, as Israel did at that time, must surely be on the way out. *Cf.* Isaiah 59:16 ; 63:5, where by contrast the continuing absence of 'a man to intervene' leads the Lord to gain the victory with His own right hand. For Ezekiel, however, this state of affairs was but the prelude to the imminent and final act of judgment on the citizens of Jerusalem, when their own way would be recompensed upon their own heads (31).[1]

n. Oholah and Oholibah (23:1–49)

The allegory of Israel's history which occupied chapter 16 is continued in this chapter in a slightly different form and in even more repulsive detail. It tells of two sisters, Oholah and Oholibah, who represent Samaria and Jerusalem. While not described specifically as brides of Yahweh, some such relationship is clearly implied in verse 4, 'They became mine', and in verse 5, 'Oholah played the harlot while she was mine'. The chapter deals with their intrigues with foreign powers, described in the crudest of pornographic terms, and with their downfall. Despite the distasteful theme and the indelicate language, the reader of these verses must appreciate that this is the language of unspeakable disgust and must try to recognize Ezekiel's passion for God's honour and his fury at the

[1] For the thought of a man who will stand in the breach, *cf.* 13:5. Some see this phrase as a contradiction of Ezekiel's view, expressed in 14:12–23, that not even the presence of three righteous men in a city will be sufficient to save it from destruction. But there is no sense in this chapter that the man to stand in the breach will save the city simply by being there : he is needed to warn the people of the coming judgment, to lead a resistance movement against the incoming tide of iniquity, to influence the people authoritatively in the direction of repentance. The issue here is quite different from that dealt with in chapter 14.

adulterous conduct of His covenant people. The feeling of nausea which a chapter like this arouses must be blamed not on the writer of the chapter nor even on its contents, but on the conduct which had to be described in such revolting terms. At the same time it is possible to see that Ezekiel's language shows considerable awareness of the fundamental characteristics of apostasy.

The chapter may be divided into four convenient paragraphs, dealing first with each of the sisters in turn (1-10, 11-21); then follows the fate of Oholibah (22-35), and finally the abominable acts of both sisters are reviewed and their judgment is pronounced (36-49).

23:1-4. Introduction. The introductory details of the allegory must not be over-pressed. The sisters represent cities and their inhabitants, rather than tribes. In any case Judah and Ephraim were not even brothers, for Ephraim was one of the two sons of Joseph and was therefore Judah's nephew. The points being made are simply that the two cities have a close affinity from the distant past, that their origins were in Egypt, and that the beginning of their subsequent conduct can be traced back to their Egyptian pre-history.

The names, Oholah and Oholibah, derive from the Hebrew 'ōhel, meaning a 'tent'. It could be a reference to a tented place of worship, but it is not clear whether this is Israel's tabernacle in the wilderness or a pagan shrine. The name of Esau's wife, Oholibamah (Gn. 36:2), or 'tent of the high place', suggests the latter, as do the tents of the gods described in the Ugaritic texts. On the other hand, Oholah could mean 'her tent' and Oholibah almost certainly means 'my tent (is) in her', which suggests Yahweh's sponsorship of Jerusalem. But again the details must not be pressed too far. It is enough that the names had a cultic flavour.

23:5-10. Oholah. The depravity of Samaria is shown by Oholah's initiative in offering herself to her Assyrian lovers. Hosea too had made insinuations of this sort: 'They have gone up to Assyria, a wild ass wandering alone; Ephraim has hired lovers' (Ho. 8:9; *cf.* 5:13; 7:11; 12:1). The historicity of the charge is borne out by a good deal of evidence. The Black Obelisk of Shalmaneser III illustrates Jehu prostrating himself before the Assyrian king (the date would be about 840 BC, at the beginning of Jehu's reign) and offering gifts, possibly with a view to buying support against Hazael of Damascus.[1] Adad-Nirari III (*c.* 812–782 BC), in an inscription found at Nimrud, also claimed to have received tribute from 'the territory of Omri', and there is no reason to doubt the truth of this.[2] 2 Kings also describes the paying of tribute by Israel to Assyria in the reigns of Menaham (*c.* 745–738 BC) and Hoshea (*c.* 732–724 BC); see 2 Kings 15:19ff.; 17:3.

The Assyrian lovers are described vividly as *warriors* (5, RSV), following a minor emendation based on the Assyrian word *qurādu*, 'warrior',[3] and as caparisoned in gorgeous violet fabrics (Heb. *tekēlet*; see *IDB*, Vol. 1, p. 450, *s.v.* 'Blue'). *Captains* (*governors*) and *rulers* are both loan-words from Akkadian, the first meaning 'district governors', like Zerubbabel or Nehemiah (Hg. 1:1; Ne. 5:14), and the second meaning 'satraps' or any less senior officials. Israel's harlotries with them were not merely political liaisons, but involved an acceptance of Assyrian idols as well, as verse 7b makes clear. In all this, she was merely perpetuating the patterns of behaviour she had learnt in Egypt. The Hebrew had never found it easy to resist the temptations and allurements of more sophisticated civilizations than his own, whether they were the fleshpots of Egypt or the dashing gallants of the Assyrian cavalry regiments. But Israel's reward was very different from her expectation. Having been possessed and used, she was then

---

[1] See *DOTT*, pp. 48f. and plate 3.

[2] See *DOTT*, pp. 50–52. A further inscription describing tribute taken by Adad-Nirari III from Jehoash of Samaria is published in *Iraq*, XXX, 1968, p. 142.

[3] It is not impossible that the same meaning could be achieved without amending the MT, *qerôbîm*. Although this is the normal word for 'those near', 'neighbours' (hardly appropriate for Assyrians anyway), there was also a late Heb. word *qerāb*, meaning 'war', from which a form such as we have in MT could have developed. Alternatively, there was an Assyrian official called *qurbutu*, who being 'close to' the king was used on intelligence missions.

despised and exposed to public ridicule, and finally savaged and destroyed.

23:11–21. Oholibah. Jerusalem's guilt is even greater than her sister's. She aped Samaria in courting Assyria, apparently failing to learn the lesson of Samaria's fate. The obvious historical episode behind this accusation is the approach made by Ahaz to the Assyrians during the Syro-Ephraimite war (2 Ki. 16:8). This was roundly condemned by Isaiah (Is. 7:7–9) who warned Ahaz of the consequences of such foolish and faithless overtures. But Ezekiel's message concentrates on the further harlotries committed by Jerusalem with the Babylonians. Again the temptation came through the sight of gorgeously apparelled military men (14f.), not flesh and blood, but painted in glorious technicolour (in typical Babylonian style) on the walls of buildings. The glamour of the sight prompted an invitation to enjoy the sensual pleasures of adultery, and this, once taken, turned quickly to disgust (17). She was not alone in this, however, for her sensuality had also caused the Lord to turn in disgust from her. So once again the pattern of life begun in Egypt had repeated itself in Judah's later history.

Verse 17 reflects the pendulum-like swing from a pro-Babylonian policy to an anti-Babylonian policy that marked Judah's political history during the last hundred years before the exile. *Discovered* (18, AV, RV) is well translated in RSV with the words *carried on openly* and *flaunted*. The references to Egypt in 19–21 may possibly reflect contemporary pro-Egyptian intrigues (*cf.* Je. 37:5), but it is not necessary that it should be so interpreted. The dominant thought is the influence of Judah's Egyptian upbringing.

23:22–35. The fate of Oholibah. This section consists of four oracles beginning with the formula : 'Thus says the Lord God' (22, 28, 32, 35). Of these the first two and the last share a certain amount of language in common, but the third is in a class by itself and consists of a poem about the cup of judgment. The first oracle (22–27) depicts Oholibah under the judgment of her foreign lovers, who have been summoned together by God to surround her in battle-array, like an army besieging a city. They comprise *Babylonians* and *Chaldeans*, though these were not separate peoples, and special mention is made of what were probably marginal tribes on the eastern borders of the Babylonian empire, *Pekod*, *Shoa* and *Koa*. These are normally identified, though not without some uncertainty, with Puqûdu, Sutû and Qutû, Aramaean tribes to the east of the river Tigris which are known from a number of Assyrian and Babylonian inscriptions. All these peoples, together with *all the Assyrians with them* (though many would regard these words as a later insertion), are to be the instruments of God's punishment upon Jerusalem. Though they inflict the cruel mutilation and slaughter described in verse 25, it is made clear that it is ultimately the Lord's doing and that His permissive will is behind it all. Verse 26, like 16:39, may even refer back to the treatment meted out by Israel to the Egyptians at the time of the Exodus : the pigeons have come home to roost at last.

The second oracle (28–31) is less strongly worded. The Babylonians are not described as lovers but as *those whom you hate*, but the principle of reciprocity is maintained : *they shall deal with you in hatred* (29, RSV). No atrocities are described, but the results of a hostile invasion are indicated by the removal of *all thy labour*, *i.e.* the wealth which was the fruit of their labour, and by their being left *naked and bare*, as if after the destruction of their armies or their fortifications. Verse 31, reminiscent of verse 13, shows that the doom of Jerusalem is imminent. She is about to drink from the cup of God's wrath and to share in her sister Samaria's dreadful fate.

The reference to *her cup* (31) is the connecting link which leads on to the poem about the cup of Samaria (32–34). This is a strange little stanza : it does not appear to say very much that has not already been said, and its interpretation is made more difficult by textual uncertainties. Its main impact is made by its striking language and pregnant phrases, as so often in this type of Hebrew poetry. To render it in English demands so much paraphrase and interpretation that the effect, especially of the 3:2 metre, is usually lost. RSV tries to keep close to the Hebrew; JB renders it wordily but well. Its starkness may be judged by this literal rendering:

> Cup of-your-sister you-shall-drink
>   (which is) deep and-wide.
> She / it / you-shall-be for-laughter and-derision
>   much to-contain.
> Drunkenness and-anguish you-will-be-full-of,
>   cup-of-waste and-desolation.
> Cup of-your-sister, Samaria,
>   you-will-drink it and-drain (it);
> And its-pieces you-shall-break(?)
>   and-your-breasts you-shall-tear-apart.

RSV follows the Syriac 'and you shall pluck out your hair' for the first half of the last line, and this fits the parallelism well. But it is a colourless phrase and MT, though using unusual words, can be defended: the noun means 'its sherds', *i.e.* broken fragments of pottery from the shattered cup, and the verb means either 'to gnaw' (an act of insanity) or 'to break', usually of breaking bones but here of shattering the cup to pieces. It may well be that here we have a popular song about the cup of fate, which Ezekiel has tailored to the needs of his message (so JB footnote).

The final oracle (35) repeats the verdict of 22:12, that the punishment for the nation's licentiousness and promiscuity is based on their prior forgetfulness and calculated rejection of their Lord.

23:36–49. Judgment on the two sisters. This final section recapitulates and enlarges on much that has gone before. Having described their history separately, Ezekiel now classes them together and comments on the similarities of their sins and their punishment. Once again, to *judge* (36) means to *declare* and make known. The offences specified are religious (37–39) as well as political (40–44). Among the former are idolatrous associations, which are branded as *adultery*; child-sacrifice, which brings *blood upon their hands* (37); defilement of

175

God's Temple by entering it with the guilt of child-sacrifice still upon them; and the profanation of sabbaths (38). Note that *both* sisters are charged with the defilement of the Jerusalem sanctuary: a reminder that the separation of Israel from Jerusalem was still remembered with bitterness, unless this refers to the successors of the Israelites (later called Samaritans) who still travelled south to worship Yahweh at Jerusalem (*cf.* Je. 41:5), and in Ezekiel's view defiled the place by their very presence there. The invitations to foreign alliances are pictured under the figure of a harlot with painted eyes (*cf.* 2 Ki. 9:30; Je. 4:30), reclining on a couch (*cf.* Pr. 7:16), entertaining her clients. At this stage the plural gives way to the singular, for Oholibah only is intended, and the suitors are denigrated as a riff-raff of desert-dwellers or drunkards,[1] who bring bangles and bracelets as payment for their prostitutes' services (42).

45. The *righteous men* can hardly be the lovers of verses 22–24, even though the nations will eventually be the instruments of God's judgment. It must mean that those who judge the two sisters will judge them righteously. The stress is on the way the judging will be done, not on who will do the judging. The punishment will be the common penalty for all adulteresses and shedders of blood: death by stoning, to which is added destruction of their property with fire (*cf.* Lv. 20:10; Dt. 21:21). The similarity of this penalty with the state of siege of a city bombarded with sling-stones and incendiary missiles can scarcely have been coincidence. The shame of the guilty person's end under Mosaic law will be exactly matched by the fate of Samaria and Jerusalem.

o. The rusty cauldron (24:1–14)

With these verses we come to the climax of all that Ezekiel has been trying to say in the previous twelve chapters. His main purpose, as we have noted, has been to justify the coming

---

[1] Heb. has both 'brought in' (*mûḇā'îm*) and 'drunkards' (*sāḇā'îm*, which some would render 'Sabeans'), but probably this is a dittograph and one word should be deleted.

judgment upon Jerusalem. We called this collection of oracles 'Objections to Judgment' (see p. 114), and we have seen arguments raised and demolished one by one and accusations made against both the past and the present conduct of the people of Jerusalem. There is hardly anything more that can be said. The hour has come. Judgment is about to fall.

The section begins therefore with a command from God to the prophet to note down the day, for it was the day when the siege would begin (1, 2). This is followed by a poetical allegory about a cauldron being set on a fire, symbolizing the city's state of siege (3–5). Then comes a prose statement consisting of two short oracles, each beginning with the words, 'Woe to the bloody city!' (6, 9), which enlarge upon and interpret the allegory and at the same time introduce the idea of the cauldron's symbolical rustiness.

24:1, 2. Naming the day. The date is normally given as 15th January, 588 BC, and is the same date mentioned in 2 Kings 25:1 and Jeremiah 52:4. It is also known from Zechariah 8:19 that this date became a fast for the exiles, as commemorating one of the critical days in the fall of the holy city. The possibility that Ezekiel could have possessed second sight to know the actual date of an event taking place some hundreds of miles away fills many commentators with alarm. The unlikelihood of this happening is one of the main arguments for giving Ezekiel a Palestinian locale at this stage of his ministry. But there is nothing inherently wrong with his being made aware of such an event at such a distance, whether it came to him through telepathic sensitivity or through a direct supernatural revelation from God. Despite all the arguments to the contrary, the latter possibility appears to be so much more in keeping with Ezekiel's characteristic God-consciousness and would be yet another authentication of his prophetic gifts. He had foreseen this event and been living with it for so long that it would not have needed a miracle or a striking theophany for his prophetic spirit to build up within himself the deep conviction that 'today is the day'.

Many lesser men than Ezekiel have had more remarkable successes with nothing more than inspired hunches to help them.

24:3-5. The song of the cauldron. This poem has no religious language in it and could well derive originally from a household cooking-song, rather like 'Polly, put the kettle on'. To use a popular saying or story or poem from everyday life and to turn it into a message was a typically prophetic way of speaking, and many popular preachers of today still use the same technique. The imagery is reminiscent of Jeremiah's vision of the boiling pot (Je. 1:13f.), and the same language has already been employed by Ezekiel in 11:3, 7, 11, though with a different interpretation.[1] Some think that the imperative verbs are addressed to the prophet and that this is therefore another of Ezekiel's acted parables, but if that were so one would expect a concluding phrase such as 'And I did as the Lord commanded me . . .'. Nevertheless the poem is an allegory and has its detailed application to the circumstances of the day, as any acted parable would. The cauldron is Jerusalem, the fire underneath and around it is the siege, the pieces of flesh are the inhabitants of Jerusalem. The word for *cauldron* (Heb. *sîr*) normally refers to any large wide-mouthed pottery utensil used for washing or cookery, though in this instance we find in verse 11 that it is made of copper.[2] In verse 5 there are a number of textual emendations which RSV has followed. The first reference to *bones* (*ʿaṣāmîm*) should probably read *logs* (*ʿēṣîm*); the otherwise unknown cognate accusative in 'boil its boilings' (*reṭāḥêhâ*) is best altered, as in two MSS, to *its pieces* (*neṭāḥêhâ*), a word specially used of joints of meat; and the final verb can easily be altered to an imperative, *seethe its bones*, but this is less necessary. JB has 'until even the bones are cooked'.

---

[1] *Cf.* also Micah 3:2f.

[2] For further information the reader is referred to *NBD*, articles on 'Pottery', 'Vessel'; and for more specialist treatment to J. L. Kelso, 'Ezekiel's Parable of the Corroded Copper Caldron', *JBL*, LXIV, 1945, pp. 391–393; and to his fuller study, *The Ceramic Vocabulary of the Old Testament*, *BASOR*, Supplementary Studies, 5–6, 1948.

24:6–14. Woe to the bloody city! Here are two oracles dependent upon each other and on the poem of the cooking-pot. The first (6–8) deals with the blood-guiltiness of Jerusalem, harking back to the message of 22:1–16, and introduces this by making play on the corrosion which the boiling of the cauldron has brought to light, probably in the form of a rusty scum. The Hebrew *ḥel'â* (*scum*, AV; *rust*, RSV, RV) occurs only here in the Old Testament. It may be related to a root meaning 'disease' or even 'filthiness', but its meaning must be drawn mainly from its context. Out of this reddish mess the contents are to be removed *piece by piece* indiscriminately. That is to say, the inhabitants of the besieged Jerusalem are to be scattered in all directions. But Jerusalem's guilt still remains, like blood spilled *on the bare rock*, uncovered by earth in burial and therefore still crying out to God for vengeance (*cf.* Gn. 4:10; Lv. 17:13; Jb. 16:18; Is. 26:21). The dispersion of the Jews has not provided a solution to this greater issue of the nation's guilt.

The second oracle (9–14) deals with this question in a different way. In verse 5, the logs were piled under the cauldron to boil the contents of the stew; now the Lord intends to kindle a fire which will eventually melt the cauldron itself. To this end the contents are first disposed of (following RSV, *boil well the flesh, and empty out the broth*, 10), the bones of the meat are burnt, and then the empty pot is stood on the burning coals so that it may become red-hot and all its filth and rust be melted away. The first two words of verse 12, *she hath wearied* (me with her) *toil*, are not in LXX and are thought by many to be a doublet from the previous verse; but the verse goes on to show that not even this drastic treatment of Jerusalem has the desired effect. Knox paraphrases: 'So deep is that rust, even the fire will not drive it out', and he adds in an engaging footnote, 'But it is not clear that this is the meaning'! In a passage of such difficulty, details of translation must often be sacrificed for the sake of making over-all sense. And the sense *is* put clearly, at least in RSV: *Its rust is your filthy lewdness. Because I would have cleansed you and you were not cleansed from your filthiness, you shall not be cleansed any more till I have satisfied my fury upon you* (13). The appalling sufferings undergone by God's people from 588 BC onwards, in the siege and in exile, were due to their unwillingness to allow God to deal with them much earlier on in their history of disobedience. And now the sentence has been passed, the moment of execution has come. Nothing can turn it back. *I the Lord have spoken* (14). His decision and His word and His action are alike irrevocable.

p. The death of Ezekiel's wife (24:15-27)

In these verses we catch a glimpse of the inner Ezekiel which rarely appears through his apparently harsh and unyielding exterior. His austerity and rigid self-discipline, his passion for truth and for the honour of God's holy name, very nearly conceal the tender heart that lies within. While not wishing to romanticize Ezekiel in any way, it is worth commenting that often a man is seen for what he really is only when he is seen in conjunction with his wife. Whereas in the other forty-seven chapters we are impressed, if not overawed, by Ezekiel's personality, in this chapter at the heart of the book which bears his name we meet him and find him attractive with human emotions like our own. This is borne out by the phrase he uses to describe his wife : 'the desire of his eyes, the one in whom his eyes delight.' Skinner writes : 'That phrase alone reveals that there was a fountain of tears sealed up within the breast of this stern preacher.'[1] His refusal to mourn openly was no act of personal choice but a symbolical demand made upon him by God, which only accentuated for him the bitterness of his loss. E. L. Allen (in *IB*) comments that men who are called by God often have to pay a heavy price for their concern with human needs and their identification with God's purpose. 'They are called again and again to surrender their private lives to the requirements of their public responsibility.' For Ezekiel there would surely have been the added burden of being misunderstood and criticized for his show of heartlessness. Behind the laconic phrase in verse 18,

[1] Skinner, p. 210.

'And on the next morning I did as I was commanded' (RSV), there must have been long hours of sleeplessness and spiritual anguish.

16–18. The manner of his wife's death, which was apparently forecast the morning that it happened (and there is no reason to suppose that it was not within a few days of the date mentioned in 24:1), is described as *with a stroke* (AV, RV). This does not *demand* a sudden death; it could mean 'plague' or 'pestilence', or anything that strikes a person down. It would not therefore be impossible that Ezekiel's wife was already ill, and this would make more sense of Ezekiel's speaking to the people in the morning to tell them of what would happen and to warn them that he had been commanded not to mourn (18). Alternatively, we can understand the death as quite without warning (from the point of view of physical symptoms), except in so far as God's prediction of it had come to Ezekiel earlier in the day, and the opening phrase of verse 18 could be taken as meaning, 'I was about my normal business of speaking to the people in the morning, and in the evening without warning my wife died.' It is very difficult to imagine Ezekiel telling all and sundry that his wife was about to die the same day, when she was at work around the house, to all appearances hale and hearty. No doubt, she would have had something to say! It is far more conceivable to suppose that, although he was forewarned, he kept the message to himself until he should have to use the sad occasion for yet another symbolical action. The mourning customs reflected in these verses are interesting. Five aspects may be observed. (*a*) *Sigh, but not aloud* (17, RSV): the word 'sigh' is normally used of the noisy groaning of wounded men and is a reminder of the ritual lamentations that were regularly laid on for funeral occasions (*cf.* Mk. 5:38). (*b*) *Bind on your turban* (RSV): in mourning the turban, the normal headdress of the priest (*cf.* Ex. 39:28; Ezk. 44:18), though it was also the festal headgear for a layman (Is. 61:3, 10), would be removed and the head covered in dust and ashes (*cf.* Jos. 7:6; 1 Sa. 4:12; Jb. 2:12). (*c*) *Put your shoes on your feet*: the sandals were taken off in time of distress, as in 2 Samuel 15:30 (*cf.* also Is. 20:2).

(d) Covering the *lips* was compulsory for the leper (Lv. 13:45), and was a sign of disgrace (Mi. 3:7). It involved veiling the lower part of the face from the nose downwards : the word *lips* (*śāpām*) really means 'moustache', which it regularly represents in modern Hebrew. (e) *Eat not the bread of men* (RV) : this was changed by Wellhausen to 'bread of sorrows' (*'anūšîm* for MT, *'anāšîm*), and some ancient versions translate 'bread of mourners' (followed by RSV), but the more difficult MT deserves to be retained. The phrase 'of men' means 'ordinary', 'common' (according to its use in Dt. 3:11 ; Is. 8:1), so the command here is not to eat ordinary food, *i.e.* the mourners' funeral meal. *Cf.* Jeremiah 16:7. Indeed it is useful to compare these words with the whole section in Jeremiah 16:5–13, where Jeremiah was forbidden by God to enter the house of mourning and was called upon to give his reasons when he was challenged by the people.

24:19–24. The sign interpreted. When Ezekiel deliberately refrained from the customary mourning procedures, it is to his credit and to that of his fellow-exiles that they immediately suspected that it had some special significance. Their visit to his home the morning after the news of his wife's death had flashed around the settlement had probably been to offer sympathy and to give support. Instead they found themselves asking for a word from God. It was no new message, but because of the occasion which prompted it, it spoke with greater force than ever before. God was about to profane, by destroying it, His holy Temple. Just as Ezekiel's dearest one had been taken away from him by a single stroke, so the nation was to lose its dearest object, its proud boast (*the pride of your power*, RSV), the desire of its soul (*that which your soul pitieth*, AV ; meaning 'object of your soul's compassion'). The people of Jerusalem would lose their children by enemy action as well. And the message was : *you shall do as I have done* (22). Howie understands this as a condemnation of the people's incredible lack of grief or sense of repentance over the tragedies which threatened them. His lack of grief pointed up the wrongness of their lack of concern. The context, however, demands that the withholding of grief should follow the catastrophe. Ezekiel had not wept, and Israel would not weep either : because in both cases the tragedy was too deep and stunning for any expression of grief to prove adequate. As Cooke puts it : 'Mourning will be out of place in the presence of a disaster so complete.'

24:25-27. The end of Ezekiel's dumbness. The chapter ends with a further word that looks forward to the second main phase of Ezekiel's ministry after chapter 33. It deals with the impact that the destruction of Jerusalem will have upon the prophet himself; note the emphatic *And you, son of man*, which opens the paragraph. As far as Ezekiel was concerned this disaster would prove a turning-point in his life's work. His message would be vindicated and for the first time he would have ready hearers. More particularly, the ritual dumbness, which was imposed upon him at the time of his call, would be taken from his mouth, and he would be able to speak freely (*cf.* 3:26, 33:22). The sentence construction of the passage is slightly confused and it gives the impression of the writer's mind running faster than his pen. As it stands, it looks as if the phrase *in that day* of verse 26 is intended to refer to the same day as verse 25, but clearly the fall of the city and the relaying of the news by a fugitive to Ezekiel could not have happened on the same day, unless it is supposed that Ezekiel was at that time in Palestine and less than a day's journey from Jerusalem (so Herntrich). It is better to assume that the writer, writing from the standpoint of knowing what was to come, rolled the event and the recounting of the event into one episode. In support of this it is worth mentioning that the word *fugitive* (26, RSV) is really *the fugitive*, as if the writer already knew about what was coming in 33:21. So he is saying : 'when this event happens and the news reaches your ears, then your mouth shall be opened and you will be dumb no longer.' This release from the restriction imposed upon him will in itself be a portent and the people will recognize the hand of the Lord in it all (27). Then at last Ezekiel will be free. His prophecies of doom will no longer need to be uttered.

He will be able to act as a shepherd and a watchman to his people. He will be free to work constructively towards the building up of a new community, a new Israel.

V. ORACLES AGAINST THE NATIONS (25:1 – 32:32)

Although the Old Testament prophets addressed their messages primarily to their own people, or to a part at least of God's covenant community, it was characteristic of them to survey the other nations of the world in order to demonstrate the Lord's sovereignty over the heathen as well as over Israel. This is the pattern in Isaiah (chapters 13–23), in Jeremiah (chapters 46–51) and also in Amos (chapters 1, 2). The purpose of this kind of writing is twofold. First, it arises out of a belief in monotheism, and is intended to show the out-workings of monotheism. If Yahweh is the God of the whole earth, He clearly has something to say about the history and destiny of nations other than Israel. Secondly, the future prospects of Israel, whether they are thought of in terms of a day of judgment or Davidic Messianism or a new covenant, must be matched by judgment on peoples who have often flagrantly disregarded the laws by which all mankind are to be judged. Such national sins as aggression, arrogance, atroci-ties and the breaking of covenants, to name but a few, deserve God's wrath, whether committed by Jewish or Gentile powers.

There is probably some significance in the fact that in this collection of oracles, the number of nations dealt with is seven (Ammon, Moab, Edom, Philistia, Tyre, Sidon and Egypt). The same number appears in Amos, though some would regard one or two of his oracles as later additions. But bearing in mind that Ezekiel's oracles were delivered at different times and were obviously collected and inserted at this stage of the book and in the present order for some purpose, it is not unlikely that whoever was responsible for this piece of editorial work was conscious of the 'seven' factor in his compilation. A further sign of editorial planning is the geographical pattern of the oracles, beginning with Ammon to the north-east of

Jerusalem, swinging southwards through Moab to Edom in the south-east, then round to Philistia in the west, and finally going farther afield in a northerly direction to Tyre and Sidon, before ending up with the distant major power, Egypt, in the south. Inevitably, the omission of Babylon provokes comment, and this is variously explained. Cooke sees Babylon as standing apart from the other nations, inasmuch as it was the instrument of God's punishment upon Israel. Skinner goes further and regards the Babylonian invaders as being the instruments of judgment upon all the nations mentioned here, as well as on Israel. Ellison puts forward the intriguing suggestion that Tyre is to be read cryptically as Babylon.[1] He contends that any prediction of the downfall of Babylon would have brought a hornets' nest around the prophet's ears ; but Tyre was described, perhaps a little too lavishly for the time, in order that the discerning reader might see the second meaning. Certainly the concentration of so much attention on Tyre's commercial prosperity seems a little unusual, but it must be remembered that Nebuchadrezzar's next move after the fall of Jerusalem was to lay siege to Tyre and the siege was to last for thirteen years. It was therefore of very great importance to the Judean exiles that Tyre should be receiving the same treatment as they had done in Jerusalem, and they would naturally be more than interested to know how the siege would end. So, despite the attractiveness of Ellison's suggestion, it does not appear to be demanded by the context.

One further observation needs to be made. The editor, whether Ezekiel or another, has inserted these oracles between chapters 24 and 33 in order to heighten the dramatic tension of waiting for the news of the fall of Jerusalem to burst upon the doubting exiles. At the same time this section marks a clear hiatus between Ezekiel's ministry and message before 587 BC and his quite different treatment of the exiles once the

---

[1] L. Finkelstein also argued this (*The Pharisees*, vol. 1, 1938, pp. 335ff.), but it is difficult to see why so much is made of Tyre as a maritime power, if it was meant to represent Babylon, and why Nebuchadrezzar was to be responsible for its downfall.

disaster had vindicated his words and created the atmosphere of stunned repentance, in which he could begin to restore the nation's confidence in the good purposes of God.

a. Against neighbouring nations (25:1–17)

Most commentators remark on the colourless prose of these four oracles (so Cooke, May, Muilenburg, Eissfeldt, *inter alios*), and this is true in comparison with the poetic splendour of the oracles on Tyre and Egypt. It does not follow from this, however, that they are secondary material. As with Amos's oracles (Am. 1:3 – 2:3), they were written in a stereotyped form, and they follow the 'because . . . therefore . . .' pattern of the invective oracle (*cf.* 26:2 ; 34:8–10 ; 36:2, *etc.*) which appears to be peculiar to Ezekiel. They have many phrases also which are typical of Ezekiel's style, such as 'profaning my sanctuary', 'stretching out my hand', 'executing judgments', and of course the ever-present 'you shall know that I am the Lord'. This last phrase occurs at the end of both the Ammon oracles (5, 7) and at the end of the Moabite and Philistine oracles (11, 17), but in the case of Edom it is varied to 'and they shall know my vengeance'. All the oracles deal with the attitude of these four neighbour states to Judah at the time of the fall of Jerusalem.

25:1–7. Against Ammon. The Ammonites had frequently been in conflict with the Israelites from the time of the Judges onwards (*cf.* Jdg. 10 ; 11 ; 1 Sa. 11 ; 2 Sa. 10, *etc.*). They had benefited themselves at the expense of the northern kingdom around 722 BC (*cf.* Je. 49:1) and they had also joined more recently in troubling Jehoiakim (2 Ki. 24:2). After the fall of Jerusalem, their king Baalis appears to have encouraged Ishmael in the assassination of Gedaliah (Je. 40:14). Their crime in this oracle was that of gloating at Judah's misfortune (3, 6 ; *land of Israel* meaning the territory of Judah, not the old northern kingdom), and their punishment would be to be overrun by nomadic desert tribesmen (*men of the east*, 4, AV) who would use the capital city, Rabbah, as a place for grazing their camels (*pasture*, RSV, rather than *stable*, AV, RV). The second oracle (6, 7) has the same form and deals with the same offence as the first, for clapping the hands and stamping the feet was obviously 'a gesture of malicious delight' (Davidson). The punishment, however, is more specific : the Ammonites will become a prey to foreign peoples and will be completely destroyed as a nation. How the final phrase of verse 7 fits in with this is not easy to see. It may be that a knowledge of the Lord will be experienced only in the calamity of final destruction. May compares the promises of restoration *after* destruction that are found in Jeremiah (48:47 ; 49:6, 39) and thinks that this hints at pagans eventually worshipping Yahweh as the true God.

25:8–11. Against Moab. The hostility between Moab and Israel dates back to Balak and Moses (Nu. 22–24). As a nation they were closely associated with their Ammonite neighbours (*cf.* Gn. 19:30–38), but they were a more settled people and had a well-developed culture. Their crime is contempt for Judah and rejection of her claims to be a peculiar people with a uniquely powerful God. Presumably her defeat in battle was regarded as adequate justification for this view, but it was none the less culpable. Moab would share the Ammonite fate. Her *flank* (9, RSV ; lit. 'shoulder') would be exposed to attack through the destruction of her strongly-fortified cities. Three of these are named and their exact position can be seen on a good Bible atlas, or in *NBD*, p. 834, Fig. 144. Oracles against Moab occur in the writings of other prophets also (*cf.* Is. 15 ; 16 ; Je. 48 ; Am. 2:1–3 ; Zp. 2:8–11). It is worth noting that not long after this both Ammon and Moab were overrun by Nabatean tribesmen and ceased to have any independent existence as nations.

25:12–14. Against Edom. Israel and Edom had a long-standing feud, traceable back in ancient tradition to their twin ancestors (Gn. 25:23). From time to time this hatred erupted violently, as it did at the fall of Jerusalem, when the Edomites took advantage of Judah's plight in a way that earned them undying and bitter animosity of the kind reflected in Psalm 137:7–9, Obadiah 1–21 and Malachi 1:3–5 (for other oracles, see Is. 34:5–7; Je. 49:7–22; La. 4:21f.; Ezk. 35; Am. 1:11f.). What the Edomites actually did we cannot say for sure, but they certainly sided with Nebuchadrezzar against Jerusalem and after the exile there is evidence of Edomite occupation of southern Judah.[1] Their crime of acting *revengefully* is expressed by Ezekiel in the strongest terms (12), and their punishment is in the same style. Israel is to be the agent for this vengeance (14, *by the hand of my people Israel*), and it is interesting to note that although Edom proper was also overrun by Nabateans, the ancestors of the modern Arabs, Edomite survivors were later subdued first by Judas Maccabaeus and then by John Hyrcanus, who incorporated them into the Jewish race by compulsory circumcision. Ezekiel, however, does not predict that they will ever 'know that I am the Lord'.

25:15–17. Against the Philistines. These inhabitants of the southern part of the coastal strip of Palestine were also inveterate foes of Israel during her early history, but they had no ties of kinship and were originally Mediterranean 'sea peoples' from the Aegean. David finally broke their military ascendancy but they continued to cause occasional trouble during the monarchy, though we have no record other than this oracle of their hostility at the time of Jerusalem's fall. The *Cherethites*, who were regularly linked with them, may well be etymologically the same as the Cretans, as LXX translates. David employed them in his standing army of mercenaries, and it is likely that 'the Pelethites' who shared this duty with them were Philistines under a slightly different name. The punishment pronounced on them for their vengeful wrongs done against Jerusalem (doubtless they too sided with Babylon) is expressed in the form of a play on words: *I will cut off* (*hiḵrattî*) *the Cherethites* (*'eṯ kᵉrēṯîm*). After Maccabaean times, the Philistines completely vanished from sight as a people and only the names of their cities remained.

[1] See W. F. Albright, *BASOR*, LXXXII, 1941, pp. 11–15. *Cf.* also 1 Esdras 4:50.

b. Against Tyre and Sidon (26:1 – 28:26)

To say that Ezekiel in these oracles turns from the nations round about Judah to more distant powers like Tyre and Sidon and Egypt is perfectly true, but it must be said with caution. It is all too easy to forget the small scale of the geography of the Holy Land. For instance, all the territories referred to in chapter 25 can be seen with the naked eye from Jerusalem. Tyre's distance is only comparative, for it is a mere 35 miles as the crow flies from the Sea of Galilee and only 100 miles from Jerusalem. For those whose business was trade it was no more than a few days' camel-ride away.

Tyre's pre-eminence in world trade was due to her natural situation, with two excellent harbours, one on the mainland where a portion of the city was built and the other on the off-shore island which gave the city its name (Tyre, *ṣōr*= rock). The two were connected by a causeway, built in the tenth century BC by Hiram I, and this effectively doubled the trading potential of the city. At the same time, when danger threatened, it made it possible to retreat into the island stronghold which thus became both treasure-chest, warehouse and impregnable fortress for the Tyrians. As a commercial centre, Tyre was famous for her glassware and for her dyed materials, using the purple dye made from the local *murex* shell-fish. Inevitably she was a prey at which foreign powers looked greedily and she had to pay a heavy tribute to Assyria as the price for commercial freedom. Her continuing prosperity would have encouraged a sense of complacency within herself and of jealousy from her less privileged neighbours, and these attitudes are fully reflected in Ezekiel's oracles.

There are five major sub-divisions of these chapters, each beginning with 'the word of the Lord came to me' (26:1 ; 27:1 ; 28:1, 11, 20). They are : (i) the prophecy of Tyre's destruction (26:1–21) ; (ii) a lamentation over the shipwreck of Tyre, pictured as a wealthy trading-vessel (27:1–36) ; (iii) an oracle about the downfall of the prince of Tyre (28:1–10) ; (iv) a lament over the king of Tyre (28:11–19) ; (v) a prophecy against Sidon (28:20–26).

i. Prophecy of Tyre's destruction (26:1–21).[1] Once again the prophecy can be further sub-divided into separate sections, each introduced by the oracular formula, *thus says the Lord God* (26:7, 15, 19). These do, however, hold together and each adds further significance to the over-all message of the chapter. The first section (1–6) is in the typical 'because . . . therefore . . .' style of the previous chapter. The offence of Tyre is that she rejoices over the fall of Jerusalem and congratulates herself that she has lost a serious commercial competitor. *The gate of the peoples* (2) suggests that Jerusalem was at the intersection of a large number of international trade-routes and so was able to impose her own tolls. Presumably Tyre looked forward to taking these over herself.

1. The date presents a problem, having no reference to the month of the year. Verse 2 implies that Ezekiel as well as the Tyrians knew the city to have fallen and yet this was not properly known in Babylon until the tenth month of the twelfth year (33:21). There are, however, serious difficulties in this dating and it may well be right to follow those MSS which read 'the eleventh year' in 33:21. If this is so, 26:1 can stand and it would be safe to assume that the month which has dropped out is the eleventh month, which was confused with the number of the year. This oracle therefore was uttered scarcely a month after the news of Jerusalem's fall reached the exiles. It could well have been triggered off by the unsympathetic remarks of some Tyrian traders who were passing through Tel Abib when the exiles were still smarting under the news of the disaster.

4–6. The punishment on Tyre is that she will become a bare outcrop of rock (a play on its name) with no buildings and no soil for any cultivation. All she would be fit for is for fishermen to spread out their nets to dry.[2] *Her daughters* are the dependent

[1] The long siege of Tyre by Nebuchadrezzar's armies lasted *c.* 587–574 BC. On the historical details of these chapters, reference should be made to S. Smith, 'The Ship Tyre', *Palestine Exploration Quarterly*, LXXXV, 1953, pp. 97–110.
[2] An early traveller, visiting Tyre over a century ago, wrote : 'The island, as such, is not more than a mile in length. The part which projects south beyond the isthmus is perhaps a quarter of a mile broad, and is rocky and uneven. It is now unoccupied except by fishermen, as "a place

villages on the mainland which would be easy prey for an attacking army.

26:7-14. Nebuchadrezzar. He is now named as the instrument for God's judgment on Tyre and his military strategy is described in some detail (*cf.* 4:1-3; 21:22). This spelling of his name was thought to be more correct than Nebuchadnezzar, being closer to the Babylonian *Nabu - kudurri - usur*, but both forms are found in the Hebrew Bible and Nebuchadnezzar may have been the common western Aramaic form. On the *fort* (8, AV; *siege wall*, RSV) and the *mound*, see the notes on *dāyēq* and *sōlᵉlâ* on p. 75. Lifting up *the buckler* is rightly interpreted by RSV as *a roof of shields*, like the Roman 'tortoise' (*testudo*). The description of the siege comes oddly in connection with an island stronghold like Tyre, where horses could certainly not be deployed. Perhaps Ezekiel was using conventional forms without regard to reality (so May), but it is better to understand this as the description of a land-based siege, as was adopted by the Assyrians when they besieged Tyre in 673 and 668 BC. When Alexander the Great took Tyre it was after similar siege operations, following on the building of an enormous mole from the mainland to the island defences.

26:15-18. The dismay of the princes of the sea. Not the least result of Tyre's crashing fall will be the dismay felt by the rulers of neighbouring principalities, dependent on Tyrian trade for their prosperity and appalled at the destruction of such a powerful overlord. The *isles* (AV) are really the *coastlands* (RSV), *i.e.* the small city-states of the Mediterranean seaboard. Their princes will sit in mourning and raise a *lamentation* (*qînâ*), the traditional mourning-song in 3:2 rhythm, which RSV renders well.

26:19-21. Tyre's descent into the underworld. In highly figurative language the island city of Tyre is pictured

---

to spread nets upon".' Quoted in W. M. Thomson, *The Land and the Book*, 1910, p. 155n.

as submerged beneath the waves of the sea. But these become the waves of the mythological cosmic flood, the waters of chaos, which have engulfed her at last. Similar language is used of Egypt in 31:14–18; 32:13–32; and Isaiah's taunt-song over the king of Babylon deserves comparison also (Is. 14:4–21). The passage gives the impression that the *pit* (Heb. *bôr*), which is identical with Sheol, is the place of no return and of utter lostness (21). There is no hope of resurrection, simply a murky continuing existence alongside *the people of old* among the ruins of the past; a dreadful end indeed.

ii. The shipwreck of Tyre (27:1–36). This chapter consists of two separate compositions: a long poem in the *qînâ* metre (3b–9, 25b–36), and a prose catalogue which is inserted in the middle of the poem (10–25a). The poem is an extended allegory about the good ship Tyre, superbly fitted out and expertly crewed, but so laden with merchandise that in heavy seas she sinks to the bottom of the ocean. Thereupon all the sailing peoples of the Mediterranean gather on the shore to bewail her loss.

27:1–9. A stately merchantman. The description of every lavish detail of the trading vessel that represents the city of Tyre is expressed as an elaboration of Tyre's opinion of her own matchlessness: '*I am perfect in beauty*' (3). There is no hint in the poem that this is the reason for her downfall, as is explicitly stated in the following chapter (28:2–8), but the poem is so subtly constructed that the point would be recognizable to any but the dullest reader. Verse 4, *thy borders* (some would understand 'thy moorings') *are in the midst of the seas*, is similar to Ashurbanipal's description of the conquered Tyrians as those who 'dwelt in the midst of the sea'.[1] The ship's construction is as sound as it could be, with timbers from Senir, the Amorite name for Hermon (so Dt. 3:9), masts from Lebanon, oars from Bashan oaks and the decking material from Cyprus pine (follow RSV here) which was inlaid with ivory. The sails were made from finest Egyptian

[1] Pritchard, *ANET*, pp. 296f.

linen, embroidered with variegated colours, which would serve as an ensign or pennon, and her awnings were of two shades of purple which came from *Elishah*. This is probably Alašiya in Cyprus, but some would argue for a site in Syria.[1] The crew came from Sidon and from Arvad, an off-shore island a hundred miles farther north; the *pilots*, lit. 'rope-pullers', should simply be 'sailors' and they were all *skilled men of Zemer* (so RSV, 8), a city associated with Arvad (Gn. 10:18) and identified as the modern Sumra, a few miles to the south of Arvad. The most experienced craftsmen of Gebal (modern Byblos) were on board as carpenters (lit. 'repairers of the seams'), and she was attended by all the navies of the world to assist in the handling of her merchandise (9).

27:10-25a. The trade directory. This is preceded in verses 10 and 11 by mention of the mercenaries who served in the army of Tyre. They came from *Persia*, Lydia in Asia Minor (*Lud*, EVV) and *Put*, which is more likely to be Cyrenaica in North Africa than Somaliland, the traditional identification. LXX translates Put as 'Libyans' consistently, and this represents the general area. Other mercenaries hailed from *Arvad*, *Helech* (=Cilicia, Akk. *Ḥilakka*; RSV is right to repoint this word which in MT means *thy army*), and *Gamad* (probably the *Kumidi* of the Tell el-Amarna letters). The picture of the ship is still maintained, with the shields of its occupants hung up in array on either side.

12. The list of cities who traded with Tyre is given in geographical order, beginning with Tarshish in the west to Rhodes in the eastern Mediterranean and then travelling from Edom northwards to Damascus, with Arabia and Mesopotamia put last. *Tarshish* (12) has normally been identified with Tartessus in Spain, but it may have been the Phoenician name for the ancient city of Nora in Sardinia.[2] *Javan* (13) is the same word as Ionia, but it normally covered a large part of Greece. *Tubal* and *Meshech* were tribes in Asia Minor which

---

[1] See *NBD*, p. 366; and May, *IB*, *in loc.* for more detailed references.
[2] See W. F. Albright, 'New Light on the Early History of Phoenician Colonization', *BASOR*, LXXXIII, 1941, pp. 17-22.

are known both from cuneiform inscriptions and from the Histories of Herodotus, where they appear together as Moschoi and Tibarenoi. They were engaged in a flourishing slave-trade with Tyre, a fact which may not be unconnected with their role in the Gog and Magog oracles (38; 39). *Beth-togarmah* (14, RSV) was probably Armenia. *Rhodes* (15, RSV, following LXX, in preference to *Dedan* which appears also in verse 20) traded in ivory and ebony, which would have come from the African interior by way of Phoenician traders on the North African coasts. *Edom* (not *Aram*, Syria), *Judah* and *Damascus* all shared in the vast flow of trade with Tyre.

17. *Wheat, olives and early figs* (RSV) is a sensible correction for the impossible AV rendering.

19. *Dan also and Javan going to and fro* (AV) is certainly not correct and RSV omits the first word and translates *and wine from Uzal*, referring to a place-name probably identifiable with modern Sana, capital of the Yemen. Millard suggests reading $w^e \underline{d}ann\hat{e}$, 'and casks of', for $w^e \underline{d}an$, 'and Dan', and translates 'and casks of wine from Izalla', a district in Anatolia famous for the quality of its wines.[1] *Cassia* was a perfume made from an aromatic bark; it was used, with *calamus* or 'sweet cane', as an ingredient for the oil for anointing priests (Ex. 30:23, 24; *cf.* also Is. 43:24; Je. 6:20, for the cultic use of *calamus*).

20–25a. For the location of these place names, see May, *IB, in loc.*; *NBD*; or L. H. Grollenberg, *Atlas of the Bible* (1956). *The ships of Tarshish* (25, EVV) have been understood by some as 'the refinery fleet', on the basis of Albright's article in *BASOR*, quoted above on verse 12.

27:25b–36. Shipwreck and lamentation. In the very place where Tyre was thought to be supreme, *in the midst of the seas* (*cf.* verse 4), she was overtaken by disaster. The powerful *east wind* (*cf.* Ps. 48:7) broke her up and she foundered, taking with her all her crew and her armies and her merchandise (is it significant that this comes first in the list?).

---

[8] See A. Millard, 'Ezekiel XXVII, 19 : The Wine Trade of Damascus', *JSS*, VII, 1962, pp. 201–203.

The *countryside* (28, RSV; lit. the 'open spaces'; AV *suburbs*), which had supplied many of those on board, will be shattered at the sound of the sailors crying for help and all the shipping world gathers to lament the loss of such a stately craft. For the signs of mourning in verses 30, 31, see 7:17f.

32. This is the unusual case of a lamentation within a lamentation, for the whole chapter was so described in 27:2. It begins, in vivid contrast to verse 3,

> Who-is like-Tyre destroyed
> in-the-midst-of the-seas?

Ironically, the achievements of Tyre are recounted in terms of the benefits which her trading had brought to the kings of the earth: no reference is made to the vast wealth which she had amassed for herself – surely a deliberate touch on Ezekiel's part. *Now* (34, RSV) she is wrecked by the very elements which brought her prosperity. Her wares (again taking first place) and her crew have gone to a watery grave. All the seaboard princedoms gasp in astonishment, but the terror on their faces is really selfish fear for the consequences that will come to them before long. Merchants will whistle through their teeth in dismay (*hiss* does not mean 'to deride', but to let out the air through the teeth to express any vivid emotion, usually of astonishment; *cf.* 1 Ki. 9:8). They will say, literally, 'You have become terrors', or as RSV paraphrases, *You have come to a dreadful end*. The same word is used (*ballāhôt*) as concluded chapter 26.

iii. The downfall of the prince of Tyre (28:1–10). In this poem metaphor is abandoned and the *prince* of Tyre (Heb. *nāgîd*, 'ruler'), Ithobal II, is vigorously attacked for his claims to deity. This does not mean to say that Tyre necessarily held to a belief in divine kingship, for the attack is not so much a personal criticism of the ruler as a verbal onslaught on the state. Tyre regarded herself as all-powerful, superhuman and virtually eternal; she was possessed of wealth and wisdom above all other cities, and this led on to the incredible arrogance for which Tyre was notorious. The oracle begins with the claim of the prince of Tyre that *I am a god*. This claim, which is the ground of his condemnation, is repeated sporadically throughout the oracle (2b, 6, 9). Yet the prince is not a god, but a man (2, 9). His claims to wisdom, which are not denied (3–5), have caused his heart, most unwisely, to be lifted up. So he will end up by meeting death at the hands of foreigners in a manner totally out of keeping with his grandiose claims. *For I have spoken*, says the Lord God; and God always has the final word.

The *Daniel* of verse 3 must be understood as the same character as appears in 14:14, 20. Although there he is renowned for his righteousness, while here it is for wisdom, the unusual spelling (Dani'el) is common to both, and a patriarchial figure from the past seems to be intended. It is quite impossible to say dogmatically that this is the same as the Ugaritic Dan'el, but the two cannot be entirely separated (see on 14:14). It is interesting to note that both righteousness and wisdom were two of the qualities of the Daniel of the Bible (*cf.* Dn. 1:17–20; 2:47; 4:18, *etc.*), and he was a classic example of a man whose head was not turned by his success.

The most terrible of the nations (7) is the Babylonians, as in 30:11; 31:12; 32:12.

iv. Lament over the king of Tyre (28:11–19). These verses abound in allusions to Genesis 2; 3 and the Paradise story. The connecting link is doubtless in the sin of pride which both Adam and Tyre were guilty of, but it is not always clear what picture is in Ezekiel's mind. Eden is both *the garden of God* (13) and *the holy mountain of God* (14, 16), a concept not found in Genesis. The *king* (note the usual word, *melek*, which Ezekiel avoids for the kings of Israel) is pictured as an epitome of the perfect primeval Man, or Adam, but he is dressed up in precious stones reminiscent of the high-priest's breastplate (Ex. 28:17–20). MT has only nine of these, but LXX gives all twelve, and is probably right. The *anointed guardian cherub* (14, RSV) is there in Eden with the perfect man, but appears to have no function until it casts him out from *the midst of the stones of fire* (lit. 'flintstones', but probably here meaning the precious stones of verse 13). So the imagery is dependent on more than just the Genesis story, from which it diverges significantly, and rather than suppose that another version of the Eden tradition was in circulation, it seems more likely that Ezekiel's imagination wandered freely and drew on a wide variety of symbolical background all interwoven with his message of the fall of Tyre. Thus, the precious stones allude to Tyre's prosperity and the temptation to sin comes to the city not from without but from greed and pride within (15-17). In addition to the punishment of being cast out of Eden and thrown down upon the earth as a public spectacle (17), it is said that fire (the flaming sword?) comes out from within her and burns her to ashes (18). The seeds of a nation's destruction are usually to be found within herself. And the comment of those who see is once again, *you have come to a dreadful end* (*cf.* 26:21 ; 27:36).

v. Prophecy against Sidon (28:20-26). This is a very brief oracle addressed to Sidon, to which are added some words relating to the future of the house of Israel (24-26). The form of the oracle is similar to that addressed to the Ammonites (25:1), but it lacks the introductory 'because . . .' clause. No indication of Sidon's offences is given. It is couched in typical Ezekiel phraseology and describes the judgments which Yahweh will execute in Sidon as an indication of His *glory* (22). When this and all His other acts of judgment are completed, the house of Israel will be able to live free of harm from their neighbour-states (24). No longer will 'the pricking thorn and the painful brier' (Cooke) vex them. Then *they*, as well as the nations who have been punished, *will know* and acknowledge that Yahweh is God.

25, 26. Finally, in a forward look beyond the exile to the days of the return, Ezekiel foretells the gathering together of the dispersed exiles and their dwelling in safety in their own land once again. This act of God will be His way of manifesting His holiness in and through His people before the nations of the world. The holy people are the channel through whom the Holy God reveals Himself. There is no mention of judgments upon Israel : that is presumably thought of as a thing of the past. The nations against whom these oracles have been uttered will be judged, and Israel will dwell securely in simple, agricultural prosperity.

c. Against Egypt (29:1 – 32:32)

The oracles against Tyre and Sidon are followed by four chapters against Egypt. These contain seven 'words from the Lord' addressed to the nation or its ruler, Pharaoh, and all but one of them are given a specific dating (29:1, 17; 30:1, undated; 30:20; 31:1; 32:1, 17). It seems strange that a twelfth of Ezekiel's book should be devoted to an *exposé* of this one heathen power, just as it seems strange to find a section as large as this one (chapters 25–32) dealing exclusively with non-Jewish affairs. The reason, however, is not hard to find. We have already had cause to note the geographical finitude of Judah in relation to the Middle East of the time, and no commentary on the life and future prospects of her people would be complete without reference to the mighty neighbours who jostled for power around her. Judah's very existence was bound up with the foreign policies of nations like Assyria and Babylon, Egypt and Persia. They determined whether the little Hebrew kingdom was allowed to retain her independence, like a little Switzerland, or whether she should become a political satellite or a military staging-post or an international bargaining-point. They could no more be ignored than can the United States and Soviet Russia in the policies of a state in Europe or South-east Asia today.

What Ezekiel was at pains to point out, however, was that the final say in Israel's destiny was not theirs but God's – and God was Israel's God ! More than that, he said that even the destiny of the great powers, such as Egypt, was in the hands of Israel's God. Yahweh controlled everything. The situation was in fact the very reverse of what appeared to be the case. The secular historian saw Israel dwarfed into insignificance by mighty neighbours ; the religious commentator, the prophet, saw the great powers held firmly in the hand of little Israel's mighty God. The lesson for the Christian minority is not difficult to draw.

i. The sins of Egypt (29:1–16). The date for this oracle is given as January 587 BC, almost exactly a year after the day that the siege of Jerusalem was begun (see 24:1). But even though the dates for these Egyptian oracles straddle the period of the city's fall, there is little in them to indicate that the Egyptians were particularly concerned with what was going on in Judah at the time. The one clue is to be found in 29:6f., where Egypt is criticized for being poor support to Israel in her moment of need : 'when they leaned upon you, you broke.' This is a clear reference to the half-hearted response of Pharaoh Hophra to Zedekiah's appeal for help (*cf*. Je. 37:7). Little is known of this action except that it produced only a temporary lull in the siege of Jerusalem, but we can presume that it was little more than a token foray on the Egyptians' part. It may be argued that Ezekiel's repeated threatenings against Egypt in these four chapters are all attributable to this one act of faithlessness, but the limited evidence hardly justifies such a conclusion, and we are probably more correct to see in these chapters the climax of Egyptian hostility of which this one known act was simply a recent example.

3–5. Pharaoh is likened to a *great dragon* (Heb. *tannîn*, 'sea-monster'), a word which represented both the crocodile, with which the Nile was infested, and also the chaos-monster of Semitic mythology. It appears in several passages in the Old Testament, identified either as 'the serpent', or as 'Leviathan' or 'Rahab' (*e.g.* Jb. 9:13; 26:11–13; Ps. 89:10; Is. 27:1; 51:9; Am. 9:3), but it was never allowed to be regarded as a real and effective opponent of Yahweh as it was with the warring divinities of Canaanite religion. Indeed Genesis 1:21 specifically mentions the *tannînîm* as being part of God's creation, thus killing decisively the myth of their rival pre-existence. The language of mythology was frequently imported into Hebrew poetry, however, and it was a particularly apt simile for the age-old enemy, Egypt, whose sun-god, Rēʿ, claimed to be self-begotten (*I have made myself*, 3, RSV mg.). For its arrogance the monster would be caught with hooks, dragged out of the river and left high and dry to rot in the wilderness like carrion. With it would go *the fish of your streams* (4), *i.e.* the people or the mercenaries or the allies of Egypt (*cf.* the 'helpers of Rahab' in Jb. 9:13).

6–9. A second apt metaphor for Egypt, the land of reeds, is now used. Egypt is a broken reed that fails all who trust in her. The Rabshakeh's words to Hezekiah in Isaiah 36:6 (=2 Ki. 18:21) suggest that the description was almost proverbial. It does not take many instances to establish a reputation for unreliability. Verse 9b brings out yet another ground for Yahweh's declaration, *I am against you* (3, 10; *cf.* 28:22). Egypt, whose prosperity was dependent on the irrigation of the river Nile, was actually claiming to be its owner and originator.

10–16. Egypt's punishment is expressed in terms similar to Judah's, as also is her restoration (*cf.* 4:4–6). She will be made a desolation from *Migdol*, in the Delta, to *Syene*, modern Aswan, at the southern boundary of Egypt with the land of Ethiopia. For *forty years* the land would be without inhabitant (11), a symbolically long period, and then restoration would take place. Unlike Judah's restoration, however, this would be limited to a return to the land of *Pathros* (14), *i.e.* Upper Egypt, where they would continue as a weakened and *a lowly kingdom*, never again to lord it over others. In terms of literal fulfilment these threats never became reality: Egypt never endured an exile as Judah did. But her subsequent history has consisted of repeated conquest and humiliation. She has never been anything more than a 'lowly kingdom' and it is unlikely that she will ever again enjoy the glory that once was hers.

ii. Egypt and Babylon (29:17–21). This oracle is the latest in the whole of the book, being dated on New Year's Day in 571 BC. Although much later than any of the other oracles against Egypt, it is inserted at this point because it links the punishment of Egypt with the raising of the siege of Tyre, an event which took place in *c.* 574 BC. It is therefore put as near to the group of oracles against Tyre as the context will allow. Nebuchadrezzar's siege of Tyre had lasted for thirteen years, and by the end of that time *every head was made bald and every shoulder was rubbed bare*, a graphic description of the chafing of helmets and the carrying of burdens for the siege-works. We do not know whether Tyre was captured by the Babylonian force or not, though a few years later Babylonian officials were in residence in the city and Babylonian suzerainty was acknowledged. All that Ezekiel tells us is that the rewards of the siege were not commensurate with the effort involved. There was insufficient booty to pay off the army (perhaps the treasures had been evacuated by sea), and so Nebuchadrezzar was to divert his attention to the more lucrative prey, Egypt. This is seen as a gift to him from God, inasmuch as his efforts against Tyre had been at the behest of Yahweh and so he was entitled to his reward (*they worked for me*, 20). In point of fact the Babylonian expeditionary force did not attack Egypt until after the date of this oracle (*c.* 568-567 BC) and we have no contemporary records of its measure of success, because the Babylonian inscriptions recording the campaign have been damaged. Ahmose II (Amasis), who had supplanted Pharaoh Hophra in 571 BC, had to come to terms with the invaders, so we may presume that Nebuchadrezzar won the tribute to pay his armies as Ezekiel had prophesied. Jeremiah also foretold Nebuchadrezzar's campaign (*cf.* Je. 43:8–13 ; 46:1–25).

21. The chapter ends with a sentence addressed to Ezekiel, predicting that in the day of Egypt's humiliation (*on that day*) a *horn* would spring forth for the house of Israel. This may be a Messianic statement (*cf.* Ps. 132:17), but the language does not demand it and it may be a general reference to Israel's future restoration. For *horn* as a symbol of strength, see 1 Samuel 2:1 ; 1 Kings 22:11 ; Jeremiah 48:25. At the same time Ezekiel's lips will be opened to speak with greater confidence. To interpret this verse in relation to Ezekiel's ritual dumbness demands that it is taken in isolation from its context, because by the time of this oracle his dumbness was a thing of the past (*cf.* 33:22). It seems better to take it simply as a reference to the authentication of Ezekiel's prophecy through fulfilment. The oracle ends with the refrain, *then they will know that I am the Lord*, which has punctuated this chapter three times already (verses 6, 9 and 16). It is Ezekiel's overriding desire.

iii. Judgment upon Egypt (30:1-19). This, the only undated oracle of the collection against Egypt, is probably to be dated shortly after January 587 BC, the date given in 29:1. The oracle that follows it (30:20-26) is only three months later. There is nothing, however, in these verses to indicate their date, except the reference in verse 10 to Nebuchadrezzar as the agent of Egypt's doom. Cooke argues from the absence of any date, the poverty of the language (many of the lines consist of conventional Ezekiel phrases), and the haphazard enumeration of the cities, that the passage is secondary and not by Ezekiel. His points are valid, but his conclusion is much less so. If all typical Ezekiel phrases were to be denied to Ezekiel, there would be precious little of his book left! Far from poverty, the section is couched in four carefully-constructed oracles (2-5, 6-9, 10-12, 13-19) dealing with related themes, each with a distinctive contribution to the whole book, as the exegesis will show.

2-5. The *day of the Lord*, which has previously been announced only in relation to Israel (*cf.* 7:2-12), is now proclaimed as being the day when judgment by the sword will fall upon Egypt. *Cf.* also the 'sword' prophecy of 21:1-17. The passage needs to be compared with other 'day of the Lord' teaching in Isaiah 2:12-17; Joel 1:15; 2:1, 2; Amos 5:18-20; Zephaniah 1:7, 14-18. On this great day, when judgment will come upon the Gentiles (as well as upon unfaithful Israel, contrary to much popular expectation), Egypt's allies will share her punishment too. RSV is right to take MT *Chub* (5, AV) as a slip for *Lub*, or *Libya*, with many Versions, but it is not necessary to emend *hāʿereḇ*, *the mingled people* (AV, RV), to *hāʿⁿrāḇ*, *the Arabians*. The Hebrew word is used in Jeremiah 25:20 of all the 'foreign folk' in Egypt, the mixed multitude; and so may be used here of mercenaries or of resident aliens.

6–9. The next oracle enlarges on the fate of Egypt's allies and satellites : *all her helpers are broken* (8). Throughout the length and breadth of the land they will fall by the sword (on *Migdol* and *Syene*, see note on 29:10), and the nearby Ethiopians, who dwell securely in the lee of their powerful neighbour, will be terrified as messengers go forth to them *in ships* (9, AV, RV ; there is no need to emend to *swift*, RSV) up the waterways of the Nile to tell them of Egypt's downfall. They will be sent *from me*, *i.e.* from the Lord, because He will be present in Egypt working His destruction upon her cities.

10–12. The agent of this judgment is now named as Nebuchadrezzar, but it is not to be his action alone. He will cause the destruction of the people in Egypt (11), but it is God Himself who will *dry up the Nile* and be responsible for the devastation which will be brought about. Behind the *hand of foreigners*, who appear to act as His agents, is the word of God (*I, the Lord, have spoken*), which is the all-powerful ultimate agent which can turn spoken prophecy into actual fact.

13–19. Finally, in a grand display of geographical knowledge, the complete devastation of the land of Egypt is expressed by means of a welter of place-names. This was a favourite mode of Hebrew expression (*cf.* Is. 10:27–32 ; Mi. 1:10–15 ; Zp. 2:4) and Cooke's description of it as 'haphazard enumeration' sums it up well but proves nothing about its authorship. If anything, its typicality authenticates it as good prophetic style. The place-names deserve comment. *Noph* (13, 16 ; AV, RV) is the classical *Memphis* (RSV), modern Mit Rahneh. It used to be the capital of Lower Egypt and remained an important centre until the conquest by Alexander the Great. There was a colony of Jews living there in Jeremiah's time (*cf.* Je. 44:1). *Pathros* (14) is the region of Upper Egypt extending southwards to Aswan. *Zoan* (14) was an important city in the eastern region of the Nile delta ; its classical name was Tanis. It has been variously identified with Avaris, the northern capital of the Hyksos dynasty, and with Raamses, the store-city (Ex. 1:11), but with no certainty. *No* (14, 15, 16 ; AV, RV) is the classical *Thebes* (RSV), modern Karnak and Luxor ; it was the capital of all Egypt for much of Egypt's history, and was the cultic centre for the sun-god, Amon. Nahum calls it No-Amon (Na. 3:8). *Sin* (15, 16; AV, RV) is *Pelusium* (RSV), modern Tel Farama, on the Mediterranean coast not far from Port Said, and a strategic defence-post against invasion. *Aven* or *On* (17) is the classical Heliopolis, the city of the sun-god and one of the oldest cities in Egypt. Joseph's father-in-law, Potiphera, was high priest there (Gn. 41:45). Jeremiah calls it Beth-Shemesh, 'the house of the sun' (Je. 43:13). Its pointing as Aven (Heb. *'āwen*), meaning 'wickedness', may well have been a punning commentary on the religion it stood for. *Pi-beseth* (17) is the modern Basta, north-east of Cairo. *Tehaphnehes* (18), or Tahpanhes, is the Greek Daphnai, modern Tel Defenneh, ten miles west of Qantara on the Suez Canal. It is famous as the frontier-city to which Jeremiah was taken after the assassination of Gedaliah (Je. 43:7; *cf.* 44:1).

iv. The arm of Pharaoh is broken (30:20–26).

The date of this oracle is April 587 BC, but the allusion is to the event of the previous year when Pharaoh Hophra's army, sent to Jerusalem in response to Zedekiah's plea, was repulsed by the Babylonian troops who were besieging the city (*cf.* Je. 37:1–10). This defeat is described as a breaking of Pharaoh's arm (21), and Ezekiel adds that the damage will not be repaired : there will be no bandaging of the broken limb so that it can wield a sword again. Instead God will break *both* Pharaoh's arms and completely debilitate him, and will strengthen Nebuchadrezzar and give him His sword so that he can be the agent of His judgment upon the Egyptians (25). By the time Nebuchadrezzar invaded Egypt, after the siege of Tyre was ended, Hophra had been killed in civil war. He had conducted a disastrous campaign in Libya, which brought on a major revolt from a rival faction under Ahmose, who was eventually responsible for doing him to death. We are not to interpret an oracle like this one of Ezekiel in too personal terms, but it clearly fits in admirably with Hophra's fate. Once again we are faced with uncertainty about the outcome of Nebuchadrezzar's Egyptian campaign, but this is only a problem to those who insist on finding literal fulfilments for every prediction in Scripture. We should not always expect this to occur, though the broad outline of events is usually fulfilled, and we must admit that we are still waiting for the fulfilment of the statement that all Egypt *will know that I am the Lord* (26).

v. The great cedar tree (31:1–18). This chapter has a clear unity, indicated both by its subject-matter, the allegory of the cedar tree and its fall, and by the introductory and closing phrases in verses 2a and 18d. It is in three sections: the poem of the magnificent tree to which Pharaoh is likened (2–9), and two prose oracles describing its downfall at the hand of foreigners (10–14) and its descent into Sheol (15–18). The date given in verse 1 is a further two months on from that of the previous oracle (30:20) and is June 587 BC.

2–9. The use of a cedar of Lebanon as an allegory for a mighty nation is no new thing. Ezekiel used the same idea in 17:1–10, 22–24, and other echoes of the language of this chapter may be found in 19:10–14; 26:19–21; 28:11–19. Isaiah's description of the descent of the king of Babylon into Sheol has distinct similarities (Is. 14:4–21), and Daniel's description of Nebuchadrezzar's dream uses much the same imagery (Dn. 4:1–12, 19–27). Some of the language is even carried over into the New Testament, as in the parable of the mustard seed (Mt. 13:31f.). The reference to *Assyria* (3, AV, RV) is clearly a mistake, because that nation has no place in an allegory addressed to Pharaoh. RSV emends the text from Hebrew *'aššûr*, 'Assyria', to *'ašweḵā, I will liken you*, a change of only one consonant; but there is much to be said for interpreting the Hebrew word as a variant form of *te'aššûr*, an evergreen tree correctly identified by Zohary as the cypress (*Cupressus sempervirens*).[1] In this case it is used in apposition to the word for *cedar*, and we would translate 'Behold a cypress, a cedar in Lebanon, with fair branches and woody shade'. Its roots are nourished by an abundance of water (4), in language

---

[1] See his article in *IDB*, vol. 2, *s.v.* 'Flora', p. 292. The identification of *te'aššûr* with the box-tree (*Buxus longifolia*) seems to be no longer tenable on geographical grounds (as in *NBD*, p. 1293).

reminiscent both of the watering of the garden of Eden (Gn. 2:10–14) and, more directly, of the network of streams which irrigate Egypt from the river Nile. The wide spread of her branches provides shelter for birds and animals, symbolizing the nations of the world who at various times enjoy Egypt's patronage. The flattering language of verses 7–9 must not be taken too literally, unless it is intended to reflect the adulation which a Pharaoh like Hophra received from his satellites, Zedekiah included. Its effect, however, is to heighten the sense of downfall when eventually this takes place, as with the similarly extravagant description of the good ship Tyre (27:3–9). Nothing whatsoever could compare with it in beauty, not even the finest trees in Eden, *the garden of God.* Here is another echo of the Genesis narrative (Gn. 2:8f.), which appeared also in the lamentation on the king of Tyre (28:12–19), and it further illustrates Ezekiel's willingness to draw on the symbolism of the past, a symbolism which his readers or hearers were presumably expected to understand.

10–14. This oracle gives the reasons for the cedar's downfall (10), describes its ruin (11, 12) and adds the intention that motivated God in effecting such a catastrophe (14). The all-too-familiar pattern of pride preceding downfall comes out in verse 10 (*cf.* Tyre, 28:2; Babel, Gn. 11:4), and this is described as *wickedness* (11), a positive wrongdoing which incurs guilt, not simply a human failing to which all are excusably prone. The result is that God casts it out, just as He expelled Adam and Eve from the garden of Eden. So, deprived of God's favour and protection, the cedar is a prey to *the most terrible of the nations* (12; *cf.* 28:7; 30:11; 32:12) and is cut down and scattered all over the land. The birds and beasts which once sheltered under its branches will prey on its remains (13), and the event will prove an object-lesson to all other nations not to aspire to such heights, because nations are human and human beings have no end but that which is common to all, the nether parts of the earth and the pit (14). Death is the great equalizer and the surest antidote to an excess of ambition. Even the Egypts of this world, who have success-stories despite their godlessness, need to be taught the lesson that may be hidden in verse 9 that *I* (Yahweh) *made it beautiful.* The prosperity of the wicked is, in the last analysis, all due to the mercy and goodness of God.

15–18. The concluding oracle deals with the reactions of her contemporaries to Egypt's demise. As with the sinking of the Tyrian merchant-ship, there is general consternation that a nation so mighty could be so humbled. What chance had lesser nations like themselves? The world of nature will mourn for her : the *deep* (Heb. *teḥôm*) grieves and the *many waters* are stopped ; Lebanon is clothed in mourning and the trees wither away as in a drought (15). The nations, too, shake with the reverberation of its fall ; all the noblest kingdoms, typified by the phrase, *the trees of Eden* (16), take comfort from the realization that just as they have flourished and died, so the great cedar-tree of Egypt has come to a similar end. The picture of trees going down to Sheol is a strange one, and May suggests that this reflects some myth of the descent of the trees of Eden to Sheol after the fall of man. He compares the tradition in *Enoch* 25:4–6 of the transplanting of the tree of life from Eden to a high mountain of God in the north-west until later it should be removed to the temple for the righteous. The idea has much to commend it but cannot of course be proved. The alternative is to see in these verses a mixing of the symbols of the downfall of states, represented by trees, and the descent into Sheol of great men, representing the nations they ruled. The confusion is particularly noticeable in verses 16 and 18. The final insult is reserved for the final verse of the chapter : Egypt, who was not to be compared with her neighbours in glory and greatness, will now lie alongside the lowliest of the dead in Sheol, namely with the uncircumcised and those *slain by the sword.* This is interpreted by Eissfeldt as the murdered and the executed, and by Cooke as those who received no burial rites. Either way, they were accorded an inferior position in Sheol, and *Pharaoh and all his multitude* would share it with them (18).

vi. A lament over Pharaoh (32:1–16). The last two oracles against Egypt, which comprise this chapter, are both dated in the *twelfth year*, *i.e.* 586/5 BC, a short time after the news of the fall of Jerusalem had reached the exiles (*cf.* 33:21). Cooke suggests that this may account for the bitterness of the prophet's tones : Egypt had failed Jerusalem in her hour of need. This argument must not, however, be over-pressed, because Ezekiel has already given up hope of any support from 'the broken reed' which is Egypt (*cf.* 29:6f.), and the tenor of his oracle here is no more virulent than the conventional style of the 'taunt-song' or *lamentation* (*cf.* Is. 14, and earlier examples from Ezekiel, as in chapter 19).

1. The date is March 585 BC, according to the reading of MT. The Versions vary between the twelfth year and the tenth month (LXX, Vaticanus ; Lat.), the eleventh year and the twelfth month (LXX, Alexandrinus ; Syr.), and the tenth year and the twelfth month (Aquila, according to Jerome). The confusion appears to have arisen out of a desire to keep all Ezekiel's dates in chronological order and to make the dates in 32:1 and 32:17 earlier than that given in 33:21. This is quite unnecessary. It is not unreasonable to expect the Egyptian collection of oracles to be chronologically arranged (with the obvious exception of 29:17, which is explained above), but the text is not to be emended to suit other patterns imposed upon it. The Hebrew reading, followed by EVV, should therefore stand.

2–8. On *lamentation* (Heb. *qînâ*, 'dirge'), see note on 19:1–14. The general style of the *qînâ* is to be found in this poem, but it is often impossible to trace the typical 3:2 metre which the word usually implies. The poem begins with the same simile as 19:2, where it was addressed to the princes of Israel. Although the *lion* was a figure associated with the house of David (*cf.* the lion of Judah ; Gn. 49:9), it was not exclusive to Israel, and May observes that the Egyptian sphinx was a lion-bodied creature.[1] So it is not necessary to emend the text, as do Fohrer and Bertholet, to get rid of it. Ezekiel's point is that Pharaoh is not the lion-like creature that he fancied himself to be, but a *tannîn*, a *dragon*. The word is the same as is used in 29:3, and again shares the double

[1] *IB*, p. 238.

inference of the Egyptian crocodile and the mythological chaos-monster, Tiamat, which was slain by the god Marduk after being captured in a net.[1] Neither simile is intended to be flattering. Like a crocodile, the king of Egypt wallows in the muddy waters of the Nile, making them even muddier by his movements, and like Tiamat, he is going to be ensnared and hauled out on to dry ground, where his carcase will be a prey for the scavengers of the earth and sky. The whole land will be drenched with his blood (6), and the heavenly luminaries will cease to give their light (7, 8). Such phrases suggest the accompaniments of the day of the Lord, as in Isaiah 13:10; Joel 2:30f.; 3:15; Amos 8:9. But it is also worth noting that they echo the language of the plagues of Egypt (Ex. 7:20–24; 10:21–23), as if to imply that Pharaoh's final hour of judgment will follow a pattern similar to God's earlier confrontation with him through Moses.

9–15. This section begins with a prose interpolation (9, 10), which abandons the figurative language that has gone before and describes the consternation which will be felt by other nations when they see the fate of the Egyptians. The combination of captivity (9; RSV *carry you captive* is preferable to *bring thy destruction*, AV, RV, especially as the words that follow imply some kind of exile) and the *sword* (10) is enough to make the nations fear for their own lives in case they are the next victims due for judgment. This leads in to the next poem (11–15) which takes up the well-used theme of the sword of the Lord (*cf.* 21:9; 30:25) which is put into the hands of the king of Babylon to be wielded against the Egyptians. So great will be the slaughter and devastation that Egypt will be uninhabited by either man or beast, and verses 13–15 vividly describe the land in such a state. The waters will be unruffled by foot of man or hoof of beast; they will be clear and will flow as smoothly as oil through the devastated countryside. There will be no man left in Egypt to *know that I am the Lord* (15), so unless we take this as a conventional, stereotyped ending to an oracle of this kind, we must suppose it to refer

---

[1] *Enuma elish*, IV, line 95; quoted in *DOTT*, p. 9.

to the watching nations who alone will benefit from the sight of such an act of God.

16. The professional wailing women of the nations are finally commissioned to chant the words of this lamentation over Egypt and all her people (*cf.* Je. 9:17–20), as a feature of their funerary rites.

vii. Pharaoh's descent to Sheol (32:17–32). The collection of oracles against Egypt concludes with this remarkable description of Pharaoh in the underworld and of the shadowy nations of the world which he sees lying there, suffering the same humiliation as himself. The language is highly poetical and the details must not be taken too literally. This is not the chapter to turn to if one wishes to understand the Bible's teaching about the after-life. It does, however, illustrate something of the concept of death which was common to Near Eastern thought and from which the Old Testament was constantly striving to break free. Sheol, the place of the departed, was thought of as a vast burial-chamber to which every grave was somehow, conceptually if not spatially, linked. As Pedersen puts it : 'Sheol is the entirety into which all graves are merged. . . . Where there is grave, there is Sheol, and where there is Sheol, there is grave.'[1] Within this shadowy abode individuals continue to maintain some sort of existence, though by reason of the poetical nature of the passages describing Sheol it is impossible to produce any consistent picture of what this existence was thought to be like. To some it was all silence and darkness (Jb. 10:20f. ; Ps. 115:17), to others there was conversation and limited activity (*cf.* Is. 14:10). Ezekiel paints a picture of compartments in Sheol, where nations lie together in graves gathered around their king or national representative. Different status-levels are recognized and warriors who have had a proper burial seem to enjoy a position of greater honour than their less fortunate neighbours (27). But again this must not be pressed : Job says there are no distinctions in Sheol (Jb. 3:17–19). Clearly Israel had no hard and fast doctrine of Sheol.

[1] Pedersen, *Israel, Its Life and Culture, I–II*, 1926, p. 462.

What the Old Testament writers did achieve was to make Sheol less and less a place beyond the realms of God's concern and authority. God had power over Sheol and He could even, in the case of His choicest servants, by-pass Sheol and translate men like Enoch and Elijah into His immediate presence. This also seems to be the hope of the psalmist in Psalms 49:15 and 73:24. For most, however, the righteous included, Sheol was the common lot, until later prospects of resurrection brought a brighter hope for those who were acceptable to God by reason of their faith, integrity and obedience to His will.

17. The date omits the number of the month and RSV follows LXX in supplying *the first month*. It is more natural to suppose that this should be 'the twelfth month', as at 32:1, and that it was either omitted deliberately (it being the same as given earlier) or it dropped out through confusion with *the twelfth year*. The date would then be a fortnight later in March 585 BC.

18–21. As this section is another funeral dirge (*cf.* 32:16), Ezekiel is commanded to chant it as a kind of incantation which will have the effect of sending Egypt and her multitude down into the nether world. *The daughters of the majestic nations* (18, RSV) must mean those who will go down to Sheol with Egypt, *i.e.* her satellites, but a very slight change of pointing produces the better sense that these are the womenfolk who are to join in the lament with Ezekiel : *you and the women of the mighty nations* (Moffatt). As happened with Tyre (28:8f.), the much-vaunted grandeur of Egypt will appear as nothing when she stands at the entrance to the underworld and is drawn down to lie with the uncircumcised who were slain by the sword (20). Her arrival is greeted by mocking words of welcome from the mighty chieftains who are already there (21b should be in direct speech, as in RSV).

22–32. Now begins the conducted tour of the nations in Sheol : 'the mighty conquerors of history pass in review' (Muilenburg). There is much repetition of phrases, of the sort usually found in poetry, but it is impossible to put these words to metre without virtually rewriting the text (as

Hölscher does; see Cooke, p. 350), and we must be content to describe it as rhythmic prose. First to be mentioned is *Assyria* (22), the great tyrant of the past, whose only epitaph is that she once *spread terror in the land of the living*. *Elam* (24) was an ancient nation to the east of Babylon, known for its warlike traditions and formerly absorbed into the great Assyrian Empire. She survived the shockwaves of the fall of Nineveh in 612 BC, which brought Assyria to her knees, and apparently was still a power to be reckoned with, for she later contributed to Cyrus's armies which overthrew Babylon. She too had spread terror, but now was bearing her shame. *Meshech and Tubal* (26) seem a strange choice of nations. May suggests that they represented the traditional 'foe from the north', but we at this remove know relatively little about them except that they harried the Assyrians on their northern frontier (see on 27:13). They were not allowed to lie in Sheol with the fallen warriors who had been buried with full military honours (27), though some commentators follow LXX in omitting the *not* at the beginning of the verse, which would therefore cancel out this little piece of discrimination. In verse 28, the person addressed is not Meshech and Tubal, but Pharaoh. *Edom* (29) has a place, with her kings and princes, as have *the princes of the north*, presumably the rulers of the Phoenician cities north of Palestine, and the *Sidonians* (30). All these will be seen by Pharaoh, and he will take what little comfort he can from the thought that he is in good company with other nations who in their day caused terror and have now been brought low.

In these eight chapters it must have been noticed that every nation but Babylon has been singled out for mention. We must suppose that this was a deliberate silence: a direct onslaught on one's captors would be too glaring a provocation. But Ezekiel's hearers and readers must have drawn the obvious conclusion that, if these countries were due for the judgment of God, Babylon could not herself escape scot-free. There was comfort here for the exiles as well.

VI. ORACLES RELATING TO THE FALL OF
JERUSALEM (33:1 – 37:28)

a. The watchman's duties restated (33:1–20)

After the long hiatus of chapters 25–32, following closely on the death of Ezekiel's wife with its symbolic parallel in the tragic fall of Jerusalem, one would have expected this new section to begin with the episode of 33:21, 22. For some reason, however, Ezekiel keeps us in suspense a little longer while he repeats two statements dealing with human responsibility, both of which have already appeared in a slightly different guise. The first of these, 33:1–9, concerns the prophet's responsibility to warn his people of approaching danger, and is to be compared with 3:16–21. The second is about the hearers' responsibility to make an individual act of repentance in order that they may live and not die, and has close similarities with 18:21–29. The fact that these two themes introduce this chapter indicates that we are dealing here with a new phase in Ezekiel's ministry, for which these links with his former ministry represent a kind of recommissioning. During the period covered by the first twenty-four chapters of his book, his main concern was with Jerusalem as it was and as it had been. From chapter 33 onwards, he is mainly interested in what it will be. As he prepares himself for this new phase in his life's work, God reminds him once again of his awful responsibility as a watchman, a lonely figure who is committed to the task of standing apart from his fellow-men in order that he can keep a constant vigil and warn his people of dangers that lie ahead. At the same time, his hearers are held responsible for acting in accordance with the watchman's warnings. They are neither to trust in their own righteousness nor to despair and with a fatalistic shrug of the shoulders to give in to their unhappy circumstances. Nor are they to take the easy way out by blaming all their misfortunes on the injustice of God. Every man has his chance and every man must act according to God's word to him. These are Ezekiel's terms of reference, and only when they have been clearly enunciated does the news break upon the waiting exiles that the city has fallen and Ezekiel's word has been proved true.

33:2–6. The watchman's duty. The illustration is drawn from what was common practice in time of war. The man deputed by his city to act as its watchman and to give warning of the approach of an enemy force had a heavy responsibility. He was to sound the alarm, so that the inhabitants of the city who were farming the lands around the city could retreat within the walls and prepare for battle. If any man disregarded the warning, he was virtually signing his death-warrant, but no blame would attach to the watchman. If, however, the watchman failed in his duty to warn, he would be held responsible for the deaths of any who were caught unawares. The *trumpet* (Heb. *šôpār*; 3ff.) was a long horn, curving upwards at the end, which was used extensively in Israel for both military and religious occasions (*cf.* Jos. 6:4; 2 Sa. 2:28; Ps. 81:3; Joel 2:15; Am. 3:6). It is still used in Jewish synagogues, especially at the New Year. The phrase, *his blood I will require* (6), reflects the concept of blood-guiltiness, which is common to much Old Testament thought, whereby the shedding of a man's blood by another, whether done deliberately, accidentally or by some failure in responsibility, involves the blood-shedder in a state of guilt and the kinsman of the deceased in a duty to avenge his death.

33:7–9. The prophet's duty. The danger which the prophet has to warn his people about is the threat of judgment by the word of the Lord (7). When this speaks in condemnation of the wicked man, the prophet must pass on the message or be held responsible. The exposition of the prophet's duties is briefer than in 3:16–21, where there is specific reference to warning the righteous man as well as the wicked, but the principle remains the same in both passages.

33:10–16. An invitation to repent. For the first time since the book opened, we are shown here that the exiles are conscious of their own sin (10). This does not appear in AV (*If our transgressions and our sins be upon us . . . how should we then live?*), but the better rendering, *Truly our transgressions and our sins are upon us* (RV mg.), suggests both a deep conviction of sin and an overwhelming feeling of despair. Earlier expressions of guilt laid the blame on other shoulders (*cf.* 18:2), but now at last Ezekiel's insistent teaching has taken effect. The prophet's immediate reaction is not, however, to rub their noses in their sins, but to proclaim God's forgiveness for those who will repent. He has no delight in judgment but He longs for men to repent (11; *cf.* 2 Pet. 3:9), and this cardinal feature of Ezekiel's theology needs to be written underneath every oracle of judgment which his book contains. The prophet's proclamation of judgment is with the ultimate purpose of repentance and salvation (*cf.* 18:21; 33:5b; Je. 1:10), though Jonah's struggle with himself suggests that this idea often went against the grain (Jon. 4:1ff.). On the same basis of man's freedom to repent, however, comes the corollary that the righteous man too needs to repent when he falls into sin : he may not trust in his former righteousness to save him (12, 13). Verse 13 does not mean to say that the godly man forfeits his salvation by committing sin : it has nothing to do with the early church's fear of post-baptismal sin or with more recent issues of 'once saved, always saved'. It simply states in reverse the principle of individual responsibility. Repentance is incumbent upon all men ; unwillingness to repent is a denial of the true spirit of faith in God's mercy. The evangelical doctrine of assurance should always be balanced by the cautionary word 'let any one who thinks that he stands take heed lest he fall' (1 Cor. 10:12). For the meaning of the phrase, *the statutes of life* (15), see 20:11, 13 (*cf.* Lv. 18:5). To be genuine, repentance has to show itself in a quality of life which is marked by obedience to God's laws.

17-20. As with the similar words in 18:25-30, the complaint of the people that *the way of the Lord is not equal* (AV, RV) or *just* (RSV) uses an unusual metaphor taken from weighing in scales. The verb means literally 'is not adjusted to the right standard', which is the action of a dishonest salesman. The boot, however, is on the other foot. It is the people who are untrue, and God will judge them one by one and show that they are found wanting (20). Their guilt is individual and personal, as well as national and corporate.

b. The city falls but the people are unrepentant (33:21–33)

At long last the blow fell and the news reached the exiles that Jerusalem had fallen. Although this came with the force of a tragedy to the exiles, Ezekiel himself was fully prepared to receive it. He of course had been given prophetic fore-knowledge of the event (*cf.* 24:2), but he had also been in an ecstatic state the previous evening and his ritual dumbness had been somehow relieved. According to 24:27, this release from his divinely-imposed silence was an indication that the day of the tragic news was about to dawn. It meant that he was now able to speak publicly and freely of all the things that had been brewing up inside him. When he did speak, his first remarks consisted of messages about the people who were left in the land of Judah (23–29) and about his fellow-exiles (30–33).

21. The date here appears to be a full eighteen months after the city's fall, and most commentators regard this as being too long and unrealistic a time-lag. Some MSS and Syriac read 'eleventh year' for MT *twelfth year*, and this is much more likely, especially as the two words differ only by one consonant in written Hebrew and hardly at all in speech. Ezra and his company took four months to make the journey over a century later (Ezr. 7:9), and so a six-month trip by an exhausted fugitive is not unreasonable for the present context. May would retain the MT reading and account for the discrepancy by the confusion between a vernal and autumnal calendar.

33:23–29. Oracle to those remaining in Judah. It looks as if those who survived the ravages made by the Babylonian forces, and whom Jeremiah described as 'the poorest of the land' who were left to be 'vinedressers and ploughmen' (Je. 52:16), were quietly annexing unclaimed properties and regarding themselves as the inheritors of the promises given to their forefathers. This was no new thing, for those who were spared the exile in 597 BC had made similar claims (*cf.* 11:15). Then they had claimed that those in exile, having gone far from the Lord, were no longer entitled to the privileges of land-ownership in Judah; now, they were making the incredibly facile plea that if one man, Abraham, had inherited the land of Canaan, *a fortiori* they who numbered a few thousands had a far greater right. The passage illustrates with remarkable aptness the overweening arrogance of the minority who wake up one morning and find themselves in the majority. Moreover, like so many minorities, they live in the past and endeavour to draw on ancient precedents to buttress insubstantial claims for the present. Our Lord had to answer similar claims from the Jews of His time (Jn. 8:33–40), as did John the Baptist before Him (Lk. 3:8). Ezekiel's answer was the bitter accusation that morally and religiously they had not a leg to stand on (25, 26). Their sins were the very same sins as had brought destruction upon the inhabitants of Jerusalem (22:6–12; *cf.* 18:10–13). Therefore their chances of escaping scot-free were nil. 'Abraham's title to the land was his righteousness' (Stalker). The difficult phrase, *Ye stand upon your sword* (26, AV, RV), is well interpreted by RSV, *You resort to the sword* (Ellison, 'you live by violence'). The charge is confirmed by the action of Ishmael and his henchmen in assassinating Gedaliah the governor at Mizpah (2 Ki. 25:25; Je. 41:1–3). What right, asks Ezekiel, have men who commit such crimes to *possess the land* (26)? Instead there will come the sword, wild beasts and pestilence, the traditional vehicles of judgment (27), and the land will be made completely desolate.

33:30–33. The people and the prophet. The issue under discussion in the previous section (23–29) was the identity of the true Israel, as between the cream of the land who were in exile and the people of the land who remained in Judah.

Jeremiah dealt with the same conflict in his vision of the two baskets of figs, and he was shown that the Lord's choice was to be found among the exiles, the good figs, and not among Zedekiah and the remnant in Jerusalem (Je. 24). Ezekiel clearly sided with Jeremiah's verdict. He was sceptical, however, of the depth of sincerity of the exiles, particularly at a time when he was being lionized and listened to as the prophet whose words had come true. Everyone was talking about him (30; not *against* him, as in AV) and encouraging each other to go and listen to what he had to say. Religious meetings were never so well attended. But was the message going deep? Ezekiel concluded that it was not : the people listened well and spoke with *much love* (31), but they betrayed themselves by their actions, which showed up their true priorities, *their heart is set on their gain*. As with Simon Magus (Acts 8:18), their receptivity to the word of God was distorted by the inner feeling of 'what is there in this for me?' Despite the prospect of future blessing and restoration that the prophet was holding out to them, their attitude was one of self-seeking. They listened to Ezekiel as men listen to *a lovely song* (lit. 'a song of love', especially of a highly sensuous kind) and *a pleasant voice* and one who *plays well on an instrument*. The grammatical relationship between these phrases is not clear and translations vary slightly, but the sense is clear. Popular music in every age has been renowned for its ability to move its hearers only fleetingly. May wonders if Ezekiel ever chanted his oracles to an accompaniment of music (*cf.* 1 Sa. 10:5 ; 2 Ki. 3:15), but there is no other evidence for this.

33. *When this comes.* The words are a typical crisis statement, usually foretelling judgment, but here they must refer to the crisis of restoration which from now on is Ezekiel's theme. Though pleasant to listen to, they are no more heeded than were his prophecies of doom. But they will as certainly be fulfilled, and in the fulfilment Ezekiel's status as a prophet will be vindicated. Ours is not the only age that treats God's spokesmen as if they are public entertainment.

c. The shepherds of the past and the Shepherd of the future (34:1-31)

It is not unusual, either in the Old Testament or in other writings from the Ancient Near East, to find rulers designated as shepherds (*cf.* Is. 44:28; Je. 2:8; 10:21; 23:1-6; 25:34-38; Mi. 5:4, 5; Zc. 11:4-17). Moses and David are given this description (Is. 63:11; Ps. 78:70f.) and it is not without significance that both these men received their call to leadership while they were actually serving as shepherds of a flock. The word 'shepherd' suggests leadership and caring, and it was therefore an appropriate metaphor to use for hereditary monarchs who might otherwise think only in terms of lording it over their people. Israelite history shows how rarely this ideal of responsible leadership was achieved, and Ezekiel was particularly conscious of the failures of the most recent kings before the exile (*cf.* 19:1-14; 21:25). He therefore precedes his promise of good leadership to come with a searing attack on the greed and selfishness of the leaders of the past. They had exploited the people as if the flock belonged to them, the shepherds. But the people were the Lord's flock (*my sheep*, 6) and the kings ruled them by the Lord's appointment (*my shepherds*, 8). Therefore the shepherds would be punished and the sheep, scattered by exile, would be rescued and returned to their own pastures and cared for by God as their good Shepherd. He would judge them righteously and would appoint His servant, David, as His vicegerent and prince (24), and all would be peace and harmony, blessing and prosperity. The passage is illustrative of a high ideal of kingship in the Old Testament and of the place of Yahweh as the true *melek*-king of Israel from whom the kingship of the house of David was derived. It is also worth noting that the close connection between the king and the shepherd-motif justifies us in seeing a certain kingly quality in such well-known passages as Psalm 23 (where the rod in verse 4 is the same word as a royal sceptre) and John 10.[1]

[1] See the discussion of this by Raymond Brown in his commentary on *John I-XII* (Anchor Bible), pp. 396-398, where he insists, against Bultmann, that 'Ezekiel's portrait of God (or the Messiah) as the ideal shepherd . . . served as the model for Jesus' portrait of himself as the ideal shepherd'.

34:1–10. Condemnation of the shepherds. The three accusations levelled against the kings of Israel are, first, that they cruelly exploited the people who were under their care, fleecing them and fattening themselves at their expense (2, 3); secondly, that they showed none of the pastoral qualities that were required of them in caring for the weak and defenceless members of the community (4); and thirdly, that instead of keeping the flock together in safety they allowed them to be *scattered* over all the earth (the word occurs three times in verses 5 and 6, and is a favourite word of Ezekiel to describe the dispersion of the exiles). This meant that they were an easy prey for wild beasts, representing here the hostile nations of the world. They were in that most pathetic of all states, at least to the eastern mind : they were as sheep without a shepherd (*cf.* 1 Ki. 22:17; Mt. 9:36).

Because of all this, God declares that He is against the shepherds, even though they ruled by His dispensation. Having failed in their responsibilities, they would not be allowed to rule any more; the flock would be taken out of their care and they would be deposed from office. This is a rather milder verdict than appeared in Jeremiah 23:2, where punishment was threatened to the shepherds. Ezekiel does not at this stage prophesy the punishment of the rulers, but only the rescue of the people from their voracious grasp. In point of fact, the exile had already removed many Israelites from the jurisdiction of their national rulers, but the phrase in verse 10b seems to imply that the yoke of kingly rule (Gedaliah perhaps?) was to be taken away even from those who were left in the land of Judah.

34:11–16. The good Shepherd. A flock of sheep must be looked after by someone, and here God represents Himself as taking on the role of Shepherd to His people. His job will be to find the straying, to rescue the lost, and to feed and tend the whole flock, giving particular attention to the weak and ailing members. The picture of the shepherd searching out the wanderer, in verse 12, is a remarkable foreshadowing of the parable of the lost sheep (Lk. 15:4ff.), which our Lord doubtless based on this passage in Ezekiel. It illustrates as clearly as anything can do the tender, loving qualities of the God of the Old Testament, and strikes a death-blow at those who try to drive a wedge between Yahweh, God of Israel, and the God and Father of our Lord Jesus Christ. Nor is it the only passage that speaks of the tender shepherd (*cf.* Pss. 78:52f.; 79:13; 80:1; Is. 40:11; 49:9f.; Je. 31:10). The reference to *a day of clouds and thick darkness* (12, RSV) has eschatological overtones (*cf.* Ps. 97:2; Joel 2:2; Zp. 1:15) and suggests that this deliverance is to be the day of the Lord for Israel, that is to say, the day when the Lord acts in salvation and judgment to usher in a new age of His righteous rule on earth.

16. RSV emends the Hebrew, which has *the fat and the strong I will destroy* (RV), to read *the fat and the strong I will watch over*. This follows LXX, Syriac and the Latin Versions and is commended by many commentators as being 'more appropriate to the Shepherd' (Cooke). But the fact remains that all but two MSS have the harsher reading and it fits in much better both with the phrase that immediately follows (*I will feed them in justice*, or 'as is fitting') and with the tenor of verses 17–22, where the fat and the strong ones of the flock oppress the weak and are condemned for doing so. Keil is therefore probably right to conclude that 'the destruction of these oppressors shows that the loving care of the Lord is associated with righteousness' (Keil, *in loc.*).

34:17–22. Judgment among the flock. So far Ezekiel has pronounced God's judgment only upon the bad shepherds, *i.e.* the kingly rulers. The good Shepherd now turns judge and deals with the bad sheep within the flock, *i.e.* the oppressive nobles or the bullying merchant-classes. A confusion of interpretation has arisen here because of the inclusion of the *rams* and the *he-goats* in verse 17. Comparison with Matthew 25:31–33 has led some to impose the New Testament pattern of a separation between sheep and goats upon this figure in Ezekiel. But the distinction is between the fat and strong, and the weak and helpless (20). The flock in biblical times, as today in the Middle East, regularly consisted of a mixture of sheep and goats, and the Hebrew word *śeh* in 17, 20, 22 (translated equally misleadingly as *cattle*, AV, and *sheep*, RSV) simply meant a member of the flock, whether a sheep or a goat. Ezekiel is saying that the powerful and prosperous citizens, who had been greedily taking for themselves all the good things of the land and denying the benefit of them to their fellows, were going to be judged by the Shepherd.[1] The flock will in fact be purified, not only of its bad leadership but also of its bad members. The language of this metaphor sets Ezekiel fairly and squarely in the prophetic tradition of Amos, for whom social justice and freedom from oppression of the poor by the rich were the two main planks of his message. It would be interesting to know whether Ezekiel had any specific examples of oppression in mind as he uttered these words. The shoddy treatment of the Hebrew slaves during the siege of Jerusalem was certainly an apt example of the truth of his allegations (Je. 34:8–11).

34:23, 24. The Messianic Shepherd. Every new paragraph of this chapter opens out the analogy still further. If the chapter is taken as a whole it will appear full of inconsistencies, but if each section is taken separately it will be obvious that new ideas are being added all along. These verses seem to abandon the concept of God as the one good Shepherd, as He plans to install His own chosen nominee to act as shepherd of His people. The context is the consummation of the present age and the opening of the new age. The scattered flock have been gathered to their own land in an eschatological act of deliverance, not without its element of judgment. United and purified, they now enter upon the supernatural golden age of peace and prosperity. Over them is set the Messianic figure who is variously described as *my servant, prince* and *David*. Who is this person? He is not, as some would believe, the historical

---

[1] May's suggestion that the distinction here is between Israelite and pagan sheep, on the grounds that the oppressors are contrasted with *my sheep* and *my flock* (19, 22) and are held responsible for scattering the flock in exile (21), seems to be incorporating altogether new and alien ideas into the metaphor.

David resurrected, nor is he a human king of the Davidic line, for we are dealing with a superhuman figure who will reign for ever (*cf.* 37:25). He is the servant of the Lord, represented as an idealized David : for David was the man whom God chose and in whom He delighted; the king who triumphed against all his foes and who extended his kingdom in all directions; the man of Judah under whose genius the whole nation was for a time united. These features of the Messianic leader's person and kingdom are more significant to Ezekiel than the physical succession of the line of David's kings. He saw no future for kings of that sort over Israel. They were condemned, and Zedekiah's fate only served to seal that condemnation. So this new Messianic figure is described not as king, but as *prince* (*nāśî'*), and in that capacity he will be the righteous ruler of the saved community of Israel.[1] Christians can see the fulfilment of this expectation in the character of Christ's future Messianic rule of which the present Christian era is a mere foreshadowing, but the Davidic lineage of Jesus relates to Old Testament prophecies other than those of Ezekiel (*e.g.* Is. 11:1 ; Je. 23:5).

34:25-31. The covenant of peace. The new age is to be marked by a new covenant which will banish wild animals from the land and ensure safety, fertility and productivity for those who dwell in it. The absence of wild animals does not quite give the same picture as is found in Isaiah 11:6-9, because for Ezekiel the security of the inhabitants is based on the removal of danger, as in Leviticus 26:6, whereas for Isaiah there was a real harmony between traditional enemies (*cf.* Ho. 2:18). The abundant fertility of the land, however, is paralleled in other golden-age prophecies, such as Hosea 2:22 ; Joel 3:18 ; Amos 9:13f. ; Zechariah 8:12, all of which see God's future blessings in terms of agricultural prosperity.

Relationships are frequently described in terms of covenant,

---

[1] The use by Ezekiel of the term *nāśî'* (lit. 'one lifted up') was not meant to indicate a great difference of *function* from that of the *melek*; it is attributable mainly to his desire to avoid the association of the latter word with the Judean monarchy. There may however be a subtle hint of a distinction in the use of *among them* instead of 'over them' in verse 24.

and the phrase *covenant of peace* (25; *cf.* 37:26; Is. 54:10) means simply 'a covenant that works'. The word *peace* is used to describe the harmony that exists when covenant obligations are being fulfilled and the relationship is sound. It is not a negative concept, implying absence of conflict or worry or noise, as we use it, but a thoroughly positive state in which all is functioning well. The area of safety promised to God's people includes both the *wilderness*, the uncultivated pastureland, and the *woods*, the scrubland which was usually a place of some danger by reason of wild beasts. But it was centred on Mount Zion (*my hill*, 26), as in most prophecies about the Messianic age. *The showers in their season* refer to the former rains, which break the summer drought in late October and November, and the latter rain (*gešem*), which soaks the ground between December and March. On their regularity and copiousness depended the fertility of the whole land of Palestine.

29. *Plant of renown* (AV; lit. 'a planting-place for a name'). If this is correct, the meaning must be that God will provide for His people plantations which will bring them renown among the nations by reason of their abundant produce. But the phrase reads awkwardly and RSV and many commentators follow LXX, Syr. in transposing two letters to make 'plantations of peace', or 'prosperity'.

31. RSV is undoubtedly right to omit *men*, with LXX, Lat.

d. Denunciation of Edom's treachery (35:1–15)

The Edomites received a brief reference in the oracles against the nations (25:12–14), and the question is inevitably raised why a whole chapter is devoted to them at this particular stage in the development of the book, when the restoration of Israel is the overriding theme. The easy answer is to regard it as interpolated, but that will not bear examination because the oracle has close links with chapter 36, both in the invective style of its prophecies ('because . . . therefore') and in the contrasting addresses to the mountains of Edom and Israel (35:3; 36:9). The probable answer is that the Edomites are known to have betrayed their relationship with Israel by plundering their land at the moment when Jerusalem was on the point of collapse, and that this action would account for the virulence of the prophecy as well as its position just after the news of the fall of Jerusalem. Also, if a preliminary to Israel's restoration was to be the removal of her hostile neighbours (the 'wild beasts' of the land, of 34:25?), then again the prophecy of the desolation of Edom is well placed here. The word 'Edom', of course, never occurs in this chapter: it is always *Mount Seir*. This refers to the mountainous region east of the Arabah, the rift-valley running south from the Dead Sea, in the heart of which is to be found the rose-red city of Petra (biblical Sela). The colour of the porphyritic stone was almost certainly the origin of the name Edom (Heb. for 'red'), though one traditional explanation was associated with Esau's appearance at birth (Gn. 25:25). In this mountainous area lived the Edomites, the descendants of Jacob's twin brother, and they maintained a constant hostility towards their Israelite kinsmen (the *perpetual hatred* of verse 5). In all fairness it must be added that the fault was not entirely all on one side. (For a biblical survey of their relationship, see Gn. 25:22ff.; 27:1–41; Nu. 20:14–21; 2 Sa. 8:13f.; 2 Ki. 8:20f.; 14:7; Ps. 137:7; Is. 34; Je. 49:7–22; La. 4:21f.; Am. 1:11f.; Ob.; Mal. 1:2–5.)

The inhabitants of Mount Seir are accused on three counts: (*a*) because of their perpetual hatred and for their attacks on the children of Israel *in the time of their calamity* (5); (*b*) because of their aspirations to territorial aggrandizement, which may well have led them to barter their support for Nebuchadrezzar for the promise of parts of Judah and Israel (10); (*c*) because of their arrogant boasts and cruel gloating over the downfall of Jerusalem (12–15). The particular heinousness of these offences is expressed in verses 10, 12 and 13. In reply, Ezekiel states that Edom's claims to land were invalid because Judah and Israel were God's territory (*the Lord was there*, 10), and unauthorized peoples possessed it at their peril (*cf.* the fate of the Assyrian colonists of the northern territory in 2 Ki. 17:24–28). And the arrogant insults hurled at the people of Judah were tantamount to blasphemies against the Lord, which He had heard. In each case the judgment pronounced by God was in the form of retribution. The *lex talionis* is invoked to bring slaughter in return for the bloodshed Edom had caused; hatred for hatred, and desolation for desolation.

3. *A desolation and a waste.* The Hebrew phrase is the alliterative *šᵉmāmâ û-mᵉšammâ*, found also in 6:14; 33:28, 29.

5. *The time of their calamity* must refer to the events of 587 BC, and not to some supposed later destruction of Jerusalem by the Edomites, hinted at in Nehemiah 1:3, as some contenders for a late date have maintained. The parallel phrase, *at the time of their final punishment* (RSV is preferable to AV here), indicates that the judgment of 587 was the culmination of Jerusalem's sufferings, as Isaiah 40:2 also makes clear. On the incident alluded to here, compare Obadiah 10–14.

6. The blood-guilt, in which Edom's treachery involved her, was all the more serious because of her primitive kinship with Israel. Although the text of this verse is not entirely clear, the fourfold reference to *blood* (*dām*) may be a deliberate word-play on the unmentioned name of Edom.

7. *Him that passeth and him that returneth:* a Hebraism, like 'he who buys and he who sells' (7:12) and 'he that goes out and he that comes in', implying 'all without exception' (*all who come and go*, RSV).

9. The hatred of verse 5 is matched by the punishment of *perpetual desolation.* This is a much harsher fate even than was inflicted on nations like Egypt and Ammon, who at least had a prospect of restoration held out to them (29:14; Je. 49:6).

10. The *two nations* are Israel and Judah. The Edomites, shut away in their mountain fastnesses, must often have cast greedy eyes at the more fertile lands to the north-west of them. But their only chance of success lay in Judah's weakness, and this they attempted to exploit. It is interesting to note that, even in the hour of Judah's judgment, God is still regarded as being there in the land and is shown to identify Himself with His people (12).

14. The meaning of RSV is that as Edom has rejoiced over Jerusalem, so God will make Edom a desolation so that

all the earth may exult over Edom. The sense of this is preferable to AV which takes it as if Edom will be the only nation
not to rejoice when all the earth is jubilant.

e. A restored land and a transformed people (36:1–38)

Ezekiel's promises of restoration for Israel began in chapter 34
with the prospect of new leadership in the person of the Lord
as the good Shepherd and the Davidic Messiah as His nominee.
The future hope is now taken up again with the prospect,
first, of a new land and then finally of a renewed people to
dwell in it. The order of leader, land and people is an interesting indication both of the recognition of the importance of
national leadership in Israel, and also of the inseparable
relationship between a people and the physical contours of the
land where they dwelt. The first point we readily recognize
today, but the second is much less easy for us to appreciate.
It does not necessarily imply a belief in localized deities,
though the Old Testament did have a high regard for the
locations of sanctuaries where God appeared to their forefathers, *e.g.* El Beth-el, the God of Bethel (Gn. 31:13; 35:7).
But it is to be set alongside such facts as the place of Canaan,
the promised land, in the Abrahamic and Mosaic covenants,
and the selection of Jerusalem or Mount Zion as the place
where the Lord was thought particularly to dwell and where
His worship was to be carried on. To those who feel that this is
altogether too materialistic a concept of God and too con-
stricting for the God of the whole earth, the enlightened
Israelite would probably answer that it is no more unreasonable than that the God of all time should declare one
day in seven as His own and that the God of all nature should
claim a tenth of its produce for Himself. Authority over the
whole is witnessed to by the surrender of the part. So the
Hebrews regarded the actual land where they lived, the
mountains, the valleys, the plains and the rivers, as a kind of
God's acre in the world, and its welfare was intimately bound
up with the welfare of God's people who lived in it. Just as
this applied in chapter 35 to Mount Seir, and by implication

to its inhabitants, so now God addresses the mountains of Israel (1–15), and this leads on to oracles concerning the people of Israel (16–38).

The structure of the chapter is as follows. (*a*) The oracle addressed to the mountains of Israel has two parts to it. Verses 1–7 promise that the nations round about Israel, and Edom in particular, will suffer reproach for the way they have treated Israel. Verses 8–15 speak more positively of the prospect of fruitfulness for the mountains of Israel and repopulation of the land by the homecoming exiles. (*b*) The second main section consists of an introductory flashback over Israel's past, showing that it was concern for His holy name which prompted the Lord to punish His people (16–21), and this is followed by three oracles dealing with the new blessings which the people are to receive and enjoy (22–32, 33–36, 37, 38).

36:1–7. The enemies of the mountains of Israel. The sentence structure is confused and critics have tried, with little agreement among themselves, to separate the original wording from later accretions. It seems more satisfactory, however, to see the confusion of expression as a mark of heightened emotion, as the prophet blazes out his indignation. One older critic comments : 'Ezekiel is seized with unusual fire, so that after the brief statement in ver. 2 "therefore" is repeated five times, the charges brought against these foes forcing themselves in again and again, before the prophecy settles calmly upon the mountains of Israel, to which it was really intended to apply.'[1] The occasion for this fiery harangue was the exultant claim of Judah's enemies that *The ancient heights have become our possession* (2, RSV). The use of the word *bāmôṯ* (lit. *high places* ; so AV, RV) is anomalous as a description of the highlands of Judah because of its idolatrous associations. But the word could bear a neutral interpretation and so there is no need to follow LXX and emend to *šemāmôṯ*, 'desolations' (*cf.* Dt. 32:13 ; Am. 4:13). The adjective *ancient* (lit. 'of eternity') underlines the belief that the land was Judah's by

---

[1] Ewald, quoted in Keil, Vol. II, p. 102. Notice also the excited repetition in verse 3 : *because, yea, because* (RSV).

reason of primeval promises, and so makes the enemy's claims all the more infuriating to Ezekiel. They were challenging not simply Judah's territorial boundaries, but the Lord's long-standing promises, and that was the next thing to blasphemy. It was this which aroused His *hot jealousy* (5, RSV) and *jealous wrath* (6, RSV), the ardour that burns within the man who is deeply wounded by another's words or actions. It led God to swear with a very strong oath ('with an uplifted hand', 7; *cf.* 20:5) that the contempt which the heathen nations had heaped upon Judah would instead return upon their own heads.

36:8–15. The blessing of the mountains of Israel. The contrast with what has gone before is marked by the emphatic introductory words, *But you.* The promises of being fertile and densely populated are the very opposite of the fate held out for the mountains of Edom (35:3, 7, 15). And the benefits of the land's fruitfulness will be enjoyed by the exiles, *for they will soon come home* (8, RSV).[1] No contradiction is to be seen here with Ezekiel's statement, expressed in 4:6, that the punishment of the house of Judah would last for forty years. Now that Jerusalem's punishment has been fulfilled, Ezekiel sees nothing but the imminent fulfilment of the promise of restoration, in a kind of prophetic foreshortening of the immediate future. This is because God is *for you* (9), *i.e.* on Israel's side, in contrast with His attitude to Israel in former times (6:2, 3b) and with His attitude to the nations round about (26:3; 28:22; 29:3; 35:3). And for this reason, He is going to repopulate the mountains of Israel with *all the house of Israel*, presumably with both Israel and Judah, and the ruined cities will be rebuilt and re-inhabited, and the waste-lands will once again be cultivated and bring forth produce. As so often, when God acts in blessing, He does *more good to you than ever before* (11).

It is not easy to see how the mountains of Israel could be

---

[1] The AV rendering, *for they are at hand to come*, takes the subject, not as Israel, but as the blessings which have been promised. This is perfectly possible, but the context seems to favour the RSV translation.

said to *bereave* the land of children (12) and to *devour men* (14). Some commentators think in terms of causing famine through drought (Davidson, May), or death through famine and wild beasts (Cooke), or the decimation of the people through war and invasion (Stalker). Skinner, less specifically, refers to Numbers 13:32, where the spies reported that the land was a 'land that devours its inhabitants', and concludes that 'the land, in mysterious sympathy with the mind of Jehovah, had seemed to be animated by a hostile disposition towards its inhabitants. . . . Its inhospitable character was known among the heathen. . . . But in the glorious future all this will be changed'.[1]

36:16–21. Historical retrospect. Once again Ezekiel repeats his assertion that Israel's sins deserved God's punishment. The people had defiled their land and made it unclean, like the uncleanness of a menstruous woman (17 ; a figure for idolatry, see note on 7:19). For this God had scattered them among the nations and judged them : He could do no other. Then, however, His act of judgment had rebounded upon His own good name, for the heathen had been astonished that such a fate should happen to the people of the Lord and it had caused them to think lightly of a God who allowed His people to be treated so. The doctrine expressed in the phrase, *I had concern for my holy name* (21, RSV), represents the utmost humiliation for the sinner. There is no consideration for him, no respect for his feelings, no love for him as a human being. He stands condemned because of his sins, and he forfeits all claim on God. He is simply a pawn on the chess-board of the world, in which God's prime concern is that all men and nations may know that He is the Lord. To put it like this in all its starkness may seem harsh and a contradiction of Christianity, but it is an aspect of the truth of God as revealed in the Old Testament. It is the aspect which is basic to Paul's statement in Romans 5:8, 'While we were yet sinners . . .' We had no claim on God, we were His enemies, we were helpless to do anything to save ourselves : but God acted in salvation.

[1] Skinner, pp. 332f.

In so doing He showed His love to us, and to all the world. But the humiliation of Ezekiel's doctrine is needed first, in order that we may appreciate the amazing grace of Romans 5.

36:22–32. God vindicates His holiness in restoring Israel. In this chapter we are at the heart of Ezekiel's salvation theology. He tells us not only what God will do but why He is acting in this way. As we have seen, the two focal points of God's purposes are His own name and the nations of the world, and these two are related. He wants His name to be great, so that the nations may regard Him not as an ineffective tribal god, but as the Lord of the whole earth. And Israel is to be the channel through which this vindication is going to be achieved (*through you*, 23). It must have been very difficult for Israel to accept this role, and the only hint that some in Israel were able to accept it is to be found in the so-called Servant Songs of Isaiah 40–55, where Israel as the Servant of the Lord fulfils His mission among the Gentiles through suffering.[1] The church also finds it a difficult role to accept, but in an age when God's power is all too often discredited by reason of His people's failures, the church needs to be prepared to be treated harshly for the sake of God's greater glory in the world.

24–30. In the case of the exiles, however, God is now going to vindicate His glory, not through their sufferings, but through their restoration. In a series of prophetic statements, Ezekiel describes what God will do. First comes the sheer physical act of returning the exiles to their native land (24). That is followed by a number of moral and spiritual changes, for which a variety of images is used. Sprinkling with *clean water* (25) means more, for instance, than just forgiveness of sins. Its symbolism is derived from ritual washings with water which were intended to remove ceremonial defilement (*cf.* Ex. 30:17–21 ; Lv. 14:52 ; Nu. 19:17–19), and this is applied to the

---

[1] This does not of course exhaust the interpretation of these songs (viz. Is. 42:1–4; 49:1–6; 50:4–9; 52:13 – 53:12), for they have strong Messianic overtones, but this is an element which must not be overlooked in the desire to see them solely as prefigurings of Christ.

people's cleansing from the defilement of idolatry (*from all your idols I will cleanse you*, 25).[1]

The terms *heart* and *spirit* (26) also need careful understanding. They are not so much parts of man's make-up as aspects of his total personality. The *heart* includes the mind and the will, as well as the emotions; it is in fact the seat of the personality, the inmost nature of man. The *spirit* is the impulse which drives the man and regulates his desires, his thoughts and his conduct. Both of these will be replaced and renewed: the heart that is stubborn, rebellious and insensitive (*a heart of stone*) by one that is soft, impressionable and responsive (*a heart of flesh*), and the spirit of disobedience by the Spirit of God. It goes without saying that there is nothing in the Hebrew word 'flesh' which suggests the corrupting tendency of the Greek *sarx*, as used in the New Testament and particularly by the apostle Paul in Romans 8. The result of this psychological transplant will be that Israel will experience a real 'change of heart' and will become, by God's gracious initiative, the kind of people that they have in the past so signally failed to be. The implanting of God's Spirit within them will transform their motives and empower them to live according to God's *statutes* and *judgments* (27). Jeremiah, in the similar passage in his prophecy on which Ezekiel's appears to be based (Je. 31:31–34), makes no reference to the gift of the Spirit but his reference to putting 'my law within them' and writing it 'upon their hearts' clearly produces the same results. The enduement with the Spirit was a sign of the Messianic age (*cf.* Is. 42:1; 44:3; 59:21; Joel 2:28f.), and Ezekiel was aware of this and mentioned it on later occasions (37:14; 39:29). For him therefore the restoration of Israel was the beginning of the last days, the age of the Messiah. In keeping with that idea, therefore, the covenant relationship between God and Israel would be renewed (*you shall be my people, and I will be your God*, 28), and in addition to cleansing from the uncleanness of the past there would be the Canaan-like prospect of a superabundance of natural prosperity (29).

[1] It is the same ritual which developed variously into the frequent lustrations of the Qumran sect and into the Christian practice of baptism.

31, 32. These concluding verses seem distinctly off-key, after the list of benefits that have gone before, but they represent an essential link with the theological premiss on which the blessings of the new age are given. Underlying everything is Ezekiel's view that the actions of God were not intended to benefit His people, but to set forth His glory in the world. Israel's reaction will be that she will be shamed by God's goodness into a state of repentance and self-loathing (*cf.* 20:43), and will therefore acknowledge God in a way that she had failed to before.

36:33–36. The nations learn through Israel's history.
Now at last the purpose behind God's actions finds its proper fulfilment. The rebuilding of the devastated cities of Israel and the reclaiming of abandoned farmlands will cause those who see it to marvel, and they will reckon that the Lord has done it in order to keep His word. *I, the Lord, have spoken, and I will do it* (36). The statement of verse 35 is in striking contrast to the earlier verdict of verse 20. It tallies with the teaching of much 'golden-age' prophecy that the glorious days to come will be like a return to the bliss of Eden before the Fall (*cf.* Is. 11:6–9 ; 51:3 ; Joel 3:18 ; Am. 9:13–15. It will be just as much an act of God's creation as was the original garden of Eden. God, not man, will be responsible for the consummation of this present age.

36:37, 38. Increase of population.
As a postscript to the promise of restored lands and cities comes this assurance that they will abound with men to work them and live in them. The imagery, which is similar to that used in chapter 34, is probably drawn from the sight of droves of sacrificial victims thronging the narrow streets of Jerusalem at festival time. *Holy flock* (38, AV) is literally 'flock of holy things' and evidently refers to animals intended for sacrifice. Just as these filled Jerusalem in their thousands (*cf.* 2 Ch. 35:7), so the rebuilt cities of Israel would be filled with throngs of men. The sacrificial simile would have come easily to Ezekiel the priest. It is tempting to wonder whether he thought beyond

the mere numerical similarity to the picture of a people who were ready to be offered, like the sheep, as living sacrifices in the service of God.

f. The spiritual rebirth of the people (37:1–28)

The familiarity of this most well-known chapter of all in Ezekiel can easily blind readers to its real meaning. The vision of the valley of dry bones has been taken by some as teaching an Old Testament doctrine of bodily resurrection, and by others it has been seen simply as an analogy for spiritual regeneration. The symbol of the two sticks has been used both to advance and to refute the theories of the British Israelites.[1] But the key to understanding this chapter aright is to see it in its context. Ezekiel had been promising his people a change in their fortunes: new leadership, a restored land, rebuilt cities, and many of the features of the Messianic era. It is not surprising that he was met with scepticism: the fall of Jerusalem had meant the break-up of their faith and it was not going to be restored as easily as that. They looked at the shattered remains of their people in exile and they could only say, 'Our bones are dried up, and our hope is lost. Can these bones live?' The answer appeared to be unmistakably 'No'. Ezekiel, however, believed that it could happen. If God's purpose was to restore Israel, He would do it by however great a miracle. Both the vision and the oracle of the two sticks conveyed this message. In the case of the first (1–14), the nation was shown that God's Spirit had the power to turn what looked like a host of skeletons into an effective army of men, a picture of Israel restored to life again and filled with the Spirit. In the second (15–28), Ezekiel shows that the old divisions between Israel and Judah will pass away: the new nation will unite the remnants of both peoples in one land under one king, and without their traditional animosity.

37:1–14. The vision of the valley of dry bones. The bones represent the Israelites in exile. They have been there

[1] See the discussion in Ellison, pp. 131ff.

for more than ten years now, and what glimmerings of hope they had when first they arrived have now been altogether extinguished. Their hope was lost : as bones, they were very dry.

The vision is a fair reflection of the despondency with which Ezekiel was faced, though it must be admitted that his earlier prophesyings had, in part at any rate, contributed to the people's despair. Now, however, when the prophet prophesied, the bones clicked into place and became living beings : Israel came alive. In the vision this happened in two stages. In the first, Ezekiel is told to *prophesy to these bones* and to command them to *hear the word of the Lord*. This results in only a partial restoration : scattered skeletons are transformed into individual corpses, but they are still just as dead. At the second stage, Ezekiel has to *prophesy to the wind* (the word is *rûaḥ*, 'breath' or 'spirit') and appeal to it to come and *breathe upon these slain, that they may live* (9). This time the corpses come alive and stand on their feet, and the miracle is complete.

What is the significance of the two stages? The difference between them is surely to be found in the *direction* of Ezekiel's prophesying ; first to the bones, telling them to hear, and secondly to the spirit, invoking its inspiration. The first must have seemed to Ezekiel very much like his professional occupation, exhorting lifeless people to listen to God's word. The effect was limited : true, something remarkable happened, but the hearers were still dead men. The second action was tantamount to praying, as Ezekiel besought the Spirit of God to effect the miracle of re-creation, to breathe into man's nostrils the breath of life (*cf.* Gn. 2:7). This time the effect was devastating. What preaching by itself failed to achieve, prayer made a reality.

The stress in this section, however, is not so much on the means as on the fact of the revival of these bones. This is made clear in the explanatory verses at the end of the vision (11–14), where the two stages of the vision are ignored. Instead a new metaphor is invoked, that of resurrection of the dead from their places of burial. There is a real inconsistency here, because the bones of the earlier vision were unburied. But this only proves that the metaphors are there to reinforce the fact of what God is planning to do, namely to effect the revival of His dispirited people, Israel. The figures of speech do not have validity in their own right. This passage does not therefore teach a doctrine of resurrection from the dead, either general, national or individual. Nor does it even imply a belief in resurrection on the part of Ezekiel or his hearers. All that can be said of it is that Ezekiel uses the language of resurrection to illustrate the promise of Israel's return to a new life in her own land from the deathlike existence of the Babylonian exile. Some would doubt whether Ezekiel was even aware of the possibility of a physical resurrection, as described in Daniel 12:2, and they would trace the origin of his metaphor either to the cultic enactment of the myth of the dying and rising god,[1] or, within the Bible, to the Yahwistic narrative of the creation of man in Genesis 2.[2] This may be overstating the case because, as Skinner has observed,[3] 'that God by a miracle could restore the dead to life no devout Israelite ever doubted', and he goes on to cite 1 Kings 17 and 2 Kings 4:33ff.; 13:21, as instances of this rare miraculous occurrence. But there is no evidence that Ezekiel either believed in or taught or showed knowledge of a doctrine of the resurrection of the dead. For Jewish and Christian commentators to read this back into chapter 37 is to attribute to Ezekiel interests that were not his and to miss the essential point of his message. When Tertullian, for instance, tried to refute the Gnostics, who held that Ezekiel 37 referred only to the restoration of Israel, and not to personal resurrection, it is probable that for once the heretics were in the right.

1, 2. The *valley* is the same word as the 'plain' in 3:22 (Heb. *biq'â*), and probably the same location is intended. Where Ezekiel saw his vision of the majesty of God, he also saw the desolation of the exiles, their bones bleached white by the desert sun, like the sight of a battlefield some months after the

[1] H. Riesenfeld, *The Resurrection in Ezekiel xxxvi and in the Dura-Europos Paintings*, 1948.
[2] See R. Martin-Achard, *From Death to Life*, 1960, pp. 93–102.
[3] Skinner, p. 348.

event. The vision may have been prompted by the actual memory of seeing the Israelite dead strewn outside Jerusalem or scattered along the desert road that led Ezekiel and his companions into exile.

3. The way in which the question is couched, *Can these bones live?*, coupled with the description of them as *very dry* (*i.e.* dead long since), indicates that the obvious answer is 'No'. However, the fact that the question comes from God, the God who kills and makes alive (Dt. 32:39), is enough to make Ezekiel guarded about his answer. He had the knowledge not to deny God's ability, but he lacked the faith to believe in it. Martin-Achard concludes that 'the prophet's words bear witness to the fact that in the age of Ezekiel the possibility of resurrection of the dead was not entertained in Israel; several centuries later, the attitude of Martha, the sister of Lazarus, will be very different (Jn. 11:23ff.).'[1]

5. Part of the artistry of this chapter is the skilful use of the Hebrew word *rûaḥ*. This appears in three different translations: as *Spirit* in verses 1 and 14, as *breath* in verses 5, 6, 8, 9 and 10, and as *wind* or *winds* in verse 9. But in reality it is the same word every time, and no English translation can do justice to its variety of meaning. The Greek word, *pneuma*, shares the flexibility of the Hebrew, and LXX was able to use it consistently in this passage. It is the same word that lies behind the double meaning of wind and Spirit in John 3:8. At its root *rûaḥ* denotes the sense of 'air in motion', *i.e.* wind or breath. This can extend from a gentle breeze to a stormy wind, or from a breath that is breathed to a raging passion. It comes to mean both man's spirit, or disposition, and also emotional qualities like vigour, courage, impatience and ecstasy. It covers not only man's vital breath, given to him at birth and leaving his body in his dying gasp, but also the Spirit of God who imparts that breath. Such is the rich variety of the word used here by Ezekiel.[2]

7. The *shaking* (AV) is interpreted by RV as an *earthquake*,

---

[1] Martin-Achard, *op. cit.*, pp. 95f.
[2] For a fuller study of *rûaḥ*, see Aubrey Johnson, *The Vitality of the Individual in the Thought of Ancient Israel*, 1964, pp. 23-37.

which accompanied the miracle, and by RSV as a *rattling*, the noise of the bones coming together. Either is possible and both meanings occur in Ezekiel (see 3:12f.; 12:18; also 38:19).

9. The *four winds* represent the four corners of the earth (*cf.* 7:2). Notice that, throughout this vision, Ezekiel has acted under orders and has even described his own implicit obedience to God's commands (7, 10). In so doing he emphasizes that this work of revival is God's work from start to finish. If man plays any part in it himself, it is only in obedience to God's direction. The same can be said of man's contribution to any spiritual revival.

11–14. There is perhaps a slight play on words in that the word for *bones* is etymologically connected with a root meaning 'strength'. Thus the metaphorical use of this word in a well-used phrase, like the dismal slogan quoted here, could conceivably have governed the shape of the vision as it developed in the prophet's subconscious mind. The phrase, *we are cut off our forparts* (11, AV; Heb. *niḡzarnû lānû*, lit. 'we-have-been-cut-off for-us'), makes little sense; LXX gives the one-word translation 'we are lost'; RSV appears to emend to 'we-are-cut-off all-of-us' (*kullānû*), without acknowledging the correction. The best solution is that of Perles who alters the word division to *niḡzar nôlēnû*, 'our-thread-of-life has-been-cut-off'. The balance with *our hope is lost* is then complete.[1]

37:15–28. The oracle of the two sticks. Once again the prophet speaks his word with the aid of a symbolical action (*cf.* 4:1; 5:1). He is told by the Lord to take two sticks (lit. 'pieces of wood') and to mark them with the words, *For Judah* and *For Joseph*. These represent the two kingdoms of former days, before Samaria fell to the Assyrians under Sargon II (722/1 BC) and Israel, the northern kingdom, lost her identity. He is to take one of them in his right hand, concealing one end of it in his clenched fist. Then he is to take the other stick and join it to the first one, end to end. His

[1] F. Perles in *Orientalische Literaturzeitung*, xii, 1909, pp. 251f., quoted in Koehler.

clenched fist will thus grasp the place where the two sticks meet, and it will appear as if he is holding one long stick in the middle. Understood in this way, it is not necessary to postulate any kind of miracle in the symbolic act. The meaning of the action is that in the restored Israel, the old divisions of north and south will be abolished and the nation will be united in God's hand. The interpretation of this, however, raises a number of controversial issues. If the inhabitants of Israel/Samaria were scattered throughout the Assyrian Empire, is there any prospect of their descendants being literally brought back, with the exiles from Judah, into the promised land? Or are we to understand 'Israel' as consisting simply of those men of northern tribal origin who had associated themselves wth Judah from time to time? Do we allegorize it all and see it simply as a picture of the church, the new Israel, united in the future kingdom of God? The problems become particularly acute, when the reader approaches this passage with the question foremost in his mind : 'Has this prophecy been fulfilled?' The fulfilment of prophecy is a question which must always take second place after the issue of correct exegesis has been settled. What, then, does Ezekiel say?

The explanation given in 21–28 is futuristic. It describes the ideal, Messianic kingdom of the last days. The children of Israel will be gathered from among the nations where they have been dispersed (21); they will be resettled in their own land; they will be one kingdom, under one Davidic king (22, 24); they will no longer practise idolatry, but they will be purified from all their defilement (23). They will live a life of obedience to the Lord and will enjoy an everlasting covenant with Him (24, 26). The Lord will establish His sanctuary in the midst of them for evermore, and the heathen will know that *I the Lord do sanctify Israel* (26–28). Now all this is the language of the golden age to which Israel looked forward as the culmination of her national religious existence. Any question of 'fulfilment' has to be related to the whole picture that is given and not to isolated features of it. The answer of the New Testament to this future hope of Israel is that it has come about, but has not been fulfilled. The golden age has dawned in the coming of Jesus the Messiah; fulfilment has begun. But it has not yet been completed. The experience of the church finds that many of the expectations of the past have become realities, but even the realities are only a foretaste of the full and final Messianic joy of the world which is to come. An over-literal interpretation of one aspect of this future hope prevents one from seeing that the prophet is mainly concerned with the ideal of unity in the Messianic kingdom, *i.e.* a spiritualized pattern of the future Israel based on the historical precedent of David's united monarchy, which was the golden age of the past.

16. *For Joseph* is the name given to the northern kingdom of Israel, or *Ephraim*. The term 'Israel' was used freely to describe the southern kingdom of Judah once the north had been overrun by the Assyrians, and so its use here would have been ambiguous. The writing on the sticks is reminiscent of Moses' similar act in Numbers 17:2ff. Compare also the oracle of the two staffs named Grace and Union (Zc. 11:7ff.), which is based on this passage in Ezekiel.

22. The same longing for a healing of the divisions between north and south was a marked feature of earlier prophecies (*cf.* Is. 11:13; Je. 3:18; Ho. 1:11).

23. For the *idols* (Heb. *gillûlîm*) and the *detestable things* (Heb. *šiqqûṣîm*), see note on 6:9. For *their dwellingplaces* (AV; Heb. *môšebōtêhem*) most commentators read (with Symmachus) *mešûbōtêhem, their backslidings* (so RSV).

24. *David* is described as *my servant*, a clear Messianic title, as well as *king* and *prince for ever* (25). We have already noted that Ezekiel avoided describing any of his Hebrew contemporaries as king (*melek*), but reserved this title for the Davidic leader of the future (*cf.* on 7:27; 12:10). The quality of permanence attaching to this future reign and expressed in the repeated phrase *for ever, for evermore* (25, 26, 28), is a strong indication that Ezekiel is here thinking not so much of a line of Davidic kings, as he had known them in the past, but of a supernatural kingly being in whom would be concentrated all the qualities of wisdom, endowment with the Spirit, righteousness and peace that were expected of God's anointed ruler.

26. *My sanctuary* in the midst of the restored people is a pledge, not of protection, but of Yahweh's election of His people. He is in covenant with them once again and dwells in their midst. This in itself will bear witness to the nations around that the catastrophe of Jerusalem has been reversed and that the people of Israel are once more Yahweh's people. The word 'to sanctify' (28) means 'to set apart as sacred', *i.e.* for God's own use and glory, and it is frequently used in parallel with words meaning 'to choose'. The restoration of the Temple is thus far more than simply a matter of repairing war-damage. It is God's way of demonstrating that He is not dead and that Israel are still His people. So the chapter concludes on a note which will readily lead on to the vision of chapters 40–48.

VII. PROPHECY AGAINST GOG (38:1 – 39:29)

These chapters can be isolated from their context in much the same way as can the prophecies against the nations in chapters 25–32. They appear to interrupt the sequence of chapters 33–37 and 40–48, which give us a picture of renewed leadership for Israel, a restored land and a reborn people, leading on to the concluding vision of the design and organization of the temple worship of this new community. How does an apocalyptic oracle of this order fit into such a pattern?

That the difficulty was felt at an early stage in the transmission of the text of Ezekiel is witnessed to by the fact that the Scheide papyri place 38–39 immediately after 36.[1] Their present position between 37 and 40 is due to the editorial work of the compiler, whoever he may have been, who assembled the material substantially in the form that has been handed down to us in the MT and Versions. The basic framework of this was chronological (with the known exception of

[1] A LXX text, dating probably from the early third century AD, containing Ezekiel 19:12 – 39:29. See *OTMS*, p. 249n.

29:17ff.), and all the undated oracles had to be fitted in where they could best be inserted. The exegete is therefore constantly having to ask himself why a certain chapter is put in its immediate context. It may be that, as 40–48 clearly hang together and are dated late ('in the twenty-fifth year of our exile', 40:1), this compels the editor to place them at the end of the whole book, and that this chronological consideration has outweighed the logical one; for one might well argue that a final overthrow of the powers of darkness should come *after* the dawning of the new age and not *before* it. The issue is an important one for those who endeavour to fit the picture of the millennium into the biblical pattern of the last things. A further difficulty is raised if we assume that the book of Ezekiel is in reality *two* books, as was apparently held by Josephus in the first century AD.[1] The most probable interpretation of this statement is that chapters 40–48 were regarded by Josephus as a separate appendix, which may even have enjoyed an independent circulation in his day, and that chapters 1–39 were the main part of Ezekiel's prophecy. Understood this way, the oracles against Gog were a suitable conclusion to chapters 1–39.[2]

We incline to the view that chapters 38 and 39 are a separate composition, written in a different literary genre, which were added to 1–37 as a kind of postscript, and that 40–48 were a later appendix which built on to the concluding chapter of the original work, 1–37. This would account both for the verbal links between 37:24–28 and 40–48, and also for the lack of such links between 38, 39 and their context.

This section consists of seven oracles, each introduced with the formula, *Thus says the Lord God* (38:3–9, 10–13, 14–16, 17–23; 39:1–16, 17–24, 25–29). They describe how Gog, the chief prince of Meshech and Tubal, will invade from the north with his hordes to despoil the land of Judah and to destroy the people who are peaceably resettled in their land once again. But the Lord will vindicate His holiness by

---

[1] Josephus, *Antiquities*, x. 5. 1 : 'Ezekiel . . . left behind him in writing two books, concerning these events.'
[2] This is well argued by Skinner, pp. 367f.

massacring the invaders, so that their bodies are scattered on the mountains of Israel to be a prey for wild beasts, and their remains will take seven months to bury in the valley of Hamon-gog. Their weapons also will provide the people of Israel with firewood for seven years to come.

Now the idea of a huge eschatological battle between the forces of evil, or the north, and the faithful people of God was no new one. Ezekiel was aware that he spoke of a fulfilment of events which earlier spokesmen had prophesied (38:17; 39:8), and his words echoed the language of others, especially Jeremiah (Je. 4:5 – 6:26; *cf.* Joel 2:20). He was in fact representing the last days in terms of the 'day of the Lord' imagery which dominated the future for prophets like Joel (Joel 2:28–32), Amos (Am. 5:18–20) and Zephaniah (Zp. 1:14–18), and which appears strongly in parts of Isaiah (Is. 29:5–8; 66:15ff.) and Zechariah (Zc. 12:1–9; 14:1–15). This is a totally different picture from the 'golden age' motif, in terms of which the return from exile to the promised land had been couched. How possible it is to reconcile the two approaches into a consistent chronological scheme must be left to others to judge, on the basis of the efforts of those who have tried. The important thing to note is that Ezekiel was apparently able to use both forms of imagery without a sense of contradiction, though he does not give any clear guidance as to how they may be balanced against each other.

A further word of caution must be spoken about the interpretation of these two chapters. The language is the language of apocalyptic: it is largely symbolical and at times deliberately shadowy and even cryptic. But though the details are vague, the main thrust is clearly and boldly expressed. Interpretation therefore needs to correspond to contents, and attempts to read too much into the incidentals of the prophecy betray the ingenuity of the speculator rather than the sobriety of the exegete.[1]

---

[1] This is particularly true of such fancies, perpetuated in the Scofield Reference Bible, as 'that the primary reference is to the northern (European) powers, headed up by Russia, all agree. The reference to Meshech and Tubal (Moscow and Tobolsk) is a clear mark of identification.' What this

a. The invasion of the armies of Gog (38:1–16)

2. *Gog* has been variously identified with Gyges, king of
Lydia, who is called Gûgu in the records of Ashurbanipal, and
with the place-name, Gagaia, referred to in the Tell el-
Amarna letters as a land of barbarians. From Ras Shamra
writings there has been found a god, Gaga, and this identification too has been suggested (*Enuma elish*, III: line 2).
Others have seen in Gog a historical figure like Alexander
the Great. The most likely suggestion is the first, but the
origin of the name is less significant than what it symbolizes,
namely the personified head of the forces of evil which are
intent on destroying the people of God.[1] The name *Magog* is
unknown in the Old Testament apart from the single reference
in Genesis 10:2 (=1 Ch. 1:5), where he is a son of Japheth
and the founder of a nation. In Revelation 20:8 Magog is a
person associated with Gog, but in Ezekiel the word is almost
certainly meant to represent the country where Gog lived
(so RV, RSV). Gog's description as *chief prince of Meshech and
Tubal* is an attempt to make sense of some awkward Hebrew.
If a place-name *Rosh* could be vouched for, RV's *prince of
Rosh, Meshech, and Tubal* would be the best translation, but in
the absence of any satisfactory identification and in view of
the frequent coupling of Meshech and Tubal (Gn. 10:2 =
1 Ch. 1:5 ; Ezk. 27:13 ; 32:26), we must suppose *rō'š* (='head',
'chief') to be in apposition to, or even a gloss on, the word
prince. The tribes mentioned are the Moschoi and Tibarenoi
(Ass. *Tabal* and *Mušku*) ; see on 27:13.

---

section is in fact dealing with is the fate, not of Israel's near neighbours,
which have been fully dealt with in chapters 25–32, but of the outlying
nations on the fringe of the known world. These can either be taken at
their face value as representing the heathen that have not even a nodding
acquaintance with the true God, or they can be seen to symbolize the
mythological forces of darkness ('the north') ranged against Yahweh and
His people. The same motif of the eschatological battle is found in Rev.
16:14; 20:7–10; and it occurs also in some pseudepigraphical writings and
in the Dead Sea Scrolls (*Book of Enoch*, 56:5–8; 4 *Esdras* 13:5–11; *War of
the Sons of Light and the Sons of Darkness*).
[1] For more detailed study, see W. F. Albright, 'Gog and Magog', *JBL*,
XLIII, 1924, pp. 378–385; J. L. Myres, 'Gog and the Danger from the
North in Ezekiel', *PEFQ*, LXIV, 1932, pp. 213–219.

38:3-9. The army musters. The opening words show that the coming invasion is not simply an enemy's plan, but that the Lord is bringing the armies of Gog against Israel for His own purposes (*cf.* verses 16, 17). The language used in verse 4 (*I will turn you about, and put hooks into your jaws*) may be a conscious echo of the mythological capture of the great sea-monster (see on 29:3-5), and if this is so it would strengthen the belief that Gog is to be understood as the personification of the cosmic forces of evil. With Gog come five other nations, of which the first three are certainly not from the north, *Cush* being Ethiopia, and *Put* being probably Cyrenaica in North Africa (*cf.* 27:10, however, where they served in Tyre's army). *Beth-togarmah* (RSV) is probably Armenia (*cf.* 27:14), and *Gomer* is usually identified with the Gimirrai of the Assyrians, or the Cimmerians of Greek literature, who came originally from north of the Black Sea. With these allies, Gog prepares to assemble his vast hordes against the tiny nation which has been gathered together and now dwells securely on the mountains of Israel. The attack will eventually come *in the latter years* (8), a clear eschatological indication, and the approach of the invading armies will be like a storm cloud (9) or like Joel's cloud of locusts (Joel 2:1-11).

38:10-13. Gog's evil intent. This brief oracle pictures the invasion as being at Gog's own initiative and his diabolical plot is contrasted with the idyllic peace and security of the Israelites, who do not even have city-walls to protect them (*cf.* Zc. 2:4) and who are therefore an easy prey for their depredations. On Israel's claim to *dwell at the centre of the earth* (12, RSV), see note on 5:5. The force of verse 13 seems to be that Gog's enterprise has roused the greed of other nations to join in the plunder, or to traffic in the stolen goods. They are typical of those who will not initiate wrong-doing, but are eager to cash in on the proceeds of it. The phrase, *the young lions thereof* (13, AV, RV), could be repointed to read *its villages* (RSV, following LXX, Syr.), but neither reading is without its problems.

38:14-16. The invasion. Whereas the previous oracle regards Gog as fully responsible for planning the operation, these verses show that God is bringing him against Israel. There is no inconsistency here : 'a divine purpose overrules, while it makes use of, the base human motive' (Cooke). The same paradox marks Isaiah's teaching on the Assyrian invasion (Is. 10:5–19) and Habakkuk's attitude to the Chaldean menace (Hab. 1:5–11). It does not mean that Gog is a luckless pawn in the hand of an all-powerful but immoral God. Gog freely acts according to the evil dictates of his lust for conquest and easy spoil, but behind everything in the universe (and especially as it relates to God's people) there is the controlling hand of God, who orders all things with a view to the ultimate vindication of His honour among the nations. What Gog imagines to be a victory for himself, the Lord turns into an opportunity for His glory (16 ; *I shall be sanctified, i.e.* I shall be recognized to be holy and to be the true God).

b. The massacre (38:17 – 39:24)

38:17-23. God rises up in anger. The defence of helpless Israel is here undertaken directly by God. He will become incensed at the unprovoked invasion by the hordes from the north and He will bring all kinds of natural disasters upon them. All these are described in the future tense, because not only is the passage predictive of what is to come in the last days, but Ezekiel is also aware that what he is saying amounts to a fulfilment of the prophecies of the past (17). Not that Gog had ever been specifically mentioned by earlier prophets, but their predictions of danger from the north were to be fulfilled in him. The weapons which will be used against Gog are earthquakes (19f. ; *cf.* Is. 24:18–20 ; Joel 3:16 ; Hg. 2:6f.), the sword (21, AV), pestilence and bloodshed (22 ; *cf.* 5:17 ; 28:23), and torrential rains, hailstones, fire and brimstone (22 ; *cf.* Gn. 19:24 ; Ps. 11:6 ; Is. 30:30 ; 34:9). All of these, except the sword, are non-human agents frequently associated with God's judgments, and this is partly why RSV follows LXX in emending 21 to *I will summon every kind of terror* against him.

But despite the difficult Hebrew, the AV rendering is fully consonant with passages such as 5:17; 6:3; 11:8; 12:14, *etc.*, and it alone makes sense of the consequent *every man's sword shall be against his brother*, as the demoralized heathen slay each other in their panic and add to the general destruction (*cf.* Jdg. 7:22; 1 Sa. 14:20; Hg. 2:22; Zc. 14:13).

39:1–16. The destruction of the invading armies. The overthrow of Gog and his forces is here retold in different language and in fuller detail. This is typical of Hebrew poetry and of the kind of semi-poetical writing which is used in these oracles. It is fond of repetition and delights to revert to previous statements and enlarge on them, even though the result is to destroy all sense of consecutive arrangement. Failure to appreciate this has led many western commentators to find doublets, contradictions and inconsistencies, and so to assume multiple authorship where this is quite unnecessary. The first two verses repeat 38:3, 4, but instead of the phrase 'put hooks into your jaws', a new word is used in 39:2 which AV wrongly conjectures to mean to *leave but the sixth part of thee*. Although the root of this verb has affinities with the Hebrew for 'six', the Versions are probably right to translate it to 'lead on', *drive forward* (RSV). The picture is of God leading His enemies forth in order to disarm and destroy them (3–5), and the ultimate indignity for them will be that their bodies will be left unburied for the wild beasts to devour (4). The oracle goes on to describe how the spoilers will be spoiled, their weapons providing firewood for the Israelites for seven years to come (9, 10), and how the remains of Gog's army will be buried in the valley of *Hamon-gog* (*i.e.* 'the multitude of Gog') to the east of the Dead Sea, and so just outside Israelite territory. This cleaning-up operation will take seven months, so great will have been the slaughter; and at the end of that time a permanent commission will be set up to search for any unburied remains, to make sure that no cause of pollution is left remaining in the land (14, 15). The repeated reference to the number 'seven' is a reminder that we are here dealing with apocalyptic symbolism, and that therefore literal fulfilment of these details is not to be sought. The purpose behind this massacre is described in terms of (*a*) the fulfilment of God's prophetic word (*I have spoken*, 5, 8); (*b*) the desire to vindicate God's holy name, which the sufferings and punishment of Israel had done so much to discredit (7); and (*c*) the illumination of the heathen (*the nations shall know that I am the Lord*, 7), though Ezekiel does not go as far as to see their eventual salvation through this knowledge, as other prophets did.

39:17–24. The great sacrificial feast. Once again the prophet reverts to an earlier statement for his theme, and 39:4 lies behind this grisly imagery of the Lord inviting birds and wild beasts to a huge sacrificial meal to feast upon the flesh and blood of the fallen warriors. Seen in this way, the inconsistency of the burial of the remains *followed* by their being eaten up, no longer exists. The idea of the Lord's sacrifice has its origin in Isaiah 34:6f.; Jeremiah 46:10; Zephaniah 1:7–9; and Ezekiel's language is followed through in Revelation 19:17–21. It is a graphic, though gruesome, picture; but the squeamish need to be reminded that atrocious acts have to be expressed in corresponding imagery, just as the blessings of God's righteous reign are symbolized by the language of the golden age. Judgment *is* a horrifying thing, and the more devastating its description is, the more men will fear it. Ezekiel was certainly never guilty of calling a spade anything but a spade. However, as Skinner comments, 'we turn with relief from these images of carnage and death to the moral purpose which they conceal' (21–24). Here the full purpose of God's action is expressed, which has hitherto only been hinted at. First and foremost, it will help Israel to know that the Lord is still their God and that the apparent rejection which their expulsion from their homeland indicated was not a permanent thing (22). Secondly, the nations of the world will learn from these events that Israel's punishment was God's intention, and not a sign of His weakness, and that the exile was a righteous God's demonstration of His righteousness for all the world to see (23, 24): a holy God punishes iniquity in His own people as well as in others. Thus, the Lord would set forth His glory among the nations, for Israel's experiences were to be a demonstration of the character of Israel's God (21), and the scandal of 36:20 would be silenced for ever.

c. God's final purposes for Israel (39:25-29)

The reference to the Exile in verse 23 leads Ezekiel back in this final oracle to his present situation. Some would say that these verses have no place in the Gog apocalypse, and it is quite true that their style and content are no longer eschatological. But they appear to be a deliberate attempt to round off the Gog oracles and to relate their message to the immediate needs of the post-587 BC generation of exiles. Nothing new is added to what Ezekiel has said on previous occasions, but as a summary of his teaching they represent a convenient conclusion to chapters 1-39, before the vision of the new temple is added in chapter 40.

25. *I will restore the fortunes of Jacob* (RSV; not as in AV, RV) is a frequent phrase, almost a technical term, for the restoration of blessing upon a person or nation (*cf.* 16:53; 29:14; Jb. 42:10; Pss. 14:7; 85:1; 126:1; Am. 9:14, *etc.*). It is put here in the context of God's mercy to both Israel and Judah (*the whole house of Israel*) and of His concern for His *holy name*.

26. *They shall forget their shame* (RSV) is a minor amendment of the MT, which has *they shall bear their shame* (so RV), a reading which is to be preferred as being more in keeping with the teaching of 6:9; 16:61; 20:43; 36:31. Cooke describes it as 'an inward feeling of self-reproach when Israel remembers the past in the felicity of the present'.

28, 29. The oracle concludes by promising a complete reversal of the exile. The exiles will be gathered into their own land; not one of them will be left among the nations (the fact that many preferred to stay in Babylon after Cyrus's edict is immaterial); and, greatest of all, *I will not hide my face any more from them*, a promise of blessing and favour in perpetuity. Finally, 36:27 is reiterated with the powerful statement, put in the prophetic perfect tense, that *I have poured out my spirit upon the house of Israel* (RV). To put this in the future (as RSV) weakens the dramatic force of this assertion. True, God had not yet done this in reality; but it was such an assured word that it could be spoken by Ezekiel as if it were an accomplished fact.

VIII. THE PLANS FOR THE NEW JERUSALEM (40:1 – 48:35)

These last nine chapters of Ezekiel, although written some years later than the rest of the book, except for 29:17–21, are an integral part of the prophet's teaching and balance certain features found in chapters 1–39. It is particularly appropriate that the book should end, as it began, with a vision. Chapters 1–3 introduced to Ezekiel the vision of God visiting His people in exile; chapters 40–48 present Ezekiel with the vision of God returning to dwell in the midst of His people, now restored and re-established in their own land. These chapters also have links with the vision of the profanation of the Temple and the departure of the glory of the Lord from Jerusalem (8:1 – 11:25), for they picture the rebuilt temple to which the glory of the Lord returns (43:5). They are therefore to be thought of not as a completely independent composition, only loosely tacked on to the end of the main body of Ezekiel's work, but as a real climax to his thought as it has been maturing through twenty years of prayer, meditation and ministry.

In his vision, Ezekiel is transported to a high mountain near to the holy city (Mount Zion is probably intended) and there he meets an angelic figure who conducts him round the temple area, measuring everything with a builder's measuring-rod. He begins with a close study of one of the gateways to the outer court (40:6–16) before entering the outer court to see the chambers which faced inwards on to the pavement around its outer wall. After looking at the two other gateways to the outer court (40:20–27), he is led to the gateway which leads from the outer court into the inner court, where only the priests are allowed to go, and once again there are three of these, on the north, east and south sides respectively (40:28–37). The temple itself stands on the western side, so there is no gateway there, either to the inner or to the outer court (see Fig. II, p. 257). A brief reference to the special sacrificial equipment and the rooms reserved for the sacrificing priests (40:38–47) prepares the way for a detailed description of the holy place (40:48 – 41:26), after which the prophet is led outside for a final survey of the temple area (42:1–20). Then, in vision, Ezekiel sees the glory of the Lord re-entering the temple and he is instructed what he must do with the information he has been given (43:1–12) ; the rest of the chapter is devoted to the measurements of the altar of sacrifice and to how the altar is to be used (43:13–27). Chapter 44 deals with various regulations relating to the ordering of the temple, in particular to the Levites and the Zadokite priests who will minister there, and this is followed by a description of the allocation of the land around the temple, with specific allotments for the temple officials and for the prince (45:1–17). Further regulations regarding feasts, offerings and sacrifices follow (45:18 – 46:24), but chapter 47 introduces a new subject, namely the flow of water from the sanctuary which pours down in the direction of the Arabah, bringing life and fertility to the barren areas of the Dead Sea valley (47:1–12). The vision concludes with a description of the boundaries of the land, and the allocation of various portions to the twelve tribes of Israel (47:13 – 48:35).

The chief problem in these chapters is that of interpretation. Four main views have been held. The first may be called the *literal prophetic* interpretation. According to this, we have here the blueprint of a temple which Ezekiel intended should be built when the exiles returned to Jerusalem : it is in fact a building specification. In defence of this theory it must be said that as Ezekiel was confidently expecting a literal return from exile, it would not be surprising for him, as a priestly as well as a prophetic figure, to outline the shape of the new temple that would surely need to be rebuilt in Jerusalem. The wording of 43:10f. (in the Heb., though not in LXX ; see commentary below) encourages those who adopt this view. On the other hand, as Hengstenberg[1] comments, 'this opinion forgets that we have here to do not with an architect, but with a prophet – with one whose department is not the hands, but the heart'. If this were an architect's specification we should have expected much more detail about materials to be used, and even though many measurements are given, the ground-plan leaves dozens of details to the imagination of any prospective builder, as those who have tried to reconstruct Ezekiel's temple have found to their cost. Moreover, this whole vision (40–48) must be taken as a unity and there are elements which are so impracticable that a completely literal interpretation of the vision must be ruled out (*e.g.* the siting of the temple on a very high mountain, 40:2; the impossible source and course of the river of life, 47:1–12; the unreality of the boundaries of the tribes which could never be worked out geographically in hilly Israel).

The second interpretation is the *symbolic Christian* one, favoured by many older commentators. They held that this vision had its fulfilment symbolically in the Christian church. Now there is truth in this view, and it is given impetus by the use made of Ezekiel's language in the book of Revelation, where the picture of the new Jerusalem is based largely on Ezekiel's pattern. But it is overstating the case to refer Ezekiel's vision *directly* to a Christian 'fulfilment', without seeing that it has a real context for the readers of his own day, and this original context must be the prime concern of the Old Testament exegete.

A variant of this, which is arrived at through similar hermeneutical principles, is the *dispensationalist* view. This is known most popularly through the Scofield Reference Bible which entitles Ezekiel 40–48, 'Israel in the Land during the Kingdom-age'. The approach is literal and futurist. It refers to the last days, when it is supposed that all the prophecies regarding the glorious future of Israel are to be literally fulfilled in a new dispensation. If it follows from this that Old Testament festivals, blood sacrifices, priesthood and worship at a temple are to be reintroduced, after the New Testament

[1] Hengstenberg, p. 350.

revelation of Christ and His finished, fulfilling work,[1] it shows how completely this view misinterprets the significance of Christ's salvation and how it casts doubt on the consistency of God's dealings with mankind. But its fault is basically in regarding Ezekiel 40–48 as prophecy and insisting on a literal fulfilment of it, if not in the past then in the future.

The fourth view is to regard these chapters, not as prophecy, but as *apocalyptic*, and to interpret them according to the canons of this style of Hebrew writing. Its features are symbolism, numerical symmetry, and futurism. We have already noted how 38–39 were couched in this style, and 40–48, although very different in content, lean in the same direction. This was Ezekiel's pattern for the Messianic age that was to come. It lay in the future, and yet it grew out of the present. It was expressed in tangible terms and yet these were merely the forms in which the general principles of God's activity were enshrined. The vision of the temple was in fact a kind of incarnation of all that God stood for and all that He required and all that He could do for His people in the age that was about to dawn. On this view, which of all the interpretations seems to take the most realistic view of the literary character of the material with which we are dealing, the message of Ezekiel in these chapters may be summarized as follows :

(*a*) the perfection of God's plan for His restored people, symbolically expressed in the immaculate symmetry of the temple building ;

(*b*) the centrality of worship in the new age, its importance being expressed in the scrupulous concern for detail in the observance of its rites ;

(*c*) the abiding presence of the Lord in the midst of His people ;

(*d*) the blessings that will flow from God's presence to the barren places of the earth (the river of life) ;

(*e*) the orderly allocation of duties and privileges to all God's people, as shown both in the temple duties and in the

[1] As Scofield's note on 43:19 implies : 'Doubtless these offerings will be memorial, looking back to the cross, as the offerings under the old covenant were anticipatory, looking forward to the cross.' The whole dispensationalist view is given a searching scrutiny in O. T. Allis, *Prophecy and the Church*, 1945.

apportionment of the land (a theme taken up in Rev. 7:4–8).

These are of course only the main themes which Ezekiel seems to be expressing in this apocalyptic sequence. There is much more which can be adduced through detailed exposition. But if the vision is interpreted on these lines, and not as prophecy in the conventional sense, readers will be spared the necessity of trying to look for some fulfilment of the words in past or future history.

a. The vision of the temple (40:1 – 42:20)

40:1–4. The man with the measuring-rod. The date is 573 BC, and *the beginning of the year* (1) certainly suggests the first month, and may have conscious associations with the Passover (Ex. 12:3) or the entry into Canaan under Joshua (Jos. 4:19). But if the year was regarded as beginning in the autumn, this would mean the seventh month, Tishri, the *tenth day* of which was the Day of Atonement (Lv. 23:27; 25:9), and there are indications that this was a New Year's Day.[1] The new age was beginning with the new year. The *very high mountain* (2) appears to be Mount Zion, as in 17:22, but if the RSV reading *opposite me* (so LXX) is preferred to MT, *on the south*, it could be taken as the Mount of Olives, which has a commanding view of the Temple area. The angelic architect (*cf.* Zc. 2:1) is similar to the scribe of 9:1–11, who acts as both guide and interpreter to the prophet in his visions, and this is typical of the apocalyptic form of revelation (*cf.* Dn. 8:15; 10:5). His supernatural character is evidenced by his appearance *like bronze* (3, RSV; *cf.* 1:4; Dn. 10:6), and he carried *a line of flax* (for measuring long distances) and *a measuring reed* in his hand. Compare Revelation 21:10–15 for an echo of this imagery. Ezekiel is told to look, to listen, to concentrate on what he is shown (*set thine heart* or *mind*, 4), and to report it in full to the house of Israel.

40:5–16. The east gateway of the outer court. Ezekiel is using the long cubit for all his measurements, *i.e.* approxi-

[1] See J. Morgenstern, *HUCA*, I, 1924, pp. 22–28; X, 1935, pp. 8, 29.

mately 20½ ins, as against the customary cubit of 17½ ins.[1] The angel's measuring-rod would thus be about 10 ft 3 ins long, and this would be the thickness and the height of the solid *wall* which surrounded the temple area, effectively marking off the sacred from the secular world outside. The

Fig. I   THE EAST GATEWAY

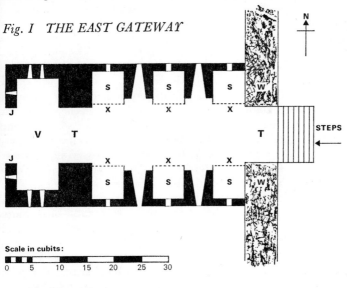

	AV	RSV
J:	Posts	Jambs (of the vestibule)
S:	Chambers	Side rooms (or guard-rooms)
T:	Threshold	Threshold
V:	Porch	Vestibule
W:	Wall	Wall (surrounding temple area)
X:	Space	Barrier (probably a low wall)

gateway that is here described bears interesting similarities with Solomon's city-gate at Megiddo, with its three recesses, or guardrooms, either side of the entrance-way.[2] It can with

[1] See D. J. Wiseman's article in *NBD*, *s.v.* 'Weights and Measures', pp. 1321f.; also de Vaux, p. 197.

[2] This is more fully discussed by G. B. Howie in *BASOR*, CXVII, 1950, pp. 13–19; and in his monograph, *The Date and Composition of Ezekiel* (*JBL*, Monograph Series IV), 1950.

only the greatest difficulty be understood without the aid of a diagram, and the reader is advised to follow the text alongside Fig. I. Ezekiel is led up the steps on to the *threshold*, or entrance hall, and he sees that the gateway consists of a passage with three square cells recessed into the walls on either side; at the end is another entrance hall, leading on to a roomy porch or *vestibule* (8 x 20 cubits in size), which in turn opens on to the outer court of the temple. Most of the measurements are intelligible in RSV, but the figures in verse 11 are confusing. The *breadth of the opening of the gateway* refers to the threshold, which is 6 cubits deep (7) and 10 cubits wide; the figure of *thirteen cubits* refers to the corridor of the gateway at its broadest point, namely at the place between the side rooms where the jambs of the recessed windows are set back one cubit behind the projecting *barrier* (12, RSV), or low partition-wall, of the side rooms. Verse 13 gives the over-all width as 25 cubits, *i.e.* 1 (thickness of wall) + 6 (side room) + 11 (corridor without the one cubit offset) + 6 + 1 = 25. The phrase, *from door to door*, suggests that a door led from each of the side rooms on to the outer court, a reasonable probability to allow the Levitical door-keepers to get to their stations to control the crowds who would throng through the gateways at festival time. Verse 14 is hopelessly corrupt, and RSV's emendations at least have the merit of making sense. The *palm trees*, engraved on the jambs (16), were a common decoration, found also inside Solomon's Temple (1 Ki. 6:29–35).

40:17–19. The outer court. Built on to the wall around the outer court, and facing inwards on to a paved area (the *lower pavement*, 18, as distinct from the upper pavement of the inner court) were *thirty chambers* (17), probably arranged in three groups of ten against the north, east and south walls, and with the gateways dividing the ten into two groups of five. Their use is not described, but they would almost certainly have been either for worshippers or for the Levites who were on duty in the temple (*cf.* Je. 35:2 for a possible use made of them). The measurement of *a hundred cubits* (19) represents the distance between the inmost part of the outer gateway and

Fig. II PLAN OF EZEKIEL'S TEMPLE AREA

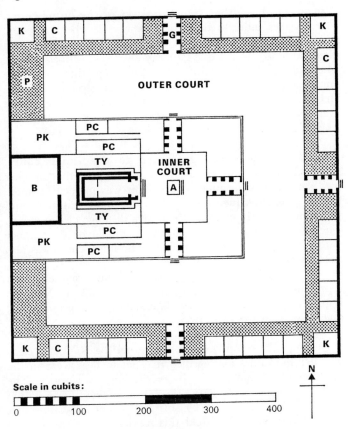

Scale in cubits:

0   100   200   300   400

A: Altar
B: Building
C: Chamber
G: Gateway
K: Kitchen

P: Pavement
PC: Priests' chambers
PK: Priests' kitchens
TY: Temple yard (AV separate place)

the threshold of the corresponding gateway to the inner court.

40:20–27. The other two gateways of the outer court. These verses indicate that the gateways in the north and south walls of the outer court of the temple area were of an identical design to the east gateway already described (7–16). They add nothing to our knowledge except that they were approached by *seven steps* (22, 26), a number omitted by the Hebrew text of verse 5, and this indicates that the temple area is thought of as a huge raised area, built up above the level of the surrounding land.

40:28–37. The three gateways to the inner court. Although it does not say so, we must suppose that another wall surrounded the inner court. This was pierced by three further gateways, identical to the three outer gateways and positioned directly opposite them at a distance of 100 cubits. The only difference was that the vestibule of these inner gates was towards the outer court. The inner court was also raised above the level of the outer court and *eight steps* (31, 34, 37) led up to the inner gateways. 'Each successive elevation represents an increasing degree of holiness' (Stalker). Verse 30 is generally agreed to be unintelligible and a dittograph of 29; several MSS and LXX omit it.

40:38–43. The equipment for sacrifice. It is not clear whether the tables for sacrifice referred to here were in the vestibule of the inner east gate or the inner north gate. The former is suggested by 46:2; the latter by one interpretation of the obscure 40:40, and by 46:19f. It is not impossible that each of the three gates had this sacrificial equipment, and that worshippers could approach by any of the three entrances. The actual siting of the twelve tables mentioned in 41, 42 is baffling; beyond the fact that eight were used for slaughtering sacrificial victims and four smaller tables were near at hand to carry the implements of sacrifice, little more positive comment can be made. Whether they were on either side of the vestibule (cramped conditions indeed) or some inside and some outside the vestibule (but how does one get to those outside?), the Hebrew does not clearly say. For 43b, LXX has 'and over the tables up above was an awning to shelter from the rain and the heat', which certainly suggests that some were out-of-doors, but the reading has no authority.

40:44-47. The priests' chambers. On the north and south sides of the inner court, adjacent to the gateways, were chambers for the sacrificing priests (not *singers*, as in AV, RV; RSV is right to follow LXX). The guide explains that those on the north side were for the priests who were responsible for the day-to-day running of the temple (45; *cf.* 44:10-14), while those on the south (facing north) were for the priests who sacrificed at the altar (46), viz. the Zadokites, whose status is further described in 44:15-21. The square of 100 cubits which makes up the inner court (47) is reckoned from the inmost threshold of the three gateways to the inner court, allowing a surround 50 cubits in depth (the length of each gateway), which may have incorporated the chambers described above and at 42:3. The altar was in the very centre of this square, opposite the temple doors. See Fig. II.

40:48, 49. The vestibule of the temple. At last the prophet is brought up the steps (*ten steps* this time, 49) to the entrance-way to the temple, where the angel-guide continues to take all the relevant measurements. LXX has preserved a better text here, which RSV follows, notably in giving the breadth of the vestibule as *twelve* and not 11 cubits, which is demanded by the other measurements. We would reverse the terms *length* and *breadth* in 49, for the vestibule was 20 cubits wide, corresponding to the width of the nave and the inner sanctuary, but Hebrew always calls the longer measurement the length, irrespective of its orientation. The *pillars beside the jambs* are not described nor are their measurements given, but Ezekiel must have had in mind Solomon's pillars named Jachin and Boaz (1 Ki. 7:15-22) which were free-standing.[1]

[1] For further discussion of these pillars, see R. B. Y. Scott in *JBL*, LVIII, 1939, pp. 143-149; H. G. May, *BASOR*, LXXXVIII, 1942, pp. 19-27; and *NBD*, art. 'Jachin and Boaz', p. 593.

41:1-4. The nave and the inner sanctuary. (See Fig.
III.) Like Solomon's Temple, Ezekiel's has three parts: the
porch or vestibule, the nave and the most holy place (Heb.
debîr, from a root meaning 'back', 'rear').[1] Ezekiel is conducted into the nave, which as a priest he is entitled to enter,

Fig. III   EZEKIEL'S TEMPLE

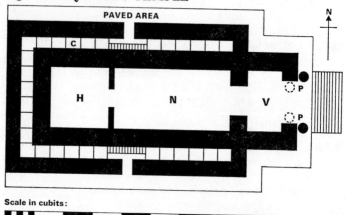

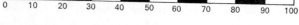

Scale in cubits:

0   10   20   30   40   50   60   70   80   90   100

C: Side-chambers (41:5-7)
P: Pillars (40:49): position not certain
V: Vestibule (40:48, 49)
N: Nave, or holy place (41:1, 2)
H: Inner room, or holy of holies (41:3, 4)
For the paved area, or platform, see 41:8-11.

but he stops short at the entrance to the inner sanctuary
where only the guide goes in (*cf.* Lv. 16; Heb. 9:7). Notice
how the breadth of the entrance-way to each room narrows
from 14 cubits (40:48) to 10 cubits (41:2) to 6 cubits for the
way in to the most holy place (41:3, RSV). The increased
narrowness symbolizes increasing sanctity.

[1] This same tripartite pattern is found throughout the Near East, notably
at Tell Tainat on the Orontes, and Hazor (see *NBD*, Fig. 13, p. 78; *BA*,
IV, 1941, pp. 20f.; XXII, 1959, pp. 3–8).

41:5-12. The side chambers. These were ranged along three sides of the temple, north, south and west, and consisted of thirty rooms in each of three storeys. They were probably store-rooms for Temple equipment and furnishings, and for the tithes and offerings that were paid to the temple servants (*cf.* Mal. 3:10). They are similar to those found in the description of Solomon's Temple (1 Ki. 6:5-10), but the measurements differ slightly. The walls of the temple against which they are built are offset one cubit each storey, so the lower chambers are 4 cubits broad (5) and in the topmost storey they would be 6 cubits broad (the wall to the adjoining temple being correspondingly thinner). They were approached by an entrance in the north and south walls (11), from which a staircase led upwards to the top (7). Surrounding the temple was a raised platform, or paved area, 6 cubits above the level of the inner court (8), and this extended for 5 cubits around the outskirts of the actual temple building (9). Between this raised platform and the chambers situated to north and south was a space of 20 cubits' breadth, described in AV as a *separate place* (12) and, equally unimaginatively, in RSV as a *temple yard* (Heb. *gizrâ*). To the west side, instead of chambers there was a large *building* (12), 70 x 90 cubits in area, which was presumably also used for storage purposes.

41:13-15a. The measurements of the temple. These may be computed as follows. The temple itself was 100 cubits long, *i.e.* jamb 5 (40:48) + vestibule 12 (40:49) + jamb 6 (41:1) + nave 40 (41:2) + jamb 2 (41:3) + inner room 20 (41:4) + wall 6 (41:5) + side-chamber 4 (41:5) + outer wall 5 (41:9) = 100. The yard and the building to the west of the temple extended a further 100 cubits, *i.e.* yard 20 (41:10) + building 70 (41:12) + two walls of building 10 (41:12) = 100. The east front of the temple and its yard was also 100 cubits, and this was matched by the over-all breadth of the building to the west (90 + two 5 cubit walls = 100 cubits). Only a man like Ezekiel could have found such pleasure in this kind of symmetrical precision. To him it meant that everything about the temple was a perfect fit : nothing was out of place.

41:15b–26. The decorations and furnishings of the temple. Much of this is obscure and rsv should generally be followed. The interior of the temple was intricately panelled and surrounded by a design of alternate palm trees (*cf.* 40:16) and two-headed cherubs, which may have been inlaid in ivory, like those found in Samaria,[1] or carved into the panelling and overlaid with gold, as in Solomon's Temple (1 Ki. 6:29–32). These covered the walls from the floor to above the level of the doors (20), that is to say, almost to the sills of the high clerestory, splayed windows that lit the nave on either side from above the level of the side-chambers. (The inner sanctuary was, of course, kept in total darkness.) In front of the double-doors which led into the most holy place was *something resembling an altar* (21f.). It was made of wood, was about 3 ft 5 ins square, and stood just over 5 ft high. This was specifically called *the table which is before the Lord* (22), but it is better known from its counterpart in Exodus 25:23–30; Leviticus 24:5–9; 1 Kings 6:20, as the table of the Presence, or the table of shewbread. It was not strictly an altar (hence its description as 'something resembling' an altar), but a table, on which were placed every sabbath twelve newly-baked cakes of fine flour to serve not only as an offering to God but also as a constant reminder that God was 'man's Provider and Sustainer, and that man lives constantly in the presence of God'.[2] The doors which separated the vestibule from the nave, and the nave from the most holy place, were double-doors, and each door consisted of *two leaves* (24) which could fold back completely on themselves. It would thus be possible for a door to be opened only a quarter of the full width of the entrance, and this would be all that was needed, for instance, when the high priest made his annual entry into the most holy place on the Day of Atonement. The wooden *canopy* (25, rsv; *planks*, av) represents an unknown Hebrew word, '*āḇ*, and is mere conjecture; it occurs also in

---

[1] See G. E. Wright, 'Solomon's Temple Resurrected', *BA*, VII, 1944, pp. 65–77. For an illustration of a similar design, see A. Parrot, *The Temple of Jerusalem*, 1957, p. 65.

[2] *NBD*, art. 'Showbread', p. 1183.

1 Kings 7:6. It could refer to a kind of canopied porch, in front of the vestibule, made from projecting beams, but we cannot be certain.

42:1–14. The priests' chambers in the temple yard.

The prophet now turns to describe the accommodation to the north and south sides of the inner court, opening on to the so-called temple yard. This is not to be confused with the side-chambers, described in 41:5–11, which abut the temple walls and which face on to these priests' chambers across the yard. Again, much of the Hebrew text is obscure and so the architectural details cannot be fully understood; RSV again leans heavily on LXX, and this is the reconstruction which we follow here. The buildings on the north side are described more fully, because those on the south side are an exact replica of them (10–12). Each side consists of two building complexes, covering a total area of 100 x 50 cubits. One of these faced on to the temple yard and consisted of changing-rooms for the priests and rooms for eating and storing the offerings given to them (13, 14). The other, separated from the first by a passageway 10 cubits wide, was a three-storeyed block facing directly on to the outer court. This was only 50 cubits in length (8) but it was continued by a *dividing-wall* for a further 50 cubits to balance the 100 cubit length of the first block of rooms (7). There was an entrance at the east end of this building, which may have allowed direct access by a private stairway from the outer court (9), but it may simply have been at the end nearest to the inner gateways. The various offerings described in 13, 14 will be studied more closely under 44:29.

42:15–20. The external dimensions of the temple area.

The Hebrew has *five hundred reeds* (AV) for the measurements of the four sides of the temple area (16–19), but this is obviously wrong: we must understand *five hundred cubits* (RSV), which corresponds with all the measurements previously given, unless we are to suppose that the reference here is to a previously unmentioned outer wall forming a square of

3,000 cubits each way (so Kliefoth, Keil), but this is most unlikely. The sum of 500 cubits can easily be reckoned from north to south by adding together : length of north gateway 50 + breadth of outer court 100 + length of north inner gateway 50 + distance across inner court 100 + south inner gateway 50 + outer court 100 + south outer gateway 50 = 500 cubits. From west to east the measurements begin with the building and yard 100 (41:13) + the length of the temple 100 (41:13) and then continue as above with the inner and outer courts and the length of two gateways. Once again we see the perfection and balance of the layout of God's sanctuary. The outer wall effectively separated the sacred within from the secular without (20).

b. The glory of the Lord returns (43:1-12)

It was nineteen years since Ezekiel had seen the vision of the glory of the Lord leaving His temple (10:18-22 ; 11:22-24). Now he sees His return, to occupy and to consecrate this new building to be His holy sanctuary. His appearance was the same as it had been before by the river Chebar (yet another link which this closing vision has with Ezekiel's earlier work) and it prompted the same response of awe and adoration. The angelic guide is still with Ezekiel and will continue to explain and instruct him in the law of the temple, but at this point there is a special word from the Lord out of the temple, which is virtually a statement of consecration.

43:1-5. The glory of the God of Israel. According to 42:15, Ezekiel was already at the east gate, and verse 1 must therefore be taken as a stylized introduction to this new section. The description of God's presence draws not only on the earlier vision of the chariot-throne borne upon the wings of the cherubim (*the sound of many waters*, 2 ; *cf.* 1:24), but also on the solar symbolism often associated with the glory of the Lord (*the earth shone with his glory*, 2 ; *cf.* Dt. 33:2 ; Is. 60:1-3 ; Hab. 3:3f.). There is further reference to the vision of the destroying angel of 9:1-11 in the phrase, *when he came to* *destroy the city* (3, RSV; not *when I came* (AV, RV) which pre-supposes that God is speaking). The glory of the Lord approaches *from the east* (2), because that was the direction in which it had been seen to depart (11:23), and enters by *the gate facing east* (4, RSV), which seems always to have had particular liturgical significance as being in direct line with the main entrance to the temple.[1] Having entered, the glory *filled the temple*, as it had done at the consecration of Solomon's Temple (1 Ki. 8:10f.; 2 Ch. 5:14; *cf.* Is. 6:1–3).

43:6–12. The Lord speaks from the temple. The kernel of what the Lord says is to be found in 7a and 12. These words state that the new temple is hallowed by becoming once again His dwelling-place, and that therefore the principle governing the layout and order of the temple is to be the principle of holiness. Wherever the Lord is, shall be most holy. The speech is enlarged by a stipulation that Israel is not to defile God's holiness, as had been done in the past (7b–9), and by an instruction to the prophet to show the details of the temple plan to the house of Israel (10, 11).

7. The words here are an echo of Solomon's prayer in 1 Kings 8:12, 13, 27. The most holy place of the temple is regarded as the Lord's throne-room (*cf.* Je. 3:17; 17:12), and as His footstool (*cf.* Pss. 99:5; 132:7), though strangely enough this idea does not seem to contradict the view that in reality the Lord dwells in heaven. The temple is simply His earthly habitation. The defilement which had previously taken place there had been by *harlotry*, *i.e.* idolatry and sacred prostitution (2 Ki. 23:7), and (apparently) by the practice of burying kings within the sacred precincts. We know from the books of Kings that fourteen kings of Judah were buried 'in the city of David', *i.e.* where the temple and royal palace were, and it appears as if the fault lay in the lack of any clear line of demarcation between what was sacred (the temple proper) and what was profane (the palace and any tombs associated with it). This separateness was Ezekiel's

---

[1] For further study the reader is referred to J. Morgenstern, 'The Gates of Righteousness', *HUCA*, VI, 1929, pp. 1–37.

great plea, as we have already observed. Verse 8 refers either to the palace buildings, which had been within the temple complex, or to the construction of royal burial-places close by. In Solomon's Temple there had been no walled-off outer court separating the Temple from the unconsecrated ground outside. Ezekiel's vision rectified this.

10–12. If the phrase, *that they may be ashamed of their iniquities*, is original and not, as some think, an addition, it echoes 16:61–63. These verses are, however, confused, as the LXX variations indicate, and it is not clear whether the command to show the plan of the temple to the house of Israel was to shame them by its demonstration of the standards of the Lord's holiness, or to encourage them to obey it by building accordingly. The *law of the temple* (Heb. *tôrâ*) is its 'pattern' of holiness; LXX translates with *diagraphē*, 'delineation', 'outline', but this may reflect a Hebrew reading *ṣûrâ*, 'form'.

c. Regulations for the worship of the temple (43:13 – 46:24)

i. The altar, its dimensions and its consecration (43:13–27). 43:13–17.

The measurements of the altar are specified as being by the longer cubit (see 40:5). Albright describes the altar as follows: 'the altar of burnt offering was built in three square stages, each with a side two cubits shorter than the stage below it; the sides of the three stages were, respectively, twelve, fourteen and sixteen cubits long. The lowest stage was set on a foundation-platform called the "bosom of the earth" (*ḥeq ha-'areṣ*). This foundation-platform was set in the pavement, its upper surface being apparently level with the surrounding pavement, but distinguished from it by a "boundary".[1] (This is the *rim* of verse 13, RSV.) The total height, excluding the horns which projected a further cubit upwards (15, RSV), was 10 cubits (2 + 4 + 4), which tallies with the height of Solomon's altar (2 Ch. 4:1). Albright goes on to say that the 20 cubits which the Chronicler stated to be the length and breadth of the altar may either be a

[1] Albright, *ARI*, p. 150.

round figure, or may reflect the size of the foundation-platform which seems to have been between 18 and 20 cubits square.[1] The shape of the altar is thus reminiscent of the Babylonian ziggurat, stepped inwards at each of its stages (see Fig. IV). Albright continues by suggesting that the pattern of the altar was ultimately derived from Mesopotamian cosmology, and he associates the 'bosom of the earth' (the *base*) with the same expression in Akkadian (*irat erṣiti*), which was used for the foundation-platform of the temple of Marduk in Babylon, and also the *altar hearth* (Heb. *har'ēl* or *'arí'ēl*) with

Fig. IV THE ALTAR OF BURNT-OFFERING

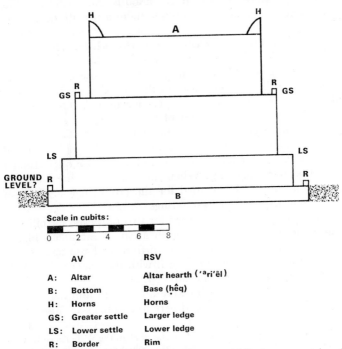

	AV	RSV
A:	Altar	Altar hearth ('^ari'ēl)
B:	Bottom	Base (hêq)
H:	Horns	Horns
GS:	Greater settle	Larger ledge
LS:	Lower settle	Lower ledge
R:	Border	Rim

[1] There is, however, no need to suppose that Ezekiel's altar was patterned on Solomon's (*pace* Albright); see de Vaux, p. 412.

the Akkadian Arallû, the 'mountain of the gods' or the underworld. This does not imply a transposition of Babylonian religious ideas into the religion of Israel, but it does bear eloquent testimony to the influence on Ezekiel of his country of exile.

The *horns* on the altar (15) were at the four corners. They were regarded as of the utmost sanctity and the sacrificial blood was smeared upon them (Ex. 29:12 ; Ezk. 43:20) ; they were also regarded as places of refuge (*cf.* 1 Ki. 1:50ff. ; 2:28ff.). A horned altar has been found at Megiddo, among other places.[1] The *steps* of the altar faced east, and we may safely assume that they were anything up to 10 cubits wide. Altar-steps were forbidden in Exodus 20:24–26, but the increased size of later altars made them a necessity.

43:18–27. The ordinances for the altar. This section contains a number of technical terms relating to sacrifice which can profitably be compared with those in the Pentateuchal legislation. But basic to the action described here is the aim of setting the altar apart for its holy function and cleansing it from every taint of the secular, a process which takes a full seven days. After the first day, when a bullock is offered as a sin-offering, a he-goat replaces it and is sacrificed daily, and in addition a bullock and a ram are offered daily as a burnt-offering (23). When this has been done for seven days, the altar may be used for the customary sacrifices of burnt-offerings and peace-offerings (27).[2]

18. The altar was to be used for two purposes, for offering burnt-sacrifice and for the application of sacrificial blood. This was done either by *throwing* it from its basin against the side of the altar or by smearing it with the finger on the four horns and other significant parts (*cf.* 20).

19. The only priests who were allowed to minister in holy things (*draw near* may be used here in a cultic sense) are those

---

[1] *NBD*, fig. 6, p. 27.

[2] Contrast Ex. 30:28; 40:10; where the altar in the tent of meeting was consecrated by anointing. The altar in Solomon's Temple was consecrated by a seven-day feast of burnt-offerings and peace-offerings (2 Ch. 7:1–9). But compare Lv. 8:14ff.

of the family of Zadok (*cf.* 40:46; 44:15ff.). Non-Zadokites were debarred from priestly office on account of their past idolatrous associations with rural shrines (44:10) and were allowed only to act as temple-servants. Ezekiel is inclined to blur the distinction between these two groups by describing them both as Levites, though this of course is strictly quite correct, but in other ways he distinguished them clearly. The *sin-offering* (*ḥaṭṭā'ṯ*) was offered in order to *cleanse* the altar (20; Heb. *ḥiṭṭē'*, lit. 'to de-sin') and to *make atonement* for it (Heb. *kippēr*, from a root meaning either 'to cover' or 'to wipe away'), and its effectiveness derived from the blood which was the victim's life sacrificed before God. The rest of the animal had to be burnt away from the sacred area (21), *i.e.* outside the camp (*cf.* Lv. 8:17; Heb. 13:11–13).

23, 24. Each day the altar was to be cleansed in this manner, and then a burnt-offering (Heb. *'ôlâ*) was offered to the Lord. This was wholly consumed in the fire and assumed the nature of a gift to God on the part of the worshippers, as they received no benefit from its death in the sense that neither they nor the priests were allowed to eat any portion of it themselves. For the sprinkling with *salt*, compare Leviticus 2:13; Mark 9:49.

27. The *peace offerings* (Heb. *šelāmîm*) were more in the nature of communal meals; only the fat parts of the animal were burnt upon the altar, leaving the flesh to be eaten by the offerers (after certain portions had been given to the priests) as an expression of communion between themselves and God. For in both of these most frequently offered sacrifices, the burnt-offerings and the peace-offerings, the religious aim was primary – that the worshippers should be accepted by God. And it was this which He promised that He would do : *I will accept you, says the Lord God.*

ii. The ministers, their duties and their entitlements (44:1 – 45:8). 44:1–3. The closed east gate. From the inner court where Ezekiel had been standing to receive his instructions about the altar (43:5), he was taken back by his guide to the east gate of the outer court and he found it shut. This

was because the glory of the Lord had entered by this way (43:4) and so no human being could use it without some degree of profanation. The only concession was that the prince was allowed to enter it (from the vestibule, *i.e.* the west end) to eat his sacrificial meal there (3). This privilege may reflect a vestige of pre-exilic sacral kingship, whereby the king was thought to occupy an important place in the cult as the representative of the Deity. Whatever degree of truth there may be in this suggestion, this privilege is but a poor consolation now that the priestly rights of the earlier kings had been stripped away from their post-exilic successors. There is no evidence that the east gate of either Zerubbabel's or Herod's Temple was closed, though its use may have been restricted to priests,[1] and the walled-up Golden Gate in the present east wall of Jerusalem reflects a later tradition and should not be related to this passage.

44:4-9. Proscription of foreigners. Ezekiel returned to the inner court by way of the north inner gateway (preparing the way for the regulation of 46:1 ?), and once again came face to face with the glory of the Lord in His temple. This time God speaks to him about who may and who may not be admitted to His sanctuary (*cf.* the ethical regulations of Pss. 15:1-5; 24:3-6), and the criterion is laid down as being membership of the covenant community. Foreigners, who were *uncircumcised in heart and flesh* (7), were not members of the covenant and therefore profaned the sanctuary by their presence. Israelites who allowed this to happen were breaking the covenant (read *you have broken*, 7, RSV; and not *they*, AV) and rendering their own offerings to God null and void. The fault was attributable to the former practice of allowing foreigners to act as temple servants, *e.g.* the Carite temple guards (2 Ki. 11:4), and this was now strictly forbidden as a profanation of *my holy things* (8). These restrictions, with the renewed emphases on holiness, the covenant and circumcision, were a feature of post-exilic Judaism and they were carried further by Haggai, Ezra and Nehemiah (Ezr. 4:1-3 ; 10:10-44 ;

[1] Mishna, *Middoth*, 1.3.

Ne. 13:1–9 ; Hg. 2:14). Herod's Temple had a warning notice put up forbidding Gentiles to pass beyond a certain point on pain of death.[1] By way of contrast, see on 47:22f.

44:10–14. Responsibilities of the Levites. Instead of the foreigners, Levites are to act as temple ministers and gatekeepers. Their duties are described (11) as (*a*) oversight of the temple gates, as part janitor and part policeman to control the crowds ; (*b*) service in the temple, involving such tasks as slaying the animals brought in for sacrifice and assisting in the kitchens (46:24) ; and (*c*) ministering to the people and helping them in their ritual duties. They therefore *stand before* the people (11, AV), while the priests stand before the Lord (15). This was a down-grading of their position, brought about because of their idolatrous behaviour in the years before Josiah's reforms in the previous century (10, 12), for these were menial tasks. Nevertheless, they were tasks which had to be done and the ordinary people were not permitted to do them, so we must beware of denigrating the duties of the Levites in Ezekiel's temple. They have their counterparts today in all aspects of church life and doubtless then, as now, many reckoned it a privilege to be attending on the people of God in the more mundane details of their religion. After all, they were doing their duties by divine appointment (14).

44:15–27. Responsibilities of the Zadokite priests. Only the sons of Zadok were allowed to minister in the sanctuary as priests. They were ultimately descended from Aaron, according to the genealogy in 1 Chronicles 6:50–53, but Zadok was a priest in David's time alongside Abiathar (2 Sa. 8:17 ; 15:24ff.) and he superseded him as chief priest by successfully backing Solomon as David's successor (1 Ki. 1:8, *etc.*). The nomination of the Zadokite line in Ezekiel is thus a clear restriction of priestly privilege and must have earned the hostility of priests of other lines. However, the Zadokite line maintained its superiority throughout the period of the second

[1] Reproduced in D. J. Wiseman, *Illustrations from Biblical Archaeology*, 1958, pp. 84, 92.

Temple and retained the high priesthood until 171 BC, when Antiochus IV transferred it to Menelaus, a Benjaminite. It is interesting to note that the Qumran covenanters looked forward to the restoration of the Zadokite line in Jerusalem.

17-19. The priestly vestments were to be made of *linen*, which was light and clean in appearance (*cf.* Ex. 39:27-29; Lv. 6:10; 16:4), and not of wool which would more easily cause the body to perspire, causing ritual uncleanness (18). The garments were to be removed, before the priests went into the outer court and mingled with the people, to avoid any suspicion of contagion between what was holy and what was common (19). A similar concern, though with a different conclusion, is to be found in Haggai 2:10-13.

20-27. A series of other regulations governing the behaviour of the priests covers the cutting of the hair (20), the drinking of wine (21) and marriage (22). In each case the purpose is to *teach my people the difference between the holy and the common* (23, RSV). The priests were by their lives to be examples of separateness; their ritual holiness was intended to promote ethical holiness among the people they were called to serve. The regulations are reminiscent of Nazirite vows (Nu. 6:1-21), which were also scrupulous about defilement through contact with a dead person (25-27). Similar regulations for priests may be found in Leviticus 21:1-9. In keeping with their duty to be examples of holiness to the people, the priests also had certain duties of a judicial character and as guardians for the proper observance of festivals and sabbaths (24).

44:28-31. Their inheritance. The opening words in AV, *and it shall be unto them for an inheritance*, suggest that the subject may be the *sin offering* of 27. This cannot be the case, however, and we must either understand MT as meaning: 'Their inheritance shall be – I shall be their inheritance', which is clumsy, or we must emend with Vulgate, RSV, to *they shall have no inheritance*. Because the Lord provides for them through His people, they need have no land of their own and *no possession in Israel* (the word is lit. a 'holding' of property). They have for their use the *cereal offering* (*minḥâ*; AV is misleading here), the *sin offering* (*ḥaṭṭā't*; *cf.* 43:19), the *guilt offering* ('*āšām*; AV, *trespass offering*; which it is virtually impossible to distinguish from the sin-offering), *every devoted* (AV *dedicated*) *thing* (*ḥērem*; something vowed to God which cannot subsequently be redeemed), and *the first* (*i.e.* best) *of all the first fruits* (*cf.* Ex. 23:19; Dt. 18:4). The prohibition of verse 31 applied to all Israelites equally (Lv. 7:24).

Fig. V APPORTIONMENT OF THE LAND

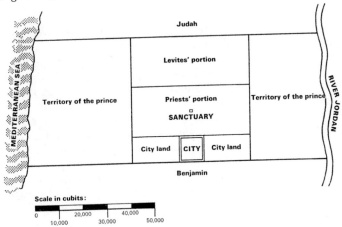

45:1–8. The allotment of the sacred portion of the land.

These verses are readily intelligible with the aid of a diagram (Fig. V). They deal only with the central portion of land, and the tribal divisions are continued in 47:13 – 48:35, with a certain repetition of this material in 48:8–22. The sacred district is called *an oblation* (1, AV, RV; Heb. *t^erûmâ*), the word normally translated a 'heave-offering' in AV, but it is more accurately designated a 'levy' or compulsory contribution.[1] This was the Lord's rightful claim on a part of what was all His land. New ideas are introduced in verse 2 with the reference to the *open space* (AV *suburbs*) which surrounds the

[1] See G. R. Driver, *JSS*, I, 1956, pp. 97–105.

temple area (a kind of 'green belt' between the sacred and profane), and also in verse 5 with a special area marked off for Levitical cities (reading RSV, *for cities to live in,* in preference to AV *for twenty chambers*), instead of the pattern proposed in Numbers 35:2–8. The *city,* or the state, is also allotted an area of land adjoining this central holy portion (6), and so is the prince (7, 8). All the rest is for the tribes to live in : there is to be no more alienation of land by royalty in the state that is to come (*cf.* Is. 5:8). The story of Naboth's vineyard is to be repeated no more (8).

iii. The offerings and other regulations (45:9 – 46:24).

45:9–12. A plea for honesty. The closing words of the previous section lead into the demand, made in true prophetic style (*cf.* Je. 22:3f., 13–17), that the princes of Israel abandon the sins which their privileged position of influence makes possible and give their attention to their real duty, the promotion of righteousness in the land (9). Even in the new restored Israel, there is the recognition that power can corrupt. A practical expression of this is to have standardized weights and measures, variations in which were a frequent cause of complaint in the Old Testament (*e.g.* Lv. 19:35f.; Dt. 25:13–16; Pr. 11:1; Am. 8:5; Mi. 6:10–12).[1] The *ephah* and the *bath* were measures of capacity, dry and liquid respectively, amounting to approximately 22 litres, or just under 5 gallons. Ten of them made up one *homer* (lit. an 'ass-load'), which was about 6 bushels or 48·4 gallons. The *shekel* was 20 *gerahs* in weight and normally amounted to 11·4 grammes, or 0·4 ounces. If, however, we follow MT of 12b, the *mina* (AV *maneh*) was to consist of 60 shekels (20 + 25 + 15, AV), instead of the more usual 50 shekels, and this may represent a devaluation of the shekel to make it accord with Babylonian usage.

---

[1] D. J. Wiseman, in his article on 'Weights and Measures' in *NBD,* writes : 'Since ancient balances had a margin of error of up to 6% . . . and no two Hebrew weights yet found of the same inscribed denomination have proved to be of exactly identical weight, the importance of this exhortation can be seen.'

45:13–17. Offerings to the prince. Specific dues are to be paid over by the people of the land to the prince, and he will have the responsibility of providing the offerings and sacrifices at all the festivals. As a regulation, this is unique to Ezekiel, and it illustrates the real (though limited) cultic responsibility allotted to the civil head of the people. The contribution is to be proportionate : a sixtieth in the case of wheat and barley (13), a hundredth in the case of oil (14), and one in two hundred of the flock (15). The *drink offering* (Heb. *nēseḵ*), or 'libation', normally accompanied the burnt-offering and usually consisted of an offering of wine, most of which was drunk at the sacrificial meal (Nu. 15:5 ; 1 Sa. 1:14 ; Ho. 9:4 ; *cf.* Ps. 116:13). Ezekiel may have envisaged that this would consist of oil and not of wine, as wine is nowhere mentioned here.

45:18–25. Some festival regulations. These are described very sketchily and presuppose that the fuller rituals were known and would be observed without needing to be elaborated here. They cover New Year's Day (18–20), Passover (21–24) and the Feast of Tabernacles (25). A number of commentators explain the regulations of verses 18–20 as being purificatory rites at the beginning of the two main divisions of the religious calendar (the first and the seventh month), preliminary to the feasts in those months. This would account for the surprising omission of the third main festival, the Feast of Weeks, but it demands that we follow LXX in verse 20 : *in the seventh month, on the first day of the month* (RV mg.). It is difficult to understand why, in MT of verse 20, a second atonement is to be made six days after the first for the sake of those who sin *through error or ignorance* (20, RSV) unless this is intended to be a modified 'Day of Atonement'. Whatever it is meant to be – a modification of former practice or a new pattern designed by Ezekiel – it illustrates the fact that in ancient Israel no less than today liturgical experimentation was demanded by new situations.[1] On the ritual of

[1] For more detailed study, see J. Morgenstern, 'The Calendar of Ezekiel 45:18–25', *HUCA*, XXI, 1948, pp. 493–496.

verse 19, compare Exodus 29:35–37. A *hin* of oil (24) is one sixth of a bath, *i.e.* 3·66 litres or 6½ pints.

46:1–8. Sabbaths and new moons. The prince had the obligation of producing the offerings, not only for major festivals, but also for sabbaths and new moons (*i.e.* the first day of the month). Just as he had privileges in connection with the closed east gateway of the outer court (44:3), so he was also allowed to enter the east gateway of the inner court and to go as far as its innermost threshold (2). There he would have a full view of what was going on at the central altar, but he was not permitted to set foot within the inner court, which was reserved exclusively for priests and Levites. The privilege was reserved for new moons and sabbaths; on working days the east gateway to the inner court would be closed (1). The sacrifices offered on these special occasions were the same : six lambs and a ram for a burnt-offering, a statutory ephah of flour for a cereal-offering to go with the ram, a further optional cereal-offering to go with the lambs, plus a hin of oil to each ephah (4, 5). In addition, on the new moon, a young bull and an ephah of flour were to be offered (6, 7). This again is a variation on the sabbath sacrifices described in the Pentateuch (Nu. 28:9f.) and those for the new moon (Nu. 28:11–15).

46:9, 10. Entry and exit. A detail is inserted here (touched off no doubt by verse 8) to ensure an orderly flow of worshippers through the limited area of the outer court. Those who enter by the north gate leave by the south gate and *vice versa*. Verse 10 appears to mean that on all non-festival days the prince will be regarded as one of the people and will come in and go out in the same way as they do.

46:11–15. General regulations. These concern various other offerings which the prince makes on behalf of the people. Three situations are dealt with : (*a*) *feasts* and *appointed seasons* (AV *solemnities*), *i.e.* major festivals and fixed occasions like sabbaths and new moons. For these it is stipulated (11) that the amount of the cereal-offering is to be an ephah of flour with a bullock or a ram, an optional amount with a lamb, and oil is to be added at the rate of one hin to an ephah (*cf.* 5, 7). (*b*) When the prince wishes to make a *freewill offering* (Heb. *nᵉḏāḇâ*), a voluntary offering over and above those stipulated, the regulation of 46:1 may be waived and the inner east gate may be opened especially for the occasion (12). (*c*) A *daily offering* shall also be made each morning, consisting of a lamb and fixed quantities of flour and oil (13–15). Ezekiel leaves no room for an evening offering (Ex. 29:38–41; Nu. 28:3–8; *cf.* 2 Ki. 16:15), but this may be due to the incompleteness of the ritual regulations that he supplies.

46:16–18. Alienation of property forbidden. The impassioned plea of 45:8f. is here expressed in terms of a regulation having divine authority. The prince is permitted to make gifts of land to his sons and they are permitted to hold it by right of inheritance. But gifts made to royal servants may be held only on a leasehold basis: they must be returned in *the year of liberty* (17), *i.e.* in the seventh year, when bondservants were to be freed (*cf.* Je. 34:14), or more probably in the fiftieth year, the year of jubilee (*cf.* Lv. 25:10–13; 27:24). In this way the prince's inheritance is safeguarded and kept within the family, and as it is further ruled that the prince is not to alienate the property of others (18), the inheritance-rights of the common people are also protected. After all, the land is not theirs but the Lord's, and both prince and people are His lessees.

46:19–24. Arrangements for cooking the sacrificial meals. In these verses we return to the conducted tour of the temple which Ezekiel was being given in chapter 42, and many would want to transpose this section to the end of 42:14. Certainly, as far as the context is concerned, somewhere in chapter 42 would be more fitting. On the other hand, it is quite understandable that verses which deal with the disposal of the sacrifices should be held over until the detailed regulations governing them have been explained.

The prophet is first shown the kitchen at the western extremity of the north row of priests' chambers in the inner court, and we may safely assume that there was a similar place on the south side of the court as well. There the priests were to boil the flesh of the guilt- and sin-offerings and to bake the flour of the cereal-offering, taking great care not to carry any of these into the outer court for fear that they may *sanctify* (AV; better, *communicate holiness to*, RSV) *the people* (20). The prophet then sees the four kitchen areas in the four corners of the outer court of the temple where the Levites (*the ministers of the house*, 24) boil the people's sacrifices for them. So the temple was a place for sacrificing, cooking and eating, as well as for prayer and so-called 'spiritual' activities. The Christian church has been the poorer when it has drawn a firm dividing-line between spiritual life and social activities. In Ezekiel's temple, at any rate, there was envisaged a healthy fusion of the two elements, and this was typical of much in Old Testament worship.

d. The life-giving waters (47:1-12)

The picture of the river flowing from under the threshold of the temple and fertilizing the barren areas of the Dead Sea valley is a clear instance of symbolism, expressive of the blessings which will flow from God's presence in His sanctuary to other parts of the land. To attempt to take this literally, as some have done, is to miss completely the point which is being made. So we need not pause over the traditions that suggest that Mount Zion, on which the temple was built, concealed beneath its rocky exterior 'an inexhaustible supply of water and underground reservoirs' (so the *Letter of Aristeas*). No amount of water-divining will confirm Ezekiel 47. The fact that this represents an idealization of God's abundant blessings is confirmed by passages such as Psalms 46:4; 65:9; Isaiah 33:20f. Blessing, fertility and water are almost interchangeable ideas in the Old Testament. The commentator is, however, justified in looking for parallels to and antecedents for this kind of symbolism, and most turn to the creation narrative in Genesis 2. The former paradise which was watered by the four-streamed river (Gn. 2:10) is here paralleled by the new creation which also has its river and its trees (7). If we add to this the fact which has already been observed (on 28:1–19) that Ezekiel seems to have known of a paradise tradition linked to a 'holy mountain of God' (28:14, 16) as well as a 'garden of God', the parallel to our present passage is almost complete.

The river grows in volume as it descends eastwards through the mountains towards the Dead Sea and before long it becomes too deep to wade through. The sheer physical impossibility of this (for no tributaries are mentioned that would swell the stream; indeed they would nullify the symbolic message that it all comes from the one true source), while it may worry us, holds no inconsistency for the writer. For this is accepted apocalyptic imagery: what it says and what that means are more important than the logic of the way it is expressed.[1]

The context of the symbolism is the continuation of Ezekiel's vision. From visiting the kitchens in the outer court, the prophet is taken back to the door of the temple (1) where he sees the water trickling from the southern corner of the temple threshold (so RSV). It flows from there past the altar of burnt-offering, still on the south side, and eventually issues from the temple area on the south side of the closed eastern gateway (2). Ezekiel has to make a detour through the north gateway in order to get to see it, for even in his vision he was earthbound. A thousand cubits eastwards from the temple wall he is led across the stream and finds it *ankle-deep* (3; Heb. *mê 'opsāyîm*, lit. 'water of ankles'). So strange did this phrase seem to the LXX translator that he virtually transliterated it and made 'water of remission' (*hydōr apheseōs*), with the result that many early Christian commentators applied this symbolism to the waters of baptism. A warning to both translators and interpreters! Similar phrases follow as the water

---

[1] Further comparison may be made with Zc. 14:8, where the waters flow from Jerusalem in both westerly and easterly directions; with Joel 3:18, and with Rev. 22:1–3, which draws heavily on Ezk. 47.

reaches to knees and loins (4), and then the river becomes impassable on foot.

The guide who shows all this to Ezekiel and measures it out with the help of his measuring-line (3; *cf.* 40:3) explains that the river flows eastwards towards the *Arabah* (8, RV, RSV; AV *desert*), which is 'the depression' (Arabic *'el-Ghôr*) of the Jordan valley, the Dead Sea and the Wadi el-'Arābā running southwards from it. Although the river is described in verses 5–9 as a *naḥal* (or 'wady', which dries up for much of the year), it is obvious that it is an ever-flowing stream which brings lasting fertility in its wake. The stagnant waters of the Dead Sea become fresh and swarm with fish (8, 9), and trees flourish on its banks, producing fresh fruit *every month* (12, RSV). Even their leaves will have medicinal properties, and the reason given for all this is that *the water for them flows from the sanctuary* (12, RSV). The temple is to be the source of life, healing and fruitfulness. By miraculous means the impossible is going to be achieved.

Before leaving this section, note that Ezekiel shows some knowledge of the Dead Sea area. *En-gedi* (10) is a town mid-way down the west coast of the Dead Sea and bears the same name to this day; *En-eglaim* is probably north of En-gedi and has been tentatively identified with 'Ain Feshka, the fresh-water spring near Qumran where the Dead Sea Scrolls were discovered. While the Dead Sea becomes a fisherman's paradise, the swamps around it retain their saltness (11), so that these rich mineral deposits can still be exploited, presumably for both domestic and liturgical use (43:24). The visionary still retains a touch of practical realism.

e. The division of the land (47:13 – 48:35)

47:13–21. The boundaries of the land. In the restored state of Israel the land was to be divided fairly between the twelve tribes in accordance with God's promises to the patriarchs (14). Levi had no portion (44:28), because in any case the Levites were provided for both by the offerings of the people and by the land in the central sacred portion to the north of the sanctuary (45:4f.; 48:13), and so Joseph was allotted *two portions* in the names of his two sons, Ephraim and Manasseh (47:13; 48:4, 5). In this way the number twelve was retained for the tribes of Israel.[1] The geographical boundaries of the land were to be the Mediterranean on the west (*the great sea*, 20) and the river Jordan on the east (18). The northern boundary was to run along a line drawn roughly from Tyre on the coast to the headwaters of the Jordan, south-west of Damascus (15–17). The place-names are impossible to identify with any certainty. *Hamath* is known as the modern Hama on the river Orontes, 115 miles north of Damascus, but probably the *entrance of Hamath* (15, RSV) was the 100-mile-long depression running in a south-westerly direction between the Lebanon and the Hermon-Antilebanon ranges (the Beqa‘). It was the northern extremity of Solomon's kingdom (1 Ki. 8:65) and an ideal frontier for defence against attack from the north via the Orontes and Leontes valleys.[2] *Hethlon* could well be modern ‘Adlun, a coastal town some 10 miles north of Tyre (the identification with Heitela, east of Tripoli, is much too far to the north). *Zedad*, *Berothah* and *Sibraim* (15, 16) may well be towns in the Beqa‘, in which case Berothah could be the modern Breitan, south of Baalbek (=Berothai, 2 Sa. 8:8) and Sibraim could be the same as Sepharvaim (2 Ki. 17:24) but its situation is unknown. *Hazar-hatticon* (16), ‘the middle Hazar’, is probably the same as *Hazar-enan* (17) and has been tentatively identified with Baniyas at the source of the Jordan (=Caesarea Philippi in New Testament times). *Hauran* is a region east of the Sea of Galilee, roughly the same as Bashan. Verse 17 describes the land lying to the north of the northern boundary as the territory (EVV, *border*) of Damascus and Hamath. Compare Numbers 33:7–9.

[1] This expedient, which antedates Ezekiel's time, has left many problems for subsequent writers who have thus had up to 14 names to choose from in naming the so-called 'twelve tribes'; *e.g.* Rev. 7:4–8, where Levi, Joseph *and* Manasseh are included, and Ephraim and Dan are left out.

[2] Y. Aharoni has recently attempted to show that 'the entrance of Hamath' was in fact the name of a city, Lebo-hamath, situated on one of the sources of the Orontes (*Land of the Bible*, 1967, pp. 65ff.).

The eastern boundary follows the Jordan south to the Dead Sea (*the eastern sea*, 18). *Tamar* was probably near to its southern end, and it marked the beginning of the southern boundary which ran westwards via *Meribath-kadesh* (*the waters of strife*, AV; *cf*. Nu. 27:14), *i.e.* Kadesh-barnea, modern 'Ain Qadeis, to the *brook of Egypt*, the wadi el-Arish, on the Mediterranean coastline. The whole area of the land deserves to be compared with the boundaries given in Numbers 34:1–12, and with the extent of Solomon's kingdom in 1 Kings 8:65.

47:22, 23. The place of aliens. An interesting example of broad-mindedness is incorporated at this stage, and it is the only indication within the vision that any but true-born Israelites can have any real place within the restored Israel of the future. The *aliens* (Heb. *gērîm*) who reside among the Israelites are to have a share in the inheritance of the tribe with which they live. This is in keeping with the regulations of the Pentateuch (*cf*. Lv. 24:22; Nu. 15:29) and with the teaching of Isaiah 56:3–8, and it is not inconsistent with Ezekiel's earlier words (*cf*. 14:7; 22:7). It is based on the principle that if these men choose to accept the standards, the religion and the way of life within Israel as a permanency, *i.e.* as proselytes who settle and have children there (22), then they are entitled to the same treatment as native Israelites.

48:1–7. The seven northern tribes. The pattern which the allocation of the land follows is that, because the central sacred portion is well to the south, seven tribes have land to the north of it and the remaining five have land to the south. The northern tribes (beginning from the north) are Dan, Asher, Naphtali, Manasseh, Ephraim, Reuben and Judah. Of these it is worth noting that the three which are farthest from the sanctuary are tribes descended from sons of Jacob's concubines, Dan and Naphtali having been born to Rachel's maid Bilhah, and Asher to Leah's maid Zilpah (Gn. 30:5–13). The fourth son by concubinage, Gad, is the farthest away from the sanctuary among the southern group of tribes (27).

Judah has pride of place immediately to the north of the central portion, as being the inheritor of the Messianic promise through the blessing of Jacob (Gn. 49:8-12), and he supersedes Reuben, the first-born, who is in the next position away on the north side. The other two places are held by the two grandsons of Rachel, the children of Joseph.

48:8-22. The central portion. Much of this is an expansion of what has already been explained in 45:1-8. The holy portion consists basically of a square of 25,000 cubits[1] in the centre, with land to the eastern and western boundaries belonging to the prince (21, 22). The apportionment of this square between the Levites, the priests and the city can best be understood with the aid of the diagram (Fig. V, p. 273). It is described as an *offering* (AV; Heb. *terûmâ*) or *portion* (RSV; see note on 45:1), or more specifically as a *portion for the Lord* (9). According to verse 9 (MT) this latter phrase describes a section of only 25,000 x 10,000 cubits, presumably the portion which is for the use of the priests, but in verse 14 the Levites' portion of the same size is added on and both are called *holy to the Lord* (14). LXX has the measurement of 25,000 × 20,000 in both 45:1 and 48:9, 13 and this would certainly be more consistent. As with the prince's territory (46:17), there is to be no alienation of this land : it is *holy to the Lord* (14).

15. The city is allotted the remaining strip of land to the south of the priests' portion. This contained the city proper, a square of 4,500 cubits, with a 250 cubit surround of *open land* (17, RSV; *suburbs*, AV, RV; Knox has 'purlieus'),[2] flanked by two stretches of arable land, 10,000 × 5,000 cubits each. This was for those who worked in the city to cultivate, both industrial and agricultural workers, who would have belonged to a variety of tribes (19). The total area of the whole of this central square, 25,000 × 25,000 cubits, would be about 50

---

[1] The word for 'cubits' is never used in MT, but AV, RV are wrong to insert *reeds* in 8, 9.

[2] The Heb. word used, *miḡrāš*, really means 'common-land', perhaps for grazing cattle.

square miles by the conventional cubit or 69 square miles by Ezekiel's longer cubit (*cf.* 40:5).

48:23–29. The five southern tribes. To the south of the holy portion are the allotted areas for the remaining five tribes. Benjamin has the privileged position nearest to the sanctuary, as his father's youngest son by Rachel; Simeon, Issachar and Zebulun come next, all born of Leah; and finally, as we have already noticed, Gad, the child of the concubine, Zilpah. It needs little imagination to realize that, apart from Judah and Benjamin, which adjoin the holy portion and which always had the closest geographical interest in Jerusalem, the other ten tribes are allotted without any regard to their original position in the land of Israel at the time of the conquest. Once again it has been a case of Ezekiel's symbolical patterning of the future according to his own inspired judgment.

48:30–35. The gates of the city. There are twelve gates to the city, three on each side, and these are named according to the twelve tribes. In this list, however, *Levi* has a place (31), and so *Joseph* (32) replaces Ephraim and Manasseh in order to keep the number steady. This does not imply different authorship for these verses; it simply illustrates the way in which the prophet devised his intricate schemes. It is not as easy to see the thinking behind this arrangement as it was in the case of the tribal divisions, but some clear indications emerge. On the north side, the side facing towards the sanctuary, the gates are named after Reuben the first-born, Judah the Davidic ancestor, and Levi the founder of the priesthood. To the south are Simeon, Issachar and Zebulun, and this pattern corresponds with their southerly geographical placing. To the west are three concubine tribes, Gad, Asher and Naphtali (34). Perhaps the least consistent trio are those on the east side, where Joseph and Benjamin, the two children of Rachel, are linked with Dan, a child of Rachel's maid.

The whole passage leads us to compare Revelation 21, with its description of a new heaven and a new earth and the vision of the new Jerusalem coming down out of heaven from God. It too had twelve gates, named after the twelve tribes of Israel, but it also had twelve foundations inscribed with the names of the twelve apostles of the Lamb (Rev. 21:12–14). The writer of Revelation owed much to Ezekiel's vivid imagery and was not afraid to Christianize it, because he saw that the symbolism still possessed meaning for the Christian church of his day as well as for the Jews of the exile.

Ezekiel's closing words gave to the city its new name: *Yahweh Shammah, The Lord is there* (35). This was a grand finale to his book and to his ministry. In his twenty-five years of exile and in the forty-eight chapters of his book, Ezekiel had seen the Lord withdraw from His temple because of the sins that were being committed there, he had met with Him by the waters of Babylon in the vision of the chariot-throne, he had promised the exiles that there would be a new covenant when God would be with His people as their God for ever, he had seen in symbolic vision the temple and the Israel of the future. Now at last the Lord would be there, with His people, for ever. For Ezekiel, the climax had been reached : but it was still only a vision. John, the exile in Patmos, who saw Ezekiel's words fulfilled in the coming of Christ as Emmanuel, God with us, also looked forward to the day when a great voice would be heard from the throne saying, 'Behold, the dwelling of God is with men. He will dwell with them, and they shall be his people' (Rev. 21:3). The glory of heaven is the ultimate fulfilment of it all.

It is to that great culmination that all Ezekiel's readers should be led.